AF342662

ON BEING A MACHINE
Volume 2: Philosophy of Artificial Intelligence

ON BEING A MACHINE

Volume 2: Philosophy of Artificial Intelligence

A. NARAYANAN B.Sc., Ph.D.
Department of Computer Science, University of Exeter

ELLIS HORWOOD
NEW YORK   LONDON   TORONTO   SYDNEY   TOKYO   SINGAPORE

First published in 1990 by
ELLIS HORWOOD LIMITED
Market Cross House, Cooper Street,
Chichester, West Sussex, PO19 1EB, England

A division of
Simon & Schuster International Group

Printed and bound in Great Britain
by Hartnolls, Bodmin

British Library Cataloguing in Publication Data

Narayanan, A.
On being a machine
Volume 2: Philosophy of Artificial Intelligence.
(Ellis Horwood series in Artificial Intelligence Foundations
and Concepts).
CIP catalogue record for this book is available from the
British Library.
ISBN 0–13–633785–6

Library of Congress Cataloging-in-Publication Data available

This volume is dedicated to Kieran

Contents

Preface

The first volume tackled the formal aspects of AI, using as starting points Turing's description of the Mathematical Objection, Lady Lovelace's Objection, and the Argument from Informality of Behaviour. We examined developments in computation theory, logic, and formal semantics which took place after Turing's paper, 'Computing machinery and intelligence', appeared in 1950. The aim of that volume was to bring the objections up-to-date by taking such developments into account.

In this volume we tackle what is for us the central question in AI, one which is best expressed by Turing as the Argument from Consciousness, namely, machines cannot think (or have emotions and experiences) because they cannot be conscious. 'According to the most extreme form of this view,' wrote Turing, 'the only way by which one could be sure that a machine thinks is to *be* the machine and to feel oneself thinking.' We present the views of four philosophers (Dennett, Searle, Davidson and Nagel) whose views on mind and consciousness have implications for AI. Sometimes these implications are explicit. When they are not, our task has been to make explicit these implications so that AI researchers are aware of the different philosophical stances which can be adopted when tackling the Argument from Consciousness. The views of Dennett, Searle and Davidson are examined in Chapter 5, and Nagel's in the last chapter.

We also examine recent developments in neurocomputing - a theme in cognitive science research which is gaining increasing prominence (not just in cognitive science but also in AI) because of the growth in popularity during the 1980s of one of its forms, connectionism (or parallel distributed processing). We argue that an examination of these developments is required in order to do full justice to the Argument from Consciousness, particularly because this objection is also concerned with how mind and brain are related. Two subdivisions of AI and cognitive science - computationalism and connectionism - are examined and compared from a conceptual point of view. A full description of the recent debates between Fodor, Pylyshyn, Minsky and Papert, on the one hand, and McClelland, Rumelhart, and the PDP group, on the other, is provided, as are attempts to reconcile the differences between these two camps. Our examination of neurocomputing issues allows us to look again at another objection which Turing identified in his 1950 paper, the Argument from Continuity in the Nervous System. Neurocomputing is examined in Chapter 6.

In Chapter 7, we take a broader view and look at the question of what AI is all about. We examine several proposals concerning the subject matter and methodology of AI, and use the thoughts of various philosophers of science (Hempel, Popper and Kuhn) in order to compare traditional views of scientific methodology with AI practice. We bring the discussion up-to-date by looking at recent methodological proposals by Marr, Peacocke, and McClelland and Rumelhart. Our discussions in this chapter lead us to a rephrasal of the Imitation Game itself - a rephrasal which we argue is a modern interpretation of Turing's original intentions.

In the last chapter, we look again at our rephrasal of the Imitation Game and this time question one of its central assumptions. We propose a framework within which it makes sense to ask the question, 'Can machines think?', and this leads us to provide criteria by which AI research is distinguished from traditional computing and psychological research.

In short, the aim of this volume (and *one* of the aims of the first volume also) is to identify the central issues which make up the area called 'the philosophy of artificial intelligence'. Our selection of headings which go into such an area is, of course, ultimately subjective, but our approach has been to start with Turing's original objections, as he phrased them, and to fan out from them. There is a limit as to the extent of the fan-out, and any major omissions which arise are a result of having to move on to the next topic. Hence, there will be much relevant literature which we cannot hope to include in a work of this kind, and wherever possible we try to refer to the appropriate sources for further reading.

Finally, the following acknowledgements are necessary. First, some of the material in this volume has appeared, or will appear, in different forms elsewhere. Parts of Sections 3 and 6 in Chapter 5 and Sections 4 and 5 in Chapter 8 are heavily edited and expanded versions of a paper called 'The intentional stance and the imitation game', delivered at the Turing 90 Colloquium at Sussex University in April 1990 and to appear in the proceedings of the Colloquium to be published by Oxford University Press. Parts of Sections 8, 9 and 10 in Chapter 5 are heavily edited and reworked versions of a paper called 'The Chinese Room Argument', which will appear in *Logical Foundations: Essays in Honour of D. J. O' Connor*, edited by Brian Carr, Macmillan (forthcoming). Parts of Sections 5 and 6 in Chapter 6 are reworked extracts of a paper called 'Memory models of man and machine', in *Artificial Intelligence: Principles and Applications*, edited by Masoud Yazdani, Chapman and Hall, 1986. Parts of Sections 9 to 14, Chapter 6, are heavily edited and rewritten versions of a paper called 'Cognitive architecture and connectionism', in *Machine Learning: Principles and Techniques*, edited by Richard Forsyth, Chapman and Hall, 1989. Parts of Sections 1 to 5, Chapter 7, are reworked versions of a paper called 'AI methodology', in *Artificial Intelligence: Human Effects*, edited by Masoud Yazdani and Ajit Narayanan, Ellis Horwood, 1984. Parts of Section 8, Chapter 7, originally appeared in 'Why AI cannot be wrong', in *Artificial Intelligence for Society*, edited by Karamjit Gill, Wiley, 1986. And part of Section 2, Chapter 8, is a heavily edited and rewritten section of a paper called 'What is it like to be a machine?', in *The Mind and the Machine*, edited by Steve Torrance, Ellis Horwood, 1984.

Secondly, to Mike Horwood and Sue Horwood, both of whom encouraged me during the last four years or so to write this work. The overall title of the two volumes - *On Being a Machine* - is due to Mike Horwood.

Thirdly, to Khalid Sattar, who provided valuable technical advice during the preparation of this book using LaTeX.

And fourthly to my colleagues - Lindsey Ford, Antony Galton, Ian Horton, Brian Lings, Wendy Milne, Andrew Palmer, Derek Partridge, Lynn Shackleton, Noel Sharkey, June Stevens, Richard Suttcliffe, Marlene Teague, Stephen Turner, Masoud Yazdani, Eby Zafari - all of whom contribute in their own way towards ensuring that the atmosphere within the Department remains buoyant and dynamic. Antony Galton's contributions, especially by way of enthusiastic discussion and comment, as well as healthy criticism, have been particularly important during the course of the book's writing.

Part III

COMPUTATIONAL MIND

Chapter 5

Theories of consciousness

5.1 INTRODUCTION

To repeat something stated in the last Chapter, one area of common and respectable interest to both philosophers and workers in the field of artificial intelligence consists of an examination of any theoretical framework, or logical mechanism, that allows ascription of mental qualities or mental predicates to computing machines (specifically, intelligent computers), whether real or imaginary, to take place on a sound and acceptable basis: 'sound', in that the framework and mechanism should provide logical criteria for such ascription, and 'acceptable', in that any such criteria should conform to the requirement of plausibility and accuracy. One constraining requirement we argued for in such an enterprise is that the ascription of mental predicates, or qualities, to an intelligent computer, if possible at all, must express the same information about the computer that it expresses about a person, otherwise the debate can be handled by, for example, having two different definitions for, say, 'intelligent': one, when it is applied to humans, and another when it is applied to computers. Although this requirement may be questioned (as it will be in the Epilogue), we nevertheless asked, as a first step, whether there could be any mechanism that allowed words like 'intelligence' to be applied to computers and humans with exactly the same meaning. Our discussion of Strawson's proposal for ascription, by one human to another, of mental qualities was meant to provide an insight into how a mechanism that permits the ascription of mental qualities to intelligent computers might be constructed. We were concerned with unpacking the *intension*, i.e. the meaning, of mental predicates and identifying the range of objects to which such predicates could be applied.

Also, we were concerned with 'persons', rather than 'human beings': by concentrating on 'persons', we tried to focus attention on the *logical* nature of the framework and mechanism. Similarly, we used the phrase 'intelligent computer' to refer to a logical entity, i.e. one which may or may not exist. There is nothing strange about the use of terms in this way: the term 'machine' (as we have seen in Part II) can also refer to a logical, or idealized, entity. A Turing Machine, for instance, can be described in logical terms using appropriate formalisms.

In this chapter, we shall start with the question (formulated by Searle (1980 and 1987)) that concluded the last chapter, namely, 'Is it the case that solely in virtue of running a computer program of the appropriate sort a machine can be said to think, or understand, or have experiences?' We claimed there that this was our way of reformulating the general question, 'Can machines think?', from the viewpoint of the Argument from Informality of Behaviour, so that it led naturally to the next objection, the Argument from Consciousness, namely, the objection that machines cannot think because they cannot be conscious. Without consciousness, no machine can have emotions, experiences or thoughts. Turing wrote that, according to one extreme form of this objection, the only way by which one could be sure that a machine thinks is to *be* that machine and to feel oneself thinking.

So far, we have only dealt with logical mechanisms for the ascription of such terms as well as the meaning such terms usually have. We have not examined the major assumptions behind such ascription mechanisms, nor examined mental phenomena *per se* (apart from some introductory remarks in the first chapter). The first volume by and large concentrated on the formal aspects of AI, where the formal aspects were unpacked in terms of various formal mechanisms. It is time to look at the concept of a thinking machine from the point of view of mental events and processes, on the one hand, and the relationship of such mental events and processes with consciousness, on the other.

We attempt to do just that in this chapter. We present the views of three contemporary philosophers who between them cover a wide spectrum concerning the nature of mind and consciousness. It is no coincidence that each of these philosophers - Dennett, Searle, and Davidson - use a form of 'mind experiment' for conceptually illustrative purposes: in the case of Dennett, a chess-playing program; for Searle, a human in a mechanical environment;

and for Davidson, a perfect android. Although we have already carefully examined Searle's Chinese Room Argument in Chapters 2 and 3, we concentrated on the negative aspects of his views, namely, his criticisms of AI. We now need to consider his positive views concerning mental events and processes.

Our main task in the Chapter is twofold: first, to provide an exposition of these philosophers' views with regard to the concepts 'think', 'understand' and 'have experiences', with critical analysis where appropriate; and secondly, in the concluding section, to reformulate the Argument from Consciousness in contemporary terms, using the views of these three philosophers as a starting point. Our overall aim is to provide modern counterparts to the Argument from Consciousness.

5.2 DENNETT'S LADDER OF PERSONHOOD

One of the interesting aspects of Dennett's philosophical framework is that it incorporates a variety of post-behaviourist concepts concerning what it is to be a person, 'post-behaviourist' in that the concepts used ('rationality', 'ascription', 'intentionality', 'reciprocity', 'meaning', 'understanding', and 'consciousness') are unpacked in a more sophisticated way than would be the case from a naive logical behaviourist viewpoint (see Chapter 1). As a result, the framework represents a form of logical end-point to which behaviourist views of mental concepts can be taken. In providing an exposition of Dennett's framework, we are thereby also presenting an up-to-date survey of recent, i.e. post-1950, developments in behaviourist philosophy.

In *Brainstorms*, Dennett (1981) proposes the following six conditions, each of which is necessary, of 'personhood'. Although Dennett is concerned with 'moral personhood', rather than personhood *per se*, '...there seems every reason to believe that metaphysical personhood is a necessary condition of moral personhood' (Dennett, 1981, p. 296). The six conditions are as follows:

rationality

intentionality

stance

reciprocity

verbal communication

consciousness

The first three are mutually interdependent:

> [B]eing rational is being intentional is being the object of a certain stance. These three together are a necessary but not sufficient condition for exhibiting the form of reciprocity that is in turn a necessary but not sufficient condition for having the capacity for verbal communication, which is the necessary condition for having a special sort of consciousness (Dennett, 1981, p. 271),

which finally is a necessary condition of moral personhood.

The first three are used for defining *intentional system*, and we shall concentrate on this concept first. Let us start with the third condition, that of stance, and then work back to the other two, interdependent conditions.

5.3 INTENTIONAL STANCE

In one of the chapters of *Brainstorms*, 'Mechanism and Responsibility', Dennett first outlines a view that he wishes subsequently to attack, namely, that in discussions concerning whether mechanism is incompatible with moral responsibility some philosophers argue that

> ...*the mechanistic displaces the purposive*, and any mechanistic (or causal) explanation of human emotions takes priority over, indeed renders false, any explanation in terms of desires, beliefs, intentions. (Dennett, 1981, p. 234, stress supplied)

Dennett's aim is to reconcile mechanism and responsibility, and to do this he examines explanations which (Dennett, 1981, p. 234) '...serve to ground verdicts of responsibility' and which

> ...are couched at least partly in terms of the beliefs, intentions, desires, and reasons of the person or agent held responsible.

> ...[Intentional explanations] cite thoughts, desires, beliefs, inten-
> tions, rather than chemical reactions, explosions, electrical im-
> pulses, in explaining the occurrence of human motions. ...[Thus]
> intentional explanations are at least not causal explanations *sim-
> pliciter*. (Dennett, 1981, pp. 234-235)

An example of an intentional explanation is 'He threw himself to the floor
because of his belief that the gun was loaded', which

> ...explain[s] a bit of behavior, an action, or a stretch of in-
> action, by making it reasonable in the light of certain beliefs,
> intentions, desires ascribed to the agent. (Dennett, 1981, p. 236)

Dennett goes on to make the following claim:

> Intentional explanations have the actions of persons as their
> primary domain, but there are times when we find intentional ex-
> planations (and predictions based on them) not only useful but
> indispensable for accounting for the behavior of complex ma-
> chines. (Dennett, 1981, pp. 236-237)

It is at this point that Dennett introduces three *stances* which

> ...one can choose to adopt in trying to predict and explain
> [a chess-playing computer's] behavior. First there is the *design
> stance*. If one knows exactly how the computer's program has
> been designed ..., one can predict the computer's designed re-
> sponse to any move one makes. One's prediction will come true
> provided only that the computer performs as designed, that is,
> without breakdown. (Dennett, 1981, p. 237, stress supplied)

The second type of stance is the *physical stance*, from which

> ...our predictions are based on the actual state of the partic-
> ular system, and are worked out by applying whatever knowledge
> we have of the laws of nature. It is from this stance alone that
> we can predict the malfunction of systems .... (Dennett, 1981,
> p. 237)

Examples of explanations from this stance are: 'If you turn on that switch you'll get a nasty shock' and 'Nothing will happen when you type in your question, because it isn't plugged in' (Dennett, 1981, p. 237). The use of sentences in the future tense allow Dennett to equate, in some sense, predictions with explanations.

There is an important feature of these two stances which needs to be brought out. It appears that when things go well with the program (i.e. when the program does not crash), the design stance can be used for prediction and explanation. When things go wrong with the program, the physical stance must be used for prediction and explanation. We shall return to this feature later.

Finally, there is the third type of stance, the *intentional stance*, which

> ...tends to be the most appropriate when the system one is dealing with is too complex to be dealt with effectively from the other stances. In the case of the chess-playing computer one adopts this stance when one tries to predict its response to one's move by figuring out what a good or reasonable response would be, given the information the computer has about the situation. Here one *assumes* not just the absence of malfunction, but the rationality of design or programming as well. ...Prediction from the intentional stance *assumes* rationality in the system, but not necessarily perfect rationality. (Dennett, 1981, pp. 237-238, stress added in both cases)

Dennett concludes the first part of his argument with the following two claims. First:

> Whenever one can successfully adopt the intentional stance towards an object, I call that object an *intentional system*. The success of the stance is of course a matter settled pragmatically, without reference to whether the object *really* has beliefs, intentions, and so forth; so whether or not any computer can be conscious, or have thoughts or desires, some computers undeniably *are* intentional systems, for they are systems whose behavior can be predicted, and most effectively predicted, by adopting the intentional stance towards them. (Dennett, 1981, p. 238, stress supplied in all cases)

And secondly:

> The presumption that we will be able to communicate with our fellow men is founded on the presumption of their rationality, and this is so strongly entrenched in our inference habits that when our predictions prove false we first cast about for external mitigating factors ... before questioning the rationality of the system as a whole. (Dennett, 1981, pp. 238-239)

Of course, Dennett's main concern is to reconcile mechanism with responsibility (and much of the remainder of his chapter relates his own views with those of other moral philosophers), and his overall conclusion to this chapter is phrased with this in mind:

> The intentional stance towards human beings, which is a precondition of any ascription of responsibility, *may* coexist with mechanistic explanations of their motions. (Dennett, 1981, p. 253, stress supplied)

In later parts of *Brainstorms*, specifically in the chapter 'Conditions of Personhood', Dennett starts to tie up his views on rationality, intentionality and stance:

> An intentional system is a system whose behavior can be ... explained and predicted by relying on ascriptions to the system of *beliefs* and *desires* (and other intentionally characterized features - what I call *intentions* here, meaning to include hopes, fears, intentions, perceptions, expectations, etc.). ... We ascribe beliefs and desires to dogs and fish and thereby predict their behavior, and we can even use the procedure to predict the behavior of some machines. ... By *assuming* the [chess-playing] computer has certain beliefs (or information) and desires (or preference functions) dealing with the chess game in progress, I can calculate - under auspicious circumstances - the computer's most likely next move, *provided I assume that the computer deals rationally with these beliefs and desires.* The computer is an intentional system in these instances not because it has any particular intrinsic features, and not because it really and truly has beliefs and desires (whatever that would be), but just because it succumbs to a certain *stance* adopted towards it, namely the intentional stance, the stance that proceeds by ascribing intentional predicates under the usual constraints to the computer, the stance

that proceeds by considering the computer as a rational practical reasoner. (Dennett, 1981, p. 271, stress supplied in all cases)

5.4   INTENTIONAL SYSTEMS

It is now time to introduce the other two, interdependent, conditions. The second condition required by Dennett is that of intentionality, i.e. the ascription to the system of beliefs and desires. Although Dennett does not state explicitly how such ascription is possible, he clearly depends on the sort of ascription mechanism formulated by Strawson in his book, *Individuals* (Strawson, 1959). For instance, when outlining the six conditions, or 'themes' as he calls them, Dennett writes:

> The second theme is that persons are beings to which states of consciousness are attributed, or to which psychological or mental or *intentional predicates*, are ascribed. Thus Strawson identifies the concept of a person as 'the concept of a type of entity such that *both* predicates ascribing states of consciousness *and* predicates ascribing corporeal characteristics' are applicable. (Dennett, 1981, pp. 269-270, stress supplied in all cases)

(We shall return to the question of ascription of a state of consciousness in the last chapter.)

The first condition is that persons are *rational beings*. Dennett unpacks this condition in two ways. First, he appeals to the rules of logic:

> The assumption that something is an intentional system is the assumption that it is rational; that is, one gets nowhere with the assumption that entity x has beliefs $p,q,r,\ldots$ unless one also supposes that x believes what follows from $p,q,r,\ldots$; otherwise there is no way of ruling out the prediction that x will, in the face of its beliefs $p,q,r\ldots$ do something utterly stupid, and, if we cannot rule out *that* prediction, we will have acquired no predictive power at all. So whether or not the animal is said to *believe* the *truths* of logic, it must be supposed to *follow* the *rules* of logic. (Dennett, 1981, pp. 10-11, stress supplied in all cases)

If the system were ideally or perfectly rational, all truths logically implied by the beliefs of the system would appear in the system, but Dennett accepts that

> ...any actual intentional system will be imperfect, and so not all logical truths must be ascribed as beliefs to any system. (Dennett, 1981, p. 11)

This reference to the imperfection of actual intentional systems identifies a theoretical weakness in Dennett's overall strategy, namely, he cannot distinguish in theory between logical conclusions and system beliefs. Instead, he relies on pragmatic considerations to make the distinction for him.

The second way of unpacking the notion of rationality is to provide some sort of status for the beliefs that a rational being holds. Dennett appeals to Griffiths (1962/63) at this point:

> For the concept of belief to find application, two conditions ...must be met: (1) In general, normally, more often than not, if x believes p, p is true. (2) In general, normally, more often than not, if x avows that p, he believes p [and, by (1), p is true]. Were these conditions not met, we would not have rational, communicating systems; we would not have believers or belief-avowers. (Dennett, 1981, p. 18)

The interesting word in the above definition is 'normally'. Taken together, these three conditions, namely, rationality, intentionality and stance, define intentional systems. Dennett states:

> So defined, intentional systems are obviously not all persons. We ascribe beliefs and desires to dogs and fish and predict their behavior, and we can even use the procedure to predict the behavior of some machines. (Dennett, 1981, p. 271)

These 'normative' aspects of Dennett's theory are subject to criticism. For example, Lycan (1982) criticizes Dennett as follows:

> Belief-ascriptions do not at all seem to *be* normative remarks. When we impute a belief to someone we do not *thereby* praise the belief as being a reasonable one. ...[I]f the beliefs posited

> by psychologists are ideal beliefs in the sense of being the beliefs
> that the psychologist thinks the subject ought to have, how is
> it that they could help us predict the subject's actual behavior,
> given that the subject in fact does not live up to the ideal in
> question? It seems these normative "beliefs" would generate the
> wrong predictions. (Lycan, 1982, pp. 25-26, stress supplied)

We shall return to the question of predictions below.

Stich (1982), in his critique of intentional systems, summarizes Dennett's
position with regard to all three conditions for intentional systems as follows:

> So *any* object will count as an intentional system if we can
> usefully predict its behavior by assuming that it will behave *ra-
> tionally*. And what is it to behave rationally? Here, Dennett
> suggest, the full answer must ultimately be provided by a new
> sort of theory, *intentional-system theory*, which will provide us
> with a *normative* account of rationality. (Stich, 1982, p. 41, stress
> supplied in all cases)

Stich then quotes Dennett from a paper unpublished at that time:

> (1) A system's beliefs are those it *ought to have*, given its
>   perceptual capacities, its epistemic needs, and its biography
>   ....
>
> (2) A system's desires are those it ought to have, given its bi-
>   ological needs and the most practicable means of satisfying
>   them. Thus [naturally evolved] intentional systems desire
>   survival and procreation, and hence desire food, security,
>   health, sex, wealth, power, influence, and so forth ....
>
> (3) A system's behavior will consist of those acts that *it would
>   be rational* for an agent with those beliefs and desires to
>   perform.
>
> (Stich, 1982, p.41, stress supplied)

Intentional systems theory, according to Dennett, is therefore a general normative theory of rationality still in its infancy:

> When the course of our argument requires some substantive
> premises about what it would be rational for a system to believe

> or do, we can follow Dennett's lead and let our common-sense intuitions be our guide. (Stich, 1982, p. 42)

Dennett claims that there are certain advantages implied in his account of intentional systems, the main one being:

> The concept of an intentional system is a relatively uncluttered and unmetaphysical notion, abstracted as it is from questions of the composition, constitution, consciousness, morality, or divinity of the entities falling under it. Thus, for example, it is much easier to decide whether a machine can be an intentional system than it is to decide whether a machine can *really* think, or be conscious, or morally responsible. (Dennett, 1981, p. 16, stress supplied)

Here we have the argument that, because trying to decide whether a machine really is conscious is difficult, the concept of intentional systems - which does not involve this question - has the advantage of simplicity over other approaches which do try to answer this question. This may indeed be an attractive aspect of Dennett's framework to those researchers who are philosophically neutral on the question of whether machines can think. However, acceptance of Dennett's framework also involves accepting, at a deeper level, the concept of intentional systems, with the implication that this concept provides an accurate analysis of what it is to ascribe rationality and intentionality to other entities.

5.5 FURTHER UP THE LADDER

Let us complete our exposition of Dennett's views by considering, briefly, the remaining three conditions of personhood. Whereas the first three are mutually interdependent in that they are not ordered, the remaining three are. The fourth condition is *reciprocity*:

> Reciprocity ..., provided that we understand by it merely the capacity in intentional systems to exhibit higher-order intentions, while it is dependent on the first three conditions, is independent of the fifth and sixth. (Dennett, 1981, p. 277)

For Dennett, a person must be able to reciprocate the stance, and this is best achieved by requiring that an intentional system itself adopt the intentional stance towards other objects. This in turn is best achieved by allowing an intentional system to ascribe beliefs, desires and intentions about beliefs, desires and intentions:

> An intentional system S would be a second-order intentional system if among the ascriptions we make to it are such as *S believes that T desires that p, S hopes that T fears that q*, and reflexive cases like *S believes that S desires that p*. (Dennett, 1981, p. 273)

The difference between animals and humans, according to Dennett, is that

> ...it is hard to think of a case where an animal's behavior was so sophisticated that we would need to ascribe second-order intentions to it in order to predict or explain its behavior. (Dennett, 1981, p. 273)

The question as to whether humans are the only second-order intentional systems is therefore an empirical one. (Dennett, 1981, p. 273)

The fifth condition is the capacity for *verbal communication*, and Dennett turns to Grice's theory of 'non-natural' meaning, where Grice attempts to define an utterer's meaning something by making an utterance in terms of the intentions of the utterer. 'Non-natural meaning', denoted by '*meaning$_{NN}$*', is distinguished from 'natural' meaning in the following way:

(a) 'Those spots mean measles'

(b) 'Those three rings on the bell (of the bus) mean that "the bus is full"'

In the case of the first sentence, *x means that p* entails p. That is, we cannot say 'Those spots mean measles, but he hasn't got measles', whereas in the case of the second sentence we can say 'Those three rings of the bell mean that "the bus is full", but in fact the conductor has made a mistake - the bus isn't full after all', i.e. in the case of the second sentence, *x means that p* does not entail p. Also, in the case of the first sentence, we cannot conclude that somebody meant something by those spots, whereas in the case of the second we can conclude that someone (the conductor) meant that the bus was full by ringing the bell three times. (Grice provides three other ways of distinguishing the first sentence from the second, but we shall not introduce them here.) The first sentence uses 'mean' in a *natural* way, whereas the second uses 'mean' in a *non-natural* way, and it is non-natural meaning, '*meaning$_{NN}$*', that Grice wants to examine.

Grice (1957) then introduced the following definition:

'U meant something by uttering x' is true if, for some audience A, U uttered x intending

(1) A to produce a particular response r

(2) A to think (recognize) that U intends (1) above

(3) A to fulfil (1) on the basis of his fulfillment of (2)

Dennett notes that (2) introduces a third-order intention: U must intend that A recognize that U intends that A produce r. For instance, in the case of the bell being rung three times on the bus, we have the following substitution:

'The conductor U meant something by ringing the bell three times' is true if, for some bus driver, the conductor rang the bell three times intending

(1) the driver to produce a particular response r (e.g. not to stop at the next bus-stop, since the bus is full);

(2) the driver to think (recognize) that the conductor intends (1) above; and

(3) the driver to fulfil (1) on the basis of his fulfillment of (2).

It is not important for us that the conductor rang the bell three times, as opposed making an utterance. For instance, the following substitution is equally valid:

'The conductor meant something by uttering "the bus is full"' is true if, for some driver, the conductor uttered "the bus is full" intending

(1) the bus driver to produce a particular response r (e.g. not to stop at the next bus-stop);

(2) the bus driver to think (recognize) that the conductor intends (1) above; and

(3) the bus driver to fulfil (1) on the basis of his fulfillment of (2).

Dennett's claim is that it is intention (2) that ascribes a third-order intention: the conductor intends that the driver recognizes that the conductor intends that the driver not stop at the next bus-stop. Dennett also argues that subsequent revisions by Grice (1968) to the basic definition above all reproduce this third-order intention, and that it is this third-order intention that results in 'genuine reciprocity'. Dennett's fifth condition therefore rests on his fourth. Dennett summarizes his invocation of Grice's definition in the following way:

> Communication, in Gricean guise, appears to be a sort of collaborative manipulation of audience by utterer; it depends, not only on the rationality of the audience who must sort out the utterer's intentions, but on the audience's *trust* in the utterer. Communication, as a sort of manipulation, would not work, given the requisite rationality of the audience, unless the audience's trust in the utterer were *well-grounded* or reasonable. Thus the *norm* is sincerity; were utterances not normally trustworthy, they would fail of their purpose. (Dennett, 1981, pp. 278-279, stress supplied in all cases)

For Dennett, one implication of adopting such a condition is that we should now see that communicating with a computer in a computing language is a very weak form of communication, although his claim is qualified somewhat:

> Achieving one's ends in transmitting a bit of [programming language] to the machine does not hinge on getting the machine to recognize one's *intentions*. This does not mean that all communications with computers in the future will have this shortcoming (or strength, depending on your purposes), but just that we do not now communicate, in the strong (Gricean) sense, with computers. (Dennett, 1981, p. 280, stress supplied)

The final condition for personhood is consciousness, and for this Dennett appeals to Frankfurt (1971), who developed the notion of 'reflective self-evaluation'. Dennett quotes Frankfurt as follows:

> 'Besides wanting and choosing and being moved *to do* this or that, men may also want to have (or not to have) certain desires and motives. They are capable of wanting to be different, in their preferences and purposes, from what they are .... No animal other than man, however, appears to have the capacity for reflective self-evaluation that is manifested in the formation of second-order desires.' (Dennett, 1981, p. 283)

Dennett summarizes his appeal to Frankfurt as follows:

> Frankfurt introduces the marvelous term "wanton" for those "who have first-order desires but ... no second-order volitions". ... He claims that our intuitions support the opinion that all nonhuman animals, as well as small children and some mentally defective people, are *wantons*, and I for one can think of no plausible counterexamples. Indeed, it seems a strength of his theory, as he claims, that human beings - the only persons we recognize - are distinguished from animals in this regard. But what should be so special about second-order volitions? Why are they, among higher-order intentions, the peculiar province of persons? Because, I believe, the 'reflective self-evaluation' Frankfurt speaks of is, and must be, genuine self-consciousness, which is achieved only by adopting towards *oneself* the stance not simply of communicator but of ... reason-asker and persuader. (Dennett, 1981, p. 284, stress supplied in all cases)

Having completed his exposition of the six necessary conditions for person-hood, Dennett concludes in the following way:

> Were these six conditions (strictly interpreted) considered suf-ficient [for moral personhood] they would not ensure that any actual entity was a person, for nothing would ever fulfill them. ... There is no objectively satisfiable sufficient condition for an entity's *really* having beliefs, and as we uncover apparent irra-tionality under an intentional interpretation of an entity, our grounds for ascribing any beliefs at all wanes, especially when we have (what we *can* always have in principle) a non-intentional, mechanistic account of the entity. In just the same way our as-sumption that an entity is a person is shaken precisely in those

> cases where it matters: when wrong has been done and the ques-
> tion of responsibility arises. For in these cases the grounds for
> saying that the person is culpable ...are in themselves grounds
> for doubting that it is a person we are dealing with at all. And if
> it is asked what could *settle* our doubts, the answer is: nothing.
> When such problems arise we cannot even tell in our own cases
> if we are persons. (Dennett, 1981, p. 285, stress supplied in all
> cases)

Hence, for Dennett, the concept of 'person' is normative, rather than descriptive, and human beings can only hope to be approximations of the ideal
person, as provided by his six conditions.

5.6   THE IMITATION STANCE

Let us pause and take stock. One of the interesting aspects of Dennett's
views is the apparent implication (not expressed by Dennett himself) that the
Imitation Game can be interpreted in a post-behaviourist way which provides
a great deal of substance and detail. That is, when Turing asks us whether
the intelligent machine will fool the human interrogator as often as the man,
we can interpret this along intentional stance lines: 'Will the interrogator
use the intentional stance with the intelligent computer as frequently as with
the human (i.e. without resorting to the design and physical stances)?' The
crucial point is that if the answer is 'Yes', all we may have agreed to, for
both human and computer, is the ascription of mental terms which are useful
explanatory and predictive devices: there is no need to infer anything to do
with the mind, or with consciousness.

So if we follow the implication through, the question, 'Can machines
think?', is to be replaced by the Imitation Game which in turn is to be
replaced by the question, 'Can machines have intentional stances applied to
them?', which when answered positively implies nothing about mental or
conscious matters. Hence, it is possible that this is all we can say when the
stance is applied to humans also, at this 'rung of the ladder'. Where we
humans differ from machines (and dogs and cats), according to Dennett's
framework, is that there are three further rungs in the ladder of personhood
which we can climb, but machines (and dogs and cats) cannot.

From the viewpoint of someone who is keen to adopt a more modern
interpretation of the Imitation Game which takes into account recent devel-

opments in behaviourist philosophy, this looks promising, since it appears to tie in quite well with what we would intuitively perceive to be a difference in the way we would justify the ascription of intentional terms to ourselves, on the one hand, and to machines, on the other. That is, when asked to justify applying an intentional term to a human, we could use a variety of other mental predicates. When asked to justify applying the same intentional term to a machine which somehow performs the same task as the human, we can appeal, not to other related intentional predicates, but to the explanatory and predictive roles that the application of the intentional term supports. In addition, when applying the intentional term to a machine, we can add the rider: 'But of course we know that it's not really doing that,' or some such phrase. That is, from our elevated position further up the ladder, we can look down on objects (Dennett's term) further down the ladder and apply this rider, and have a justification for doing so.

Unfortunately, tempting as this scenario is, it is not clear that Dennett's ladder of personhood can support such an interpretation. To see why not, we shall examine three aspects of his framework where circularity may be involved. Far from being on a ladder, we may be on a treadmill. The main point is that the areas where the circularities arise are precisely where we would expect them to were the Imitation Game to be interpreted from a traditional behaviourist point of view.

5.7 CIRCULAR INTERDEPENDENCE?

First, let us examine the role of explanation and prediction in Dennett's framework and try to give more substance to Lycan's general criticism quoted earlier concerning the relationship between belief and prediction. According to Dennett's account of the third condition - the stance - explanation and prediction perform the same role. If there is a difference, this is because explanations describe, or apply to, something that has already happened, whereas predictions describe, or apply to, something that is about to, or will, happen. Dennett's examples, where sentences using the past tense are called 'explanations' and those using the future tense 'predictions', would appear to support this view: a prediction expresses a proposition which is essentially the same as that of a post-event explanation (with a tense change in the predictive sentence from past or present to future), and an explanation expresses a proposition which is essentially the same as that expressed by a pre-event prediction (with a tense change in the explanatory sentences from future to present or past). But, it is quite possible to predict the behaviour of a system independently of any explanation either being provided or even being possible, and similarly it is quite possible to explain the behaviour of a system independently of any predictions either being made or even being possible. We must immediately qualify these claims by taking into account the difference in role of the design and physical stances, i.e. according to Dennett, when things go well the design stance is used for prediction and explanation, and when things go wrong the physical stance is used for prediction and explanation. Let us now try to justify our claim.

In the computing domain, a program, after receiving certain input, may enter a state which leads inevitably to a 'crash', i.e. the program fails. A programmer may correctly predict that every time the program is fed with this input it will enter into some physical state which is identical with a crash state. However, the programmer need have no knowledge of the internal states of the program in order to make this prediction. The only assumption the programmer must be committed to in order for the predictions to be predictions is that he or she is dealing with a deterministic program on a deterministic machine, i.e. with all other things being equal, the same program has no choice but to fail when run on the same machine with the same input and when it enters the same state on that machine. But this assumption in no way explains the cause of the crash. In order to provide such an explanation, the programmer may indeed have to look at the physical states of the system, as Dennett claims, but much more likely is that the programmer will need to look at the design of the system in addition to the logic of individual program statements and various program units. But the use of the design stance in this way, i.e. for explaining malfunctions, is not catered for by Dennett, since the design stance is used only when the program functions normally. If predictions essentially expressed the same propositions as those expressed by explanations in the computer programming domain, there would be no need to train programmers in the art of 'debugging', i.e. the skills involved in finding and eradicating faults in the design and logic of the program. Predicting a system crash would, according to Dennett, be sufficient for explaining (and therefore for correcting?) the system fault, and this is not true, certainly not in the programming domain.

Also, explaining is not the same as prediction. Again, if we look at the programming domain, it is possible to state that, for instance, in the programming language LISP to ask for the head of an empty list leads to an undefined value being returned, i.e. one can only ask for the first item of a list of one or more items. We may have a declaration, or rule, about the way a particular construct should work, and a partial explanation here where there is no malfunction as such would indeed, as Dennett claims, involve an examination of the design specifications of the LISP interpreter. However, it may not be possible to predict what will happen if a programmer were to ask for the head of an empty list when running a LISP interpreter, since different LISP interpreters handle this request differently. Sometimes, an error is reported; at other times, a spurious value is returned with no warning being given to the programmer that this is what has happened. There is no malfunction as such (i.e. the program does not crash) and therefore, according to Dennett, no need to invoke the physical stance, yet it may be only through knowledge of the physical characteristics (e.g. knowledge of the computer's architecture and physical memory system) of a particular implementation (i.e. from a physical stance) that a full explanation can be given. The nature of our first objection is therefore twofold: it denies the accuracy of the role of the physical and design stances; and it denies that predictions express essentially the same propositions as explanations.

We can generalize the objection in the following way. It is a 'fact' of computational theory that it is not possible to predict, for all cases, that a Turing Machine will halt for all possible inputs. Yet the explanation for such behaviour is intelligible and does not depend in any way on the predictions which, in any case, cannot always be made. But according to Dennett's scheme, it appears that if we cannot predict the behaviour of a Turing Machine then we cannot explain the behaviour of that Turing Machine, whereas, computationally speaking, we can provide an explanation of the behaviour of a Turing Machine using, say, quintuples, or other logical or functional primitives, without in any way committing ourselves to predicting how the machine will operate when provided with input - real or imaginary.

Similarly, we may be able to predict various phenomena without being able to explain the reasons for their occurrence. For instance, when acquiring language the child moves through various stages of learning (from babbling to forming sentences), and there is much applied work in psychology and psycholinguistics which attempts to identify the end of one stage and the beginning of the next, with the stages usually being dependent on the age of the child and other developmental characteristics. But there is as yet no agreed explanation of why it is that the child goes through these stages, or why it is that the child acquires the particular language that it does, although there are a variety of hypotheses including, for instance, Chomsky's *universal grammar* (as exemplified in the early work of Chomsky (1976)). Yet the presence or absence of these hypotheses usually does not affect the empirical work of collecting data on the basis of the observed stages of language learning. Indeed, it could be argued that the role of prediction is to identify regularities in the real world *in order that* some explanation can later be provided of why it is that these regularities occur in the first place.

We conclude out first objection with the claim that in the foundations of the intentional stance there lies a misconception concerning the nature of explanation and prediction, at the very least in the programming domain and perhaps also in the domain of science. Dennett's conception is very similar, at first sight, to Mach's, as described in *The Science of Mechanics* (1960). According to Mach, an adequate explanation in science is a generalized description which reminds us of past experiences by describing them and allows us to anticipate, or predict, future experience. The major difference is that Mach deals with theory, and Dennett with 'intentional stance'. Mach at least allows for the possibility of confirmation, or correspondence with reality, at both the descriptive and predictive levels. Dennett, however, seems to hold the view that an intentional stance need have no correspondence with reality at the descriptive level. One immediate conclusion is that if an intentional stance need not correspond to reality except by predicting, one could adopt any form of stance to an object, hoping that predictions could be used to justify the stance. Such a self-perpetuating method cannot hope to distinguish between the *justified* and *unjustified* use of a stance. That is, as long as a 'prediction' remains unconfirmed we cannot distinguish between the justified application of the intentional stance which has resulted in a prediction not yet confirmed (but confirmable in principle) and the unjustified application of the stance which has resulted in a 'prediction' which, in principle, cannot be confirmed at all.

Let us grant that the foundations of the intentional stance (i.e. the design and physical stances) are sound, however, and move to the second objection that can be levelled against it as a candidate interpretation of the Imitation Game. We need to remember that the intentional stance is just one step in the 'ladder' of personhood, in that Dennett argues that being an intentional system is not a sufficient condition for being a person and thereby having consciousness. But if the other two, interdependent conditions - intentionality based on a Strawsonian mechanism, and rationality - themselves introduce consciousness (the sixth condition), then we no longer have a stepped approach but a confused one. Let us examine whether this is the case.

Dennett has this to say on Strawson when summing up his ladder of personhood:

> The *first* and most obvious theme is that persons are *rational beings*. ... The *second* theme is that persons are beings to which states of consciousness are attributed, or to which psychological or mental or *intentional predicates*, are ascribed. Thus Strawson identified the concept of a person as "the concept of a type of entity such that *both* predicates ascribing states of consciousness *and* predicates ascribing corporeal characteristics" are applicable .... (Dennett, 1981, pp. 269-270, stress supplied in all cases)

If a Strawsonian ascription framework is really being appealed to by Dennett as the provider of the second condition, then the question arises as to how the second condition is going to cope with the following characteristic of intentional predicates (or, more generally, what Strawson calls *P-predicates* (for *person*-predicates)):

> [T]hough not all P-predicates are what we would call 'predicates ascribing states of consciousness' (e.g. 'going for a walk' is not), they may be said to have this in common, that *they imply the possession of consciousness on the part of that to which they are ascribed*. (Strawson, 1959, p. 105, stress added)

This makes it appear that consciousness is necessary for intentionality, not the other way around as in Dennett's scheme. That is, the important point is whether in the act of ascribing an intentional predicate to an object we confer consciousness to that object, or whether the object already possess consciousness and the mechanism only deals with the justification of a certain ascription. Strawson himself writes:

> There would be no question of ascribing one's own states of consciousness, or experience, to anything, *unless* one also ascribed, or were ready to ascribe, states of consciousness, or experiences, to other individuals *of the same logical type* as that thing to which one ascribes one's own states of consciousness. (Strawson, 1959, p. 104, stress added in both cases)

That is, for Strawson it appears that if we ascribe a state of consciousness, or intentional predicate, to another individual, that other individual is, logically, of the same type as ourselves, namely, *an entity with consciousness* (a person). In other words, what Strawson appears to have in mind is not 'Persons are beings to which states of consciousness *are* attributed, or to which psychological or mental or intentional predicates, *are* ascribed' but 'Persons are beings to which states of consciousness *must be* attributed, or to which psychological or mental or intentional predicates, *must be* ascribed'. What the ascription mechanism does is to provide justification for the ascription of particular mental states and intentional predicates, and in the case of both this is done with the implication that the other individual is conscious. What is in question is *which* state of consciousness that individual is in, not *whether* that individual has consciousness. (Strawson goes on to outline three different types of P-predicate, but this is of no concern here.) The question of whether an individual is conscious is equivalent to asking whether that individual is of the same type as ourselves, and this must be answered positively before - logically - individual states of consciousness and particular intentional predicates can be ascribed to that individual.

If this is the case, and if something like a Strawsonian mechanism is used as the second condition, we may have to restructure the ladder of personhood, since consciousness is introduced as the sixth condition. (We return to the question of restructuring in the last chapter.) Dennett's strategy appears to be to use a Strawson-like mechanism which necessarily implies consciousness on the part of that to which mental, intentional and psychological predicates are ascribed but then to uncouple the implication of consciousness from these predicates. The ascription of such predicates without consciousness implications is then justified on the basis of a restricted, and as we have just seen perhaps incorrect, account of explanation and prediction.

Of course, proposers of the intentional stance can claim that the main point of the exercise is precisely to separate the ascription of intentional predicates from the implication of consciousness, but if that is the case then they must declare exactly how such an ascription mechanism works, since it seems to differ from a Strawsonian mechanism in a very important way. Even if such a mechanism can be found, what we shall have is an ascription mechanism that can make no reference to consciousness, since consciousness only comes later in the ladder of personhood. The danger then is that the ascription mechanism is justified on the basis of the predictions and explanations which follow, but that takes us back to the first objection above. That is, if intentional predicates which normally imply consciousness are used in the intentional stance without that implication, we are left with the problem of explaining how, and why, such ascription is justified and therefore why it performs the useful and indispensable role that is claimed for it. If we rule out intentionality (the second of the first three, interdependent conditions), that only leaves the first - rationality - as a candidate for the provider of some clarification on this point.

Let us turn to a later paper by Dennett (1982), in which he responds to a criticism by Stich (1982) concerning the relationship between logical conclusions and beliefs, on the one hand, and explanation and prediction on the other. The two (i.e. logical conclusions/beliefs, and explanation/prediction) are related by the concept of rationality, and Stich makes the point that the relationship is not entirely clear. Dennett accepts this criticism to a certain degree, stating:

> [F]or ten years I have hedged and hinted and entertained claims [about rationality] that I have later qualified or retracted. (Dennett, 1982, p. 73)

Dennett then provides more information as to what he means by rationality:

> I want to use "rational" as a general-purpose term of cognitive approval - which requires maintaining only conditional and revisable allegiances between rationality, so considered, and the proposed ... methods of getting ahead, cognitively in the world. (Dennett, 1982, p. 76)

This brings us to our third objection. The notion of 'getting ahead cognitively' is a very interesting one. 'To get ahead cognitively' could mean that an individual's cognitive architecture is such that it does all the learning, planning, control, perception, natural language understanding, and so on, for that individual and that therefore the individual is quite passive in the cognitive process (indeed, the 'individual' as an active, dynamic and thoughtful entity could disappear altogether), but given other passages from Dennett concerning rationality (e.g. those quoted earlier in this chapter), it is clear that this is not what is implied: rationality introduces belief - beliefs concerning the truth of propositions, for example. It is obviously important for belief not to be intentional, otherwise we would end up with a complete circle, and Dennett's escape route lies in the earlier passage quoted by Stich (1982), in which Dennett claims that a system's beliefs (note, not an *individual*'s beliefs) are those it *ought* to have, given not only its perceptual capacities and epistemic needs but also, in the case of naturally evolved intentional systems, biological needs such as survival and procreation. However, this may be no escape route at all, since the phrases 'perceptual capacities', 'epistemic needs', and 'biological needs' all contain terms - *perceptual, epistemic,* and *needs* - which are intentional in nature. That is, perception, as commonly understood, involves the *recognition* of objects; epistemic needs concern the acquisition of *knowledge*, and a need is something *wanted.* If rationality is indeed normative, then all this means is that rationality provides the conditions under which certain goals that we have chosen for ourselves can be attained, or if unpacked conditionally it means that if we want a given thing, we must act in a certain way. Within the normative interpretations there are still intentional terms lurking.

There appear to be two ways to avoid complete circularity: first, to adopt a strictly biological or mechanistic interpretation, which is what Dennett wanted to avoid all along; and secondly, to have some sort of hierarchy of rationality, where some base terms are cashed biologically out of which other intentional terms are built. In the case of the latter approach, intentionality would appear to be restricted to biological entities only, and the implication is that the intentional stance not only confers intentionality to an entity but also assumes some sort of biological status. We are then back to the earlier problem concerning consciousness, except that this time the question is posed differently: does the intentional stance ascribe a particular intentional predicate to an entity which logically must be of a certain biological type, or does the ascription of an intentional predicate ascribe something which is independent of the entity's biological type?

Summarizing our objections concerning the intentional stance, we can identify three general conclusions. *First,* consciousness nowhere explicitly plays a part, except in the sixth condition, where consciousness is unpacked as reflective self-evaluation. The fact that a Strawson-like ascription mechanism is used in the second condition, with its requirement that predicates ascribable to persons necessarily imply consciousness on the part of that to which they are applied, is ignored. The relationship between this condition and the sixth, which introduces moral consciousness, is never examined.

Second, Dennett admits he is not interested in providing logically watertight conditions for personhood. Although such an approach has the advantage that the overall theory at least has some grounding in pragmatic terms (i.e. behaviour), it can also lead to circularity and vacuity, as we saw in two places: the lack of a theoretical distinction between logical conclusions and beliefs held by the system, on the one hand, and the blurring of the distinction between explanation and prediction, on the other. The two problems are related: typically, we would provide explanations of someone's behaviour by subsuming the behaviour under some belief held by that person, e.g. 'She took the umbrella with her because she believed it was raining', and the beliefs of that person would be assumed to be rational. If the beliefs were not rational, that would then raise the question as to whether the explanation was really an explanation. This then leads to the further question of what counts as rational. Our point can now be summed up as follows. If rationality is described in terms of explanation and prediction, we may have circularity. Dennett does state that his first three conditions of personhood, i.e. rationality, intentionality, and stance, are interdependent, and so prediction (via intentional stance) is dependent on rationality and intentionality, and vice versa. It is a moot point as to where interdependency gives way to circularity.

And *third*, because a mainly behaviourist theory results, Dennett is still left with the task of answering the following question: 'What if we programmed a computer (intelligent or otherwise) to satisfy the behaviourist conditions? Would we not say that such a computer has intentions and consciousness (reflective self-evaluation)?' Dennett's only answer, apart from referring to biological needs of naturally evolved systems, must be that, in the final analysis and on behaviourist grounds, we just do not know. The impression left may therefore be one of a lot of expended energy to answer a question that is either not clearly defined or is irrelevant. Although it is permissible to answer this criticism by highlighting the various ways that a Dennett-like approach clarifies aspects of the concept of person which were previously not well understood, there may be no answer to this, further criticism: if ultimately we still cannot answer the question of whether a computer can think or be conscious, because behaviourist conditions by their very nature are rule-like and computers can follow rules, this shows that the behaviourist view is essentially unimportant for answering questions dealing with any conceptual overlap between human beings and non-human beings. That is, whereas behaviourist viewpoints may be useful for associating human behaviour with concepts such as intention, desire, hope, and so on, qualities which can be unpacked behaviourally, it has little to say about the conceptual interconnections between such interesting concepts as consciousness, thought, and intention.

We have worked through the details of Dennett's six conditions in order to provide a glimpse of the way that a philosopher can combine several different theories, most of which display a behaviourist leaning, which results in an overall, hybrid view of the concept 'person'. We shall return to Dennett's framework in the last chapter, but it is now time to move on to another philosophical framework.

5.8 THE CHINESE ROOM REVISITED

Let us return to Searle's Chinese Room Argument (1980), which we described in Chapter 2, Section 10. Our only concern there was to identify, from a formal point of view, the implications of the Chinese Room Argument. However, we left some loose ends in that chapter, and we shall tidy these up as we go along. Specifically, we left until later four objections to the Chinese Room Argument, all of which Searle believed could be answered. Also, we did not explain the importance of 'same causal power as the brain' for Searle.

In order to tidy these matters up, as well as to consider some of the finer points of Searle's arguments, we shall concentrate on a subsequent paper published in 1987 (Searle, 1987), which is more informal and also more informative. In this later paper, Searle makes clear exactly what his motive was in attacking 'strong AI'. He states that there is a gap between 'intentionalist psychology' (where explanations for behaviour are couched in everyday terms, e.g. 'He voted for Mrs Thatcher because he thought she would cure inflation') on the one hand, and neurophysiology (e.g. 'He voted for Mrs Thatcher because of a condition of his thalamus'!) on the other. After claiming that 'dead carcasses of theories that were supposed to fill the gap' included behaviourism, cybernetics, structuralism, post-structuralism, and sociobiology, Searle states that the most recent candidate is cognitive science, of which AI is thought to be the central approach:

> [T]he most ambitious gap-filling theory is the one that says that work in cognitive psychology and artificial intelligence has now established that the mind is to the brain as the computer program is to the computer hardware. This is a very common equation in the literature: mind/brain = program/hardware. To distinguish this view from more cautious versions of artificial intelligence, I have labelled it 'strong artificial intelligence' ('strong AI' for short). According to strong AI, the appropriately programmed computer with the right inputs and outputs literally has a mind in exactly the same sense that you and I do. (Searle, 1987, p. 210)

One consequence of this view is this:

> [A]nything whatever, any system whatever, could have thoughts and feelings - and indeed it not only *could have*, but *must have*, thoughts and feelings - in exactly the same sense that we do, provided only that it is running the right program. That is, if you have the right program with the right inputs and the right outputs, then any system running that program, regardless of its chemical structure (whether it is made of old beer cans or silicon chips or any other substance) *must have* thoughts and feelings in exactly the same way you and I do. And this is because that is all there is to having a mind: having the right program. (Searle, 1987, p. 210, stress supplied)

One interesting point here is that Searle is ambiguous about the possibility of strong AI and its *necessity*. That is, Searle jumps from a system possibly having thoughts and feelings to a system necessarily having thoughts and feelings. This may mean that there is yet another AI thesis, one which can be expressed in Searle-type language as follows:

> If you *could have* the right program with the right inputs and the right outputs, then any system running that program, regardless of its chemical structure (whether it is made of old beer cans or silicon chips or any other substance) *could* have thoughts and feelings in exactly the same way you and I do.

Interesting as this 'average' AI thesis is, we must not be side-tracked. After naming individuals who Searle claims are strong AI researchers (Simon, Newell, Minsky and McCarthy), Searle states that his aim is to refute strong AI and 'solve the mind-body problem'. He first re-introduces his Chinese Room Argument, in which he asks us to imagine being in a room with a set of English rules for matching an input set of Chinese symbols with an output set of Chinese symbols. We are asked to imagine also that we become so good at this matching process that our answers are indistinguishable from a native Chinese speaker. (For problems with this latter piece of imagination, from a computational point of view, see Chapter 2, Section 10.) But we don't understand a word of Chinese:

> And this is the point of the story: *if I don't understand Chinese in that situation, then neither does any other digital computer solely in virtue of being an appropriately programmed computer, because no digital computer solely in virtue of its being a*

> *digital computer has anything that I don't have*. All that a dig-
> ital computer has, by definition, is the instantiation of a formal
> computer program. But since I am instantiating the program,
> since we are supposing we have the right program with the right
> inputs and outputs, and I don't understand any Chinese, then
> there is no way any other digital computer *solely in virtue of in-
> stantiating the program* could understand Chinese. (Searle, 1987,
> pp. 213-214, stress supplied in all cases)

Searle's point is simple: there is all the difference in the world between
manipulating symbols according to some rules, and actually understanding
a language. The former activity is syntactic, the latter semantic. Searle's
conclusion to his Chinese Room Argument is that mind/brain is not equal
to program/hardware:

> Instantiating the right program is never sufficient for having
> a mind. There is something more to having a mind than just
> instantiating a computer program. And the reason is obvious.
> Minds have mental contents. They have semantic contents as
> well as just a syntactic level of description. (Searle, 1987, pp.
> 214-215)

Let us briefly describe, for the sake of completeness, four objections that
Searle raises against his position (Searle, 1980). First, there is the *Systems
Reply*. According to this objection, it is not the person (computer) in the
Chinese Room that understands but the system as a whole, of which the
person (computer) is just one subpart. For instance, there is the input, the
output, the mapping between input and the symbols which is written down
somewhere, the searching of filing cabinets for the relevant information, the
writing of answers on the card, paper, pencils, and so on. Searle's reply is to
internalize the whole system in the person (computer), so that, for instance,
the person (computer) has memorized all the symbols and rules, does not
need pencil and paper, nor access to any filing cabinets. Yet we still would
not say that the person (system) understood Chinese.

Secondly, there is the *Robot Reply*. According to this objection, it is not
the program in the Chinese Room which has understanding but an imagined
robot which contains, as a subpart, a natural language program as well as a
variety of other programs, such as programs for visual and auditory perception, walking, running, eating, drinking, moving objects, and so on. Such a

robot which could affect the real world would have genuine understanding. Searle's reply to this is to apply the Chinese Room Argument to each of the other programs this imagined robot is supposed to have, thereby denying that any of the other programs, which must also manipulate symbols in a purely formal way, could have understanding.

Thirdly, there is the *Brain Simulator Reply*. According to this objection, we are asked to imagine that the program in the Chinese Room does not contain symbols at all but simulates the actual sequence of neuron firings in the brain. The simulation is based on what happens when a human processes Chinese sentences, and if we say on the basis of neural activity that the human understands Chinese, why not the computer in the Chinese Room? Searle's reply to this is to ask us to imagine the person (computer) in the Chinese Room, instead of having a filing cabinet in the Room, operates a complex set of water pipes running through the Room. These pipes have valves on them, and the person (computer) turns the valves on and off according to a rule book. The pipes, which simulate the brain of a Chinese speaker, are connected to a system which outputs Chinese symbols. But the person (computer) does not understand Chinese, nor do the pipes.

And fourthly, there is the *Many Mansions* reply, according to which Searle's Chinese Room Argument only applies to current-day knowledge of understanding (and intentionality in general), as well as current-day technology. Whatever understanding is, one day we shall build machines which understand, and this will be when the process of understanding, as well computer technology, improves. Searle's reply is to say that this redefines the problem. His concern is to attack the *thesis* that mental processes are computational processes over formally defined elements, whereas the redefinition results in a *statement* which cannot be tested. (There are two other objections that Searle answers, but they are not of interest to us.)

5.9 SEARLE'S POSITIVE THESIS

Now that we have completed our exposition of Searle's counter-objections, let us return to his more recent 1987 paper. After dismissing a misunderstanding of his position - that he is arguing that it is impossible for anything not made of biological material to duplicate the 'causal power of the brain' - on the grounds that this is an empirical question, Searle then outlines how he would fill the intentionality-neurophysiology gap - in short, he proposes to get rid of the gap altogether. That is,

> There isn't any gap between the level of intentionalistic explanations and the level of neurophysiological explanations. (Searle, 1987, p. 215)

He justifies this by first describing four 'puzzles': consciousness, intentionality, subjectivity, and intentional causation. These puzzles are expressed as questions:

a. Consciousness - How can a physical system have consciousness?

b. Intentionality - How is it that many mental states, e.g. beliefs, desires, intentions, are directed at, or about, or are of objects and states in the world?

c. Subjectivity - I have my mental states, and not yours. How are subjective, conscious mental states possible?

d. Intentional causation - How do mental states have an impact on a physical object such as a human body?

Searle's answer to these four puzzles is that mental states and processes are *real biological phenomena*. He qualifies this immediately by saying that he is not concerned to show how biological phenomena are related to neurophysiological processes in the brain but to demonstrate how 'it is even possible that mental states could be biological phenomena in the brain' (Searle, 1987, p. 217). He calls this the common-sense view of the mind and states that similar biological approaches to the mind-body problem can be found in the nineteenth century.

His defence of this view proceeds along the following lines. First, he provides a brief summary of brain physiology, pointing out that in most cases neurotransmitters at the synapses increase or decrease the rate of firing of the next neuron in line. This is to be contrasted with the widely held view that brain functions are like those of a digital computer, where either a current flows or it does not. 'Nothing could be further from the truth,' says Searle (Searle, 1987, p. 219). (We shall examine neurocomputing in greater detail in the next chapter.)

Secondly, Searle ties up the rate of neuron firings with mental states in the following way:

> [T]hese variable rates of neuron firing relative to different neu-
> ronal circuits and different local conditions in the brain *produce*
> all the variety and heterogeneity of the mental life of the human
> or animal agent. The smell of a rose, the experience of the blue
> of the sky, the taste of onions, the thought of a mathematical
> formula - all of these are *produced by variable rates of neuron
> firing*, in different circuits relative to different local conditions in
> the brain. (Searle, 1987, pp. 219-220, stress added)

Searle asks us to imagine what would happen if we fed auditory stimuli into
the visual cortex, and visual stimuli into the auditory cortex:

> [I]t seems reasonable to suppose that the auditory stimulus
> would be 'seen', that is, it would produce visual experiences, and
> the visual stimulus would be 'heard', that is, it would produce
> auditory experiences, in both cases because of specific, though
> largely unknown, features of the visual and auditory cortex re-
> spectively. (Searle, 1987, p. 220)

From this, he argues:

> *[M]ental phenomena, whether conscious or unconscious, whe-
> ther visual or auditory, pains, tickles, itches, thoughts, and all the
> rest of our mental life, are caused by processes going on in the
> brain.* Mental phenomena are as much a result of electrochem-
> ical processes in the brain as digestion is a result of chemical
> processes going on in the stomach and the rest of the digestive
> tract. (Searle, 1987, p. 220, stress supplied)

And later, he summarizes his position succinctly:

> To put it crudely ... all our thoughts and feelings are caused
> by processes inside the brain. As far as the causation of mental
> states is concerned, the crucial step is the one that goes on inside
> the head, and not the external stimulus. And the argument for
> this is simply that if the events outside the brain occurred but
> caused nothing in the brain, there would be no mental events,
> whereas if the events in the brain occurred the mental events
> would occur even if there were no outside stimulus. (Searle,
> 1987, p. 222)

He argues that his position is very different from that which holds that external causation is the essential form of causation for mental contents. According to his view, external causes affect only the central nervous system, not mental contents. Also, he differs from materialists who claim that all there is to, say, pain, is just C fibre stimulations. According to Searle's view, C fibre stimulations are not identical with pains but are *part of the causes* of certain kinds of pain. This leads him to make a second claim:

> To our first claim, namely that pains and other mental phenomena are caused by brain processes, we need to add a second claim: *pains and other mental phenomena are features of the brain.* (Searle, 1987, p. 223, stress supplied)

Searle anticipates the objection that he has contradicted himself: how can something that stands in a causal relationship to something else also be a feature of that something else? His answer is to reject the traditional view of causation which assumes two discrete events, where one may be physical and the other mental (see Chapter 1). This, in his view, leads us back to dualism. Instead, he proposes a 'more sophisticated concept of causation'. He introduces the notions of micro- and macro-properties of systems. For instance, a table is a 'system' which is composed of micro-particles. Micro-particles have features at the level of molecules, atoms, and subatomic particles. But the table as system also has certain properties, such as solidity: these are macro-properties or surface properties of the physical system. Searle goes on:

> Some of these macro-properties can be causally explained by the behaviour of elements at the micro-level. For example, the solidity of the table in front of me is (causally) explained by the lattice structure of the molecules of which the table is composed. (Searle, 1987, p. 223)

Searle accepts that not all macro-properties can be explained at the micro-level, but that is not important. The main point is that in the case of the table we can say that surface phenomena are caused by the behaviour of elements at the micro-level and at the same time the surface phenomena *just are* physical features of the system in question. Searle states:

> My preferred way of stating this point is to say that the surface feature F is *caused by* the behaviour of micro-elements M,

> and at the same time is *realized in* the system of micro-elements.
> The relations between F and M are causal but at the same time F
> is simply a higher-level feature of the very system which consists
> in elements M. (Searle, 1987, pp. 223-224, stress supplied)

Searle accepts that it is very common, especially in science, for there to be a shift from causation to definitional identity: from 'The solidity of this table is caused by the behaviour of elements at the atomic, molecular and sub-atomic level' to 'Solidity just is the lattice structure of the system of molecules', but he does not believe that much depends on this shift. The main point he wants to make is that when we say that some system of particles is solid, we cannot say that a particular particle is solid. Exactly the same principle applies with regard to the brain and mind:

> Nothing is more common in nature than for surface features of
> a phenomenon to be caused by and realized in a micro-structure,
> and those are exactly the relations that are exhibited by the
> relation of mind to brain. The intrinsically *mental* features of the
> universe are just higher-level *physical* features of brains. (Searle,
> 1987, pp. 224-225, stress supplied)

Given this conclusion, Searle then provides answers to the four puzzles mentioned earlier. First, consciousness:

> The way ... to dispel the mystery is to understand the pro-
> cesses. We do not fully understand the processes, but we under-
> stand the *character* of the processes, we understand that there are
> certain specific electrochemical processes going on in the relations
> among neurons or neuron-modules and perhaps other features of
> the brain, and that these processes are causally responsible for
> the phenomenon of consciousness. (Searle, 1987, p. 225, stress
> supplied)

Secondly, intentionality:

> [T]he way to master the mystery of intentionality is to de-
> scribe in as much detail as we can how the phenomena are caused
> by biological processes while at the same time they are realized in
> biological systems. Visual and auditory experiences, tactile sen-
> sations, hunger, thirst, sexual desire and olfactory experiences

are all caused by brain processes and realized in the structure of the brain, and all are intentional phenomena. (Searle, 1987, p. 226)

Thirdly, subjectivity:

> The solution to this puzzle can be stated equally simply. It is a mistake to suppose that the definition of reality should exclude subjectivity. If science is the name of a set of objective and systematic truths we can state about the world, then the existence of subjectivity is just an objective scientific fact like any other. If a scientific account of the world attempts to describe how things are, then one of the features of the account will be the subjectivity of mental states, since it is just a plain fact about biological evolution that it has produced certain sorts of biological systems, namely human and certain animal brains, that have subjective features. ... Thus the existence of subjectivity is an objective physical fact of biology. (Searle, 1987, p, 226)

And finally, intentional causation:

> How ... could anything as gaseous and ethereal as a thought give rise to an action? The answer is that thoughts are not gaseous and ethereal. Their logical and intentional properties are solidly grounded in their causal properties in the brain. Because mental states are physical states of the brain, they can cause behaviour by ordinary causal processes. They have both a higher and lower level of description, and each level is causally real. ... My conscious attempt to perform an action such as raising my arm causes the movement of the arm. At the higher level of description, the intention to raise my arm has the movement of my arm as its condition of satisfaction and it causes the movement of the arm. At the lower level of description, a series of neuron firings which originate in the cortex causes the release of the transmitter substance acetylcholine at the 'end plates' where the axon terminals of motor neurons connect to the muscle fibres; this in turn causes a series of chemical changes that result in the contraction of the muscle. ... [T]he same sequence of events has two levels of description, both of which are causally real and

> where the higher-level causal features are both caused by and re-
> alized in the structure of the lower-level elements. (Searle, 1987,
> p. 227)

Searle concludes with the following axioms (Searle, 1987, pp. 231-232):

Axiom 1: Brains cause minds

Axiom 2: Syntax is not sufficient for semantics

Axiom 3: Minds have contents; specifically, they have intentional or semantic contents

Axiom 4: Programs are defined purely formally, or syntactically

Conclusion 1. Instantiating a program by itself is never sufficient for having a mind (by Axioms 2, 3 and 4)

Conclusion 2: The way the brain functions to cause minds cannot be solely by instantiating a program (Axiom 1 and Conclusion 1)

Conclusion 3: Any artefact that had a mind would have to have causal powers (at least) equivalent to those of the brain (by Axiom 1, trivially)

Conclusion 4: For any artefact that had a mind, the program by itself would not be sufficient for having a mind. The artefact would have to have causal powers equivalent to the brain (by Conclusions 1 and 3)

5.10   THE MIND/BRAIN RELATIONSHIP

Let us now analyze the salient features of Searle's positive thesis on the mind-brain relationship.

First, he states that he is not concerned to show how biological phenomena are related to neurophysiological processes; rather, he wants to *demonstrate how it is even possible* for mental states to be biological phenomena of the brain. Let us use 'S' to label the proposition that mental states are biological phenomena of the brain. Our first objection is that Searle's argument does not clearly distinguish between the aims of demonstrating the *possibility* (versus *impossibility*), the *necessity* (versus *contingency*), and the *actuality* (versus *falsity*) of **S**. The *possibility* of **S** can be argued for on the basis that the opposite, **not-S**, is *not necessary*, i.e the possibility of **S** is equivalent to it not necessarily being the case that **not-S**. The *necessity* of **S** can be argued for on the basis that it is not possible that **S** is false, i.e. the necessity of **S** is equivalent to it not being possibly the case that **not-S**. The *actuality* of **S** can be argued for on the basis of empirical evidence. Our objection consists of asking whether Searle's aim of demonstrating how it is even possible for **S**, i.e. for mental phenomena to be biological phenomena, is achieved by the strategy he subsequently adopts, or whether in fact Searle has a different (and more radical) aim in mind. That is, if Searle does indeed want to demonstrate the possibility of **S**, then one accepted way would be for him to show that *it is not necessarily the case that mental phenomena are not biological phenomena of the brain.*

Going back to Chapter 1, Section 2, we saw there that there are two different logical ways of unpacking cause. If the causal relationship between brain events **B** and mental events **M** is *necessary*, i.e. if **B** is necessary for **M**, then we have the conditional statement: 'If not **B** then not **M**.' That is, if brain events do not occur, then nor do mental events. If brain events are *sufficient* for mental events, we have: 'If **B** then **M**.' That is, brain events **B** constitute, *de facto*, a sufficient condition for mental events **M**, in that if mental events do not occur then nor do brain events.

Searle does indeed claim that if events outside the brain occurred but caused nothing inside the brain there would be no mental events (i.e. brain events are necessary for mental events), as well as that if brain events occurred then the mental events would occur even if there were no outside stimulus (i.e. brain events are sufficient for mental events). This therefore leads to the interpretation that Searle sees brain events as both necessary and sufficient for mental events.

If this is true, then this lays down the conditions under which mental events can be said to be caused by brain events, but it does not *demonstrate* that it is *possible* for mental events to be caused by brain events. That is, Searle has not provided a demonstration (logical or actual) of brain events causing mental events. All he has done is to present two statements, one of which we interpret in our own causal terminology as expressing causal necessity, the other as expressing causal sufficiency, and both of which are conditional in nature. Neither has been demonstrated, by logic, to be true. Instead, Searle appeals to what might be called 'empirical facts', as opposed to logical facts, about brain functions and processes in order to provide justifications for the truth of his claims. But this will only work if he manages to tie up empirical facts with his own causal and logical arguments. But what is crucially missing from Searle's analysis - notwithstanding his reservations about the notion of brain events causing, in the traditional sense, mental events - is a clear statement *in his own causal terminology* of why and how - logically and causally - brain events are sufficient, and necessary, for mental events, as we understand the terms. Our objection is that because no such clear explanation is provided by Searle, the following questions may pose problems for him.

First, if we look at the causally sufficient connection, is it possible (i.e. is it consistently and coherently conceivable and imaginable in some world) that brain events occur without the mental event being caused? To take one ghoulish example, a person may be 'dead' in that that person's mental life has disappeared, but nevertheless may the brain still be receiving signals (possibly from the peripheral nerves but not necessarily) which in turn cause brain events which in turn cause ... nothing? If this can be imagined, then brain events may not be sufficient for all mental events. That is, Searle does not say *which* types of brain events cause mental events, and which do not, and *why* one type does and another does not. Searle needs to provide a more detailed account of what he means by 'brain events' here. Some notion of 'being mentally alive' will probably be required, but care must be taken not to come up with a brain-event description which has exactly the same ghoulish example applied to it.

Secondly, if we look at the causally necessary interpretation, we see that if B does not occur, then nor does M. Is it possible to imagine some world where mental events occur without there being any brain events? For instance, could there be a world of 'pure thought' where mental events occur without the mind having to be lumbered with a (physical) brain? If this is possible, then brain events are not necessary either.

Thirdly, if he wants to demonstrate the possibility of the sort of causal connection he has in mind by demonstrating its actuality, he is dealing with empirical matters. That is, the argument: from *it being the case that* mental states are biological phenomena it then follows that mental states *could* be biological phenomena in the brain, is a trivial one, except, of course, that it has to be demonstrated factually that mental states are biological phenomena. This could be difficult, empirically, but that does not mean that Searle should not try. However, if it is a straightforward empirical matter, one wonders what all the fuss is about.

We must make clear that we are not accusing Searle of being wrong.

However, if he does want to argue along the lines of necessary and sufficient conditions - albeit in his own causal terminology - he needs to provide reasons, i.e. he needs to *demonstrate*, that a world without the sort of causal connection between brain and mental events he envisages is impossible.

Searle may accuse us of having ignored his statements about different levels of description and he may want to claim that the sort of causal terminology and mechanism we have asked for can be found there. This leads us to our second objection. Searle, when describing consciousness, states that the conscious attempt to raise my arm causes the movement of the arm. At the higher level of description, my intention to raise my arm causes the movement of my arm since the condition of satisfaction of my intention is the raising of my arm. At a lower level of description, an account can be provided which refers only to neuron firings which in turn cause certain muscle movements. The higher level description is at the macro-level, the lower at the micro-level:

> [T]he same sequence of events has two levels of description, both of which are causally real and where the higher-level causal features are both caused by and realized in the structure of the lower-level features. (Searle, 1987, p. 227)

This may well be right, but unfortunately there is another description which appears not to have a place in this hierarchy, namely, the description of the event itself. For Searle, the event is:

> My conscious attempt to perform an action such as raising my arm causes the movement of the arm. (Searle, 1987, p. 227)

This apparently is a description which is neither high- nor low-level; indeed, it may not be a description at all but a sequence of events. The high-level description of this sequence of events is:

> ...the intention to raise my arm has the movement of my arm as its condition of satisfaction and it causes the movement of the arm. (Searle, 1987, p. 227)

Notice how 'conscious attempt' has been replaced by 'intention', and the intention has a 'condition of satisfaction', but it is not at all clear *what causes the movement of the arm*. Is it the intention, or the condition of satisfaction? If the former, the question, at the higher-level of description, is how intentions can cause anything at all. For example, someone may have the intention of writing the greatest book ever written, but that does not cause that person to write the greatest book ever written. If the latter, a person may well intend to write the greatest book ever written and may also know very well that the condition of satisfying this intention is to write the greatest book ever written, but nevertheless that person may never get round to writing such a book.

We are back to the point where it is not clear exactly what Searle has in mind. This is because he gives us little idea of what sort of relationships are possible in his causal model, and what exactly the relationship is between a sequence of events and a higher-level description of it. We can surmise that the higher-level somehow involves the use of intentions and other intentional terms, but the relationship is not spelled out. For example, how can we be sure that a higher-level description of a sequence of events is an accurate description, and is not just a redefinition of the sequence of events? Does that matter for Searle?

Two further questions now arise. There is a danger that Searle, in describing mental processes in physical terms, will be accused of providing precisely the sort of model that can be computationally replicated. That is, by using the notions of cause-effect, physical processes of the brain, rates of firing, neuronal activity, and so on, he may be providing the blue-print for the sort of computer that can have, and perhaps *must have*, mental states. If a human brain could be exactly replicated using organic material in a laboratory, and if the processes of this artificial brain correspond computationally to the sort of processes that take place in a human brain, would Searle then have any grounds for claiming that the artificial brain did not have mental states? The point here is that if brain processes can be described physically, then it may be possible to translate the physical description into a computational notation, i.e. a program, and run. If the implementors of the program could prove that the program is exactly equivalent to the physical specification, it would be interesting to see whether Searle would grant mental states to either the program, or the computer on which it is running, or both.

The other question concerns exactly what is being related in Searle's causal model. Is Searle claiming that *types* of brain event cause *types* of mental event, or only that a *token* brain event causes a *token* mental event? The former implies statements such as 'This *type* of neuronal activity causes *pain*, whereas this other *type* of neuronal activity causes *desire*', as well as 'This particular brain event causes a particular mental event', i.e. type-type identity includes token-token identity, as opposed to the latter, which implies only that a particular brain event causes a particular pain, e.g. 'This *particular* pattern of neuronal activity causes this *particular* pain I feel in my foot', i.e. token-token identity does not imply type-type identity. The impression given in his two papers (Searle, 1980 and 1987) is that Searle supports type-type cause, but this is not certain.

We repeat that we are not claiming that Searle cannot answer these points. However, they do demonstrate the gaps that exist in Searle's theory, and he needs to plug these gaps if his theory is to be accepted as a viable alternative to strong AI. The gaps occur because there is a serious omission (and deliberately so) in his framework: what exactly constitutes 'causal power of the brain'? If we look at Searle's 'axioms' and 'conclusions' described earlier, Conclusions 2 and 4 (that the way the brain functions to cause minds cannot be solely by instantiating a program, and that for any artefact that has a mind the program by itself would not be sufficient for having a mind - the artefact would have to have causal powers equivalent to the brain) restate Searle's claim that it is possible for mental states to be biological phenomena. However, Searle does not tell us what the magical, mystery ingredient that would support his claim actually consists of. There are two ways to proceed: one is to provide greater detail on this magical, mystery ingredient called 'causal power of the brain'; the other is to argue that even if Searle were to provide more information on what constitutes causal power of the brain he may still not have achieved his goal. With regard to the latter case, what is being claimed is that even if we were to know all that there was to know about the brain so that the notion of causal power of the brain could be clearly specified, this may still not satisfy Searle's philosophical objective, which is to demonstrate that mental states are biological phenomena. To see how such an argument can be formulated against a Searle-type 'mental as biological' framework, we turn to Davidson.

Before we leave Searle, we can say that he has usefully reminded us of some of the more extravagant claims made by certain AI researchers - those who belong in the 'strong AI' tradition. His categorization of strong AI and weak AI may not be exhaustive, and Searle may not mind that it is not. As we saw in the first volume, his description of strong AI, by means of the Chinese Room Argument, raises some important questions concerning the formal limits of not just AI but computation in general. His own answer, which depends on the notion of causal power of the brain, raises more questions than it answers, especially with respect to causality.

Let us turn our attention to a philosopher who has clear views on the role, and limits, of causality in the domains of the physical and the mental.

5.11   DAVIDSON ON THE MATERIAL MIND

In his paper, 'The material mind', Davidson (1973) starts at exactly the point where Searle stops:

> Suppose that we understand what goes on in the brain perfectly, in the sense that we can describe each detail in purely physical terms - that even the electrical and chemical processes, and certainly the neurological ones, have been reduced to physics. ...Let us also dream that the brain, and the associated nervous system, have come to be understood as operating much like a computer. We actually come to appreciate what goes on so well that we can build a machine that, when exposed to the lights and sounds of the world, mimics the motions of a man. ...Finally, ...let us imagine that *l'homme machine* has actually been built, in the shape of a man and out of the very stuff of a man, all synthesized from a few dollars' worth of water and other easily obtainable materials. Our evidence that we have built him right is twofold. First, everything we can learn about the physical structure and workings of actual human brains and bodies has been replicated. Second, Art (as I shall call him) has acted in all observable ways like a man: Art has had or seems to have had appropriate expressions on his or its face, has answered questions (as it seems), and has initiated motions of a human sort when exposed to environmental change. Every correlation that has been discovered between what we know of mental processes, so far as this knowledge is reflected in physically describable ways, and what goes on in the human nervous system, every such correlation is faithfully preserved in Art. (Davidson, 1973, p. 339-340)

Whereas Searle had placed some importance on separating the nervous system from the brain (since he wanted only the brain, and not the nervous system, to cause mind), for Davidson this distinction is not that important. What is important is this:

> On a particular occasion, a pin penetrates the skin or sur-
> face of Art; he jumps away, wears the expression of pain and
> surprise, makes sounds like "Ouch!" Or so we are tempted to
> describe matters. I assume we can describe the penetration of
> the skin and all of Art's motions in purely physical terms - terms
> that can be incorporated into physical laws. Knowing the rele-
> vant structure of Art, we know *exactly* how the penetration of
> the skin caused the reaction (physically described). ...Now con-
> sider one pair of descriptions: the official physical description
> of the cause (or stimulus) and the psychological description of
> the effect (bodily movement, exclamation, facial expressions or
> surprise and pain). These are ...descriptions of cause and ef-
> fect and as such the events must fall under laws. If something
> like this holds for all psychological events - and we have been
> assuming nothing less - then are we not committed to the view
> that all psychological events are strictly predictable, and even
> that, for Art, we know how to predict them? Further, since we
> know both the physical and the psychological descriptions of the
> same events, why can we not correlate physical with psycholog-
> ical descriptions systematically? How then can we deny that in
> building Art we have reduced psychology to physics, and hence
> solved all the problems specific to psychology? (Davidson, 1973,
> p. 342)

We should state that, for Davidson, psychology is

> ...a subject that deals with phenomena described by con-
> cepts that involve intention, belief, and connative attitudes like
> desire. I would include among these concepts action, decision,
> memory, perception, learning, wanting, attending, noticing, and
> many others. (Davidson, 1973, p. 340)

Davidson subsumes intentional concepts under the general heading of psychology. From our point of view, the contrast between Searle's and Davidson's views is best brought out if we interpret 'physics' (in the Davidsonian
sense) to be neurophysiology/biology (in Searle's sense), and 'psychology' (in
Davidson's sense) as the study of mental states/processes (in Searle's sense).
However, for the remainder of this section, we shall stick with Davidson's
terminology, but keep Searle's distinctions in mind.

Davidson now outlines two conclusions. First:

> Art is physically indistinguishable inside and out from a man,
> and he has reacted to change in his environment by moving in
> ways indistinguishable from human behaviour. Identifiable parts
> of the interior of Art are physically connected with his move-
> ments, in accord with everything known about the construction
> of the brain and the nervous system. All this falls short, however,
> of assuming that we have succeeded in *identifying* such things as
> beliefs, desires, intentions, hopes, inferences, or decisions with
> particular states of the brain or mechanisms in it. Of course,
> there may be reason to connect *parts* of the brain with various
> cognitive processes; but parts are not mechanisms. (Davidson,
> 1973, p. 341, stress added in the first case, but supplied in the
> second)

Davidson's first conclusion is concerned with identifying psychological phenomena with brain states. His second, related, conclusion concerns knowledge of what Art is experiencing:

> [O]ur detailed understanding of the physical workings cannot,
> in itself, force us to conclude that Art *is* angry, or that he *believes*
> Beethoven died in Vienna. In order to decide this, we would have
> first to observe Art's macroscopic movements, and decide how to
> interpret them, in just the way we decide for humans. ...The
> point is a simple one. If we want to decide whether Art *has* psy-
> chological properties, we must stop thinking of him as a machine
> we have built and start judging him as we would a man. Only
> in this way can we study the question of possible correlations
> between physical and psychological properties. (Davidson, 1973,
> p. 345, stress added in both cases)

Davidson then explores these conclusions further. He first points out that
Art was built (conceptually) not on the basis of *laws* correlating psychological
phenomena with physical, but on the basis of knowledge of the physical
correlate of *individual* acts or movements. Even though we may be able to
predict Art's physical movements when, say, a pin is pushed into his finger,
we cannot interpret the movement as, say, a response unless we are fully
aware of all the physical details. And then we would interpret the movement
as we would a human movement in the same situation and environment.

Secondly, Davidson spells out why it is that we should not expect to discover lawlike correlations or causal laws connecting psychological and phys-

ical events and states - why '...complete understanding of the workings of body and brain would not constitute knowledge of thought and action' (Davidson, 1973, p. 346). He claims that two themes emerge from the above mind-experiment concerning Art. The first is that individual, dated events are to be distinguished from sorts of events. For instance, we can say that a certain gesture means one thing in one country, and another thing in another country. What this means is that individual gestures can be identified as being of the same or different sort: we must not confuse an *individual* gesture with a *sort* of gesture. The second theme concerns the relationship between psychological and physical descriptions. Davidson is quite happy to accept that, although psychological characteristics cannot be reduced to physical ones, they are nevertheless strongly dependent on them. That is, physical characteristics of an event *determine* the psychological characteristics. In other words, '...psychological concepts are *supervenient* on physical concepts' (Davidson, 1973, p. 348, stress supplied). It is impossible for two events to agree in all their physical characteristics and to differ in their psychological characteristics. Davidson then goes on to say:

> The two themes, of the distinction between individual events and sorts, and the supervenience of the psychological on the physical, are related. For what needs to be stressed is that it is the descriptions of individual psychological events, not sorts of events that are supervenient on physical descriptions. If a certain psychological concept applies to one event and not to another, there must be a difference describable in physical terms. But it does not follow that there is a single physically describable difference that distinguishes any two events that differ in a given psychological respect. (Davidson, 1973, p. 348)

This is quite a complicated relationship. Davidson appears to have the following picture in mind. A physical event, say, a certain brain state, is associated with a physical description of that state. That physical state itself determines a single psychological event which in turn is associated with a certain psychological description, e.g. 'He's in pain'. The psychological description is therefore correlated with the physical description at that time. It can even be claimed that the physical state caused the psychological state, at that time. If the concept of pain applies to that particular event, but not to some other, that must be because there is a difference describable in physical terms between the two events. But that does not mean that there is any physically describable difference between pain events in general and, say, happiness events in general. (We have for the moment ignored the point that pain and happiness are *states* rather than events.) This is because psychological events and their descriptions are supervenient on the physical, at the individual event level. This gives us no grounds for claiming that there is any lawlike relationship between physical and psychological events, or between physical and psychological predicates. At best, there are statistical generalizations, but these do not constitute a set of scientific laws. Davidson writes:

> What I have supposed is that for any particular, dated psychological event we can give a description in purely physical terms; and so for any *given, finite* class of events, we can set up a correlation between psychological and physical descriptions. But although this can be done, it does not follow that such psychological predicates as 'x desires his neighbour's wife', or ... ' x signed a check for \$20' which determine, if not infinite classes, at least potentially infinite ones - it does not imply that such predicates have any nomologically corresponding physical predicates. ...Science is interested in nomological connections, connections that are supported by instances, whether or not the instances happen to exhaust the cases. (Davidson, 1973, p. 343, stress supplied)

5.12 EVENTS AND THEIR DESCRIPTIONS

At this point, let us try to identify some assumptions behind Davidson's arguments. With regard to the role of predicates, he writes:

> It should be easy to appreciate the fact that although every psychological event and state has a physical description, this gives us no reason to hope that any physical predicate, no matter how complex, has the same extension as a given psychological predicate - much less that there is a physical predicate related in a lawlike way to the given psychological predicate. (Davidson, 1973, p. 343)

events	ps_1	ps_2	ps_3	ps_4	ps_5	ps_6	ps_7
ph_1	e_1	e_2	e_3	e_4	e_5	e_6	e_7
ph_2	e_8	e_9	e_{10}	e_{11}	e_{12}		e_{13}
ph_3	e_{14}		e_{15}		e_{16}	e_{17}	
ph_4		e_{18}					
ph_5				e_{19}	e_{20}		e_{21}
ph_6	e_{22}		e_{23}		e_{24}		
ph_7		e_{25}	e_{26}	e_{27}	e_{28}	e_{29}	e_{30}

Figure 5.1

Taking this remark at face value, we have the following picture (*Figure 5.1*) of the way predicates are applied to events[1]. Let us assume that there are 30 events ($e_1 \cdots e_{30}$), 7 physical predicates, and 7 psychological predicates, and that these predicates can be applied to the 30 events in the way described in the above event-predicate grid. That is, the columns describe which events the psychological predicates $ps_1 \cdots ps_7$ are applied to, and the rows which events the physical predicates $ph_1 \cdots ph_7$ are applied to. What Davidson seems to be saying is that although, for instance, e_1 can be described by both ps_1 and ph_1, that does not mean that ps_1 and ph_1 have any other event in common to which they can both be ascribed. For instance, ph_1 can be applied to events e_2 to e_7, whereas ps_1 can be applied to e_1, e_8, e_{14} and e_{22}. The only event to which the two predicates can be applied is e_1. From this it would be wrong to conclude that ps_1 can somehow be equated with, or reduced to, ph_1: these two predicates may not have any other events in common, since the domain of events over which each predicate presides is different. This feature of differing domains of predicates justifies Davidson's claim that there is, and indeed can be, no lawlike relationship possible between predicates.

This is certainly an interesting view. The implications are that there is only one type of event to which predicates of both types can be applied, and that there need be no overlap in the type and range of events to which both a physical and psychological predicate apply. Also, if there is only one type of event, that means that it is only in the act of predicate ascription

---

[1] I am indebted to Antony Galton for introducing me to this way of interpreting Davidson's metaphysics.

that events can be categorized as physical or psychological (mental). That is, a psychological event, for Davidson, is an event which is described with a psychological predicate, and similarly with physical events.

5.13 METAPHYSICS

Before examining this aspect in more detail, let us introduce some metaphysics here. *Monism* is a metaphysical theory which is to be distinguished from *pluralism*. Monism's claim, very roughly, is that reality consists of only one kind of substance, whereas pluralism's claim is that reality consists of many kinds of substance. The word *substance* is used by metaphysicians to refer to objects in the world devoid of any of their *sensible* properties, i.e. properties of objects which can be sensed by us through vision, touch, and thought, for example. The reason why metaphysicians use such a term arises out of the way language appears to distinguish an object from its properties. For example, the statement, 'This rose is red', appears to pick out an object - the rose physically in the presence of the utterer - and ascribe a property to that object - that of redness. It therefore appears that we can refer to (sensible) properties of an object (say, redness) whilst using a word, or phrase, which seems to stand for the object itself (the rose). From this it is concluded that words such as 'rose' refer to an object *in itself* independently of, or separately from, the property to be ascribed to it by other parts of the statement. If it is necessary to distinguish logically between the object itself and its sensible properties, the question as to what can be usefully said about the object independently of, or separately from, its sensible properties is a *metaphysical* question, dealing as it does with the way we think, and talk, about reality. One of the subquestions in metaphysics is concerned with the number of different types of stuff that objects, in themselves, are made of. (See Carr (1987) for a modern introduction to metaphysics and its place in twentieth century philosophy.) Monism claims that all objects, where *object* is a general term which can cover events as well as entities, is made up of only one type of stuff. Another way to put this is to say that reality is made up of one type of substance. Pluralism claims, on the other hand, that reality consists of more than one kind of substance.

Monism has experienced mixed fortunes during this century, and is most frequently contrasted with one form of pluralism, *dualism*, which advocates that reality is made up of two types of substance - the material and the mental. One of monism's most famous adherents (temporarily) was Bertrand

Russell, who during the first couple decades of this century toyed with a particular form of monism. Consider the following:

> Common sense divides human beings into souls and bodies, and Cartesian philosophy generalized this division by classifying everything that exists as either mind or matter. This division is so familiar ... that it has become part of our habits, and seems scarcely to embody a theory. ... Nevertheless, almost all the great philosophers since Leibniz have challenged the dualism of mind and matter. Most of them, regarding mind as something immediately given, have assimilated to it what appeared to be 'matter', and have thus achieved the monism of the idealist. We may define an idealist as a man who believes that whatever exists may be called 'mental', in the sense of having a certain character, known to us by introspection as belonging to our minds. In recent times, however, this theory has been criticized from various points of view. On the one hand, men who admitted that we know by introspection things having the character we call 'mental' have urged that we also know other things not having this character. On the other hand, William James and the American realists have urged that there is no specific character of 'mental' things, but that the things which are called mental are identical with the things which are called physical, the difference being merely one of context and arrangement. ... We have thus three opinions to consider. There are first those who deny that there is a character called 'mental' which is revealed by introspection. These men may be called 'neutral monists', because, while rejecting the division of the world into mind and matter, they do not say 'all reality is mind', nor yet 'all reality is matter'. Next, there are 'idealistic monists', who admit a character called 'mental', and hold that everything has this character. Next, there are 'dualists', who hold that there is such a character, but that there are things which do not possess it. (Russell, 1914, pp. 129-130)

And later in the same paper, Russell makes it clear that at the time of writing he favours neutral monism (which he abandoned gradually after 1921):

> A large part of the argument in favour of neutral monism ...consists of the polemic against the view that we know the

> external world through the medium of 'ideas', which are mental. ... [F]or the present, I wish only to say that, as against this view, I am in agreement with neutral monism... The upholders of 'ideas', since they believe in the duality of the mental and the physical, infer from this assumption that only ideas, not physical things, can be immediately present to me. Neutral monists, perceiving (rightly, as I think) that constituents of the physical world can be immediately present to me, infer that the mental and the physical are composed of the same 'stuff', and are merely different arrangements of the same elements. (Russell, 1914, p. 147)

Russell therefore categorizes three types of monism - neutral, idealistic, and realistic monism - and one type of pluralism - dualism. Idealistic monism claims that there is only one type of substance, and this is mental. The argument in favour of this form of monism is that it is only through the mind and its ideas that the world can be perceived. Hence, even what we call 'physical' is 'reducible' to the primitive substance 'mental', and this substance is available to us through introspection. Neutral monism, on the other hand, denies that it is the mental which is the one type of stuff of which reality is comprised. Instead of claiming that it is the mental or the physical (material) which constitutes the one type of substance, neutral monists argue that, irrespective of what type of stuff the world is made up of, there are two ways of interpreting the substance - the mental and the physical. The mistake, from the neutral monist's point of view, is to elevate one interpretation as the only interpretation of the substance. The third form of monism - realistic monism - advocates only one substance, which is matter. The mental aspect (if any) of objects is therefore identical with its material aspects, and all mental aspects can be reduced to, or identified as being identical with, the material aspects of objects.

Let us compare this threefold distinction of Russell's with a fourfold distinction introduced by Davidson:

> It may make the situation clearer to give a fourfold classification of theories of the relation between mental and physical events. ... On the one hand there are those who assert, and those who deny, the existence of psychophysical laws; on the other hand there are those who say mental events are identical with physical and those who deny this. Theories are thus divided into four

> sorts: *nomological monism*, which affirms that there are corre-
> lating laws and that the events correlated are one (materialists
> belong in this category); *nomological dualism*, which comprises
> various forms of parallelism, interactionism, and epiphenome-
> nalism; *anomalous dualism*, which combines ontological dualism
> with the general failure of laws correlating the mental with the
> physical (Cartesianism). And finally there is *anomalous monism*,
> which classifies the position I wish to occupy. (Davidson, 1970,
> pp. 213-214, italics supplied)

(Parallelism, interactionism, epiphenomenalism and Cartesianism were introduced in Chapter 1.) The point of the quote is that Davidson adds
another form of monism to the three forms within Russell's characterization
(whilst interpreting neutral monism as a form of dualism and ignoring idealistic monism). Whereas neutral monism has nothing to say about substance
as such except that physical and mental aspects of an object are identical
with this one type of substance; whereas idealistic monism claims that the
one type of substance is mental; and whereas realistic monism claims that
the one type of substance is physical (material), anomalous monism claims
that while there is only one type of event (one type of substance) that does
not mean that mental (psychological) events can be explained in terms of
physical events, or can be reduced to physical events. This is because there
are no laws which reduce all mental events to physical events.

5.14   TYPES

The introduction of the word *events* is important for Davidson, since it
performs the role of providing the one substance out of which mental and
physical events are somehow derived. And mental and physical events are
linguistic descriptions:

> What does it mean to say that an event is mental or physical?
> One natural answer is that an event is physical if it is describable
> in a purely physical vocabulary, mental if describable in mental
> terms. (Davidson, 1970, p. 210)

An event *per se* is not physical or mental: it is only its possibility of being
described in physical or mental terms that makes it physical or mental. The

notion of mental then requires clarification: if mental events refer to events
that take place in the mind only, then we may well end up with two sorts of
substance, or events - a form of dualism - rather than one. Davidson writes
on this point:

> [T]he distinguishing feature of the mental is not that it is
> private, subjective, or immaterial, but that it exhibits what Bren-
> tano called *intentionality*. Thus intentional actions are clearly
> included in the realm of the mental along with thoughts, hopes,
> and regrets (or the events tied to these). (Davidson, 1970, p.
> 211, stress added)

Davidson provides this account of intentional actions (which he admits is
incomplete and unsatisfactory but which nevertheless may be true):

> [A]n action is performed with a certain intention if it is caused
> in the right way by attitudes and beliefs that rationalize it.
> (Davidson, 1978, p. 87)

That is, rationalization is a form of causal explanation, based on beliefs
and attitudes, of the action performed with a certain intention. As we can
see, this part of Davidson's framework is beginning to look quite complex,
especially when he includes feelings of pain and after-images as exhibiting
intentionality also.

Davidson also believes (as he must if he is not to encounter difficulties)
that laws and explanations are linguistic items:

> Mental events as a class cannot be explained by physical sci-
> ence .... (Davidson, 1970, p. 225)

> Causality and identity are relations between individual events
> no matter how described. But laws are linguistic; and so events
> can instantiate laws, and hence be explained or predicted in the
> light of laws, only as those events are described in one way or
> another. (Davidson, 1970, p. 215)

We should now have a better understanding of what exactly what Davidson
has in mind. He is attacking the view, called *Type-Type Identity Theory*,
which claims that mental or psychological event types are identical with

neurophysiological event types. It may be useful to digress for a short while to say something about types before returning to this point.

The word *type* is commonly used in both computer science and mathematical logic, and whilst there are some similarities in the way types are used in these two areas there are also some important differences. First, let us look at *type* in a computer science context, where the term is most frequently used in conjunction with the word *data*:

> The primary characteristics of the concept of type [as embodied in structured programming languages] are the following:
>
> 1. A data type determines the set of values to which a constant belongs, or which may be assumed by a variable or an expression, or which may be generated by an operator or a function.
>
> 2. The type of a value denoted by a constant, variable, or expression may be derived from its form or its declaration without the necessity of executing the computational process.
>
> 3. Each operator or function expects arguments of a fixed type and yields a result of a fixed type. If an operator admits arguments of several types (e.g. + is used for addition of both integers and real numbers), then the type of result can be determined from specific language rules.
>
> (Wirth, 1976, p.4)

For computer scientists, data types allow the specification of values which constants and variables can take, as well as determining what type of value is to be returned by operators and functions. In addition, data types must be declared in the computer program so that the value of constants, variables and expressions can be inferred from the text of the program rather than from the execution of the program. Finally, data types are used for specifying the expectations of operators or functions with regard to their arguments. (The notion of data type has led to the development of *abstract data types*, where the programmer can generate within a program unit new types and operators such that the representation of a type and the implementation of its operators are hidden from the rest of the program: the new type name and the specifications of the operations are nevertheless visible to other program units so that they too can declare within their own scope objects of the new type.)

Historically, the motivation for types in *mathematical logic* arose out of several paradoxes that Russell and other logicians noted concerning various 'self-referring' expressions (see Volume 1, Chapter 3, Section 10) and resulted in Russell's *theory of types*. Quine sums up this theory as follows:

> [T]he theory works as follows. We are to think of all objects as stratified into so-called types, such that the lowest type comprises individuals, the next comprises classes of individuals, the next comprises of classes of such classes, and so on. In every context, each variable is to be thought of as admitting values only of a single type. The rule is imposed, finally, that $(\alpha \in \beta)$ is to be a formula only if the values of β are of next higher type than those of α; otherwise $(\alpha \in \beta)$ is reckoned as neither true nor false, but meaningless. (Quine, 1953, p. 90)

The concept of type in the theory of types has implications for *type identity*, which can be expressed in several ways depending on the area in question. Let us use the following passage from Ayer to introduce a *formal language* account of type identity:

> A complete philosophical elucidation of any language would consist, first, in enumerating the types of sentences that were significant in that language, and then in displaying the relations of equivalence that held between sentences of various types. And here it may be explained that two sentences are said to be of the same type when they can be correlated in such a way that to each symbol in one sentence there corresponds a symbol of the same type in the other; and that two symbols are said to be of the same type when it is always possible to substitute one for the other without changing a significant sentence into a piece of nonsense. (Ayer, 1936, p.83)

This general statement of Ayer's brings out some of the essential characteristics about type-type identity. First, there is the difference between types and *tokens*. For instance,

(i) It is raining outside

$$
(a) \quad
\begin{aligned}
\textbf{sentence} \;&\rightarrow\; \textbf{noun verb} \\
\textbf{noun} \;&\rightarrow\; John | Mary \\
\textbf{verb} \;&\rightarrow\; sleeps | eats
\end{aligned}
$$

$$
(b) \quad
\begin{aligned}
\textbf{event} \;&\rightarrow\; \textbf{m\_description} | \textbf{p\_description} \\
\textbf{m\_description} \;&\rightarrow\; m_1 | m_2 | \cdots | m_n \\
\textbf{p\_description} \;&\rightarrow\; p_1 | p_2 | \cdots | p_m
\end{aligned}
$$

Figure 5.2

(ii) It is raining outside

are two *tokens* of the same sentence (type). That is, writing the same words in the same order is sufficient, from the point of view of types, to make it one sentence. The question then arises as to what other, sufficient conditions there are in other domains for allowing us to identify tokens as belonging to the same type. For instance,

(i) It is raining

(ii) Il pleut

are two different tokens of the same proposition, 'It is raining', but in this case examining the two tokens for a simple duplication of words is not sufficient for identifying that both tokens are tokens of the same proposition, as it was for the previous example. Something more, i.e. a semantic theory, is required in the second example in order to come up with the appropriate type-token distinctions.

According to Ayer, we could have two different tokens which differ in words belonging to the same type as long as there is a correlation of some sort which helps us identify, for every word or phrase in one sentence, a corresponding word or phrase in the second sentence which belongs to the same type as the word or phrase in the first sentence. For instance, imagine we had the a simple grammar (*Figure 5.2 (a)*) where a sentence consists of a noun followed by a verb. A noun in turn consists of either the symbol *John* or the symbol *Mary*. A verb is either *sleeps* or *eats*. According to this grammar, it is possible to consider the sentence tokens *John sleeps*, *Mary sleeps*, *John eats*, and *Mary eats* to be four tokens of the same *sentential type* **noun** (followed by) **verb**, since *John* and *Mary* belong to the same type, **noun**, and *eats* and *sleeps* belong to the same type, **verb**. Since **noun verb** is a form of **sentence**, it follows that all four tokens are of the same type, **sentence**.

The important point about this example is the way that we can work our way up the hierarchy of types, classifying tokens as belonging to the same type by correlating tokens of one sentence with tokens of another by moving up a level to the words' type. The correlation Ayer refers to is given in this case by the form and content of the grammar rules.

Let us return to Davidson and type-type identity. Davidson's claim is that it is not possible to provide such rules of correlation which will always classify a token description of a mental event as belonging to the same type as a physical description token. That is, if we rewrite the simple grammar as if it were a 'grammar of events' (*Figure 5.2 (b)*), where an event consists of a mental description (**m_description**) *or* a physical description (**p_description**), $m_1 \cdots m_n$ represent descriptions using mental predicates (i.e. mental events), and $p_1 \cdots p_m$ represent descriptions using physical predicates (i.e. physical events), the rules of the grammar are such that it is not possible to always correlate a token p_i with token m_j via the types to which the tokens belong, since there is no level within the grammar at which **m_description** is a token of **p_description**, or vice versa. Instead, according to our grammar, **m_description** and **p_description** are themselves tokens of the one type, **event**.

This does not mean that there are no identities between tokens, and in fact Davidson supports a particular form of *token-token* identity thesis, where every mental event token is identical with some physical event token, but not necessarily the other way around:

> Anomalous monism shows an ontological bias only in that
> it allows the possibility that not all events are mental, while
> insisting that all events are physical. (Davidson, 1970, p. 214)

This takes us back to the concept of supervenience introduced earlier. Two mental events of the same type are different only because there is a physical (i.e. physically describable) difference between them; hence, descriptions of individual psychological events, not sorts of events, are dependent on physical descriptions.

5.15   DESCRIBING EVENTS

That concludes our introduction to Davidson's views. We should now be able to see exactly what the point of Art was; namely, Art summarizes the logical conclusion to which neurophysiological progress can be taken. But even assuming this end-point can be reached, all that can be explained is the identity (through correlation) of particular mental states with particular brain states. But this does not allow us to conclude that mental states can be explained in terms of physical brain states, or can be reduced to physical brain states.

Lycan (1982) notes that Davidson appears to deny the possibility of explaining and predicting mental events by means of psychological laws alone, since according to Davidson there may be no such thing as psychological *laws*. Whilst this is an interesting point, let us instead highlight a possible problem for Davidson concerning the way that an event is a mental or physical event. As we have seen, a mental event is an event which is *describable* in mental terms, and a physical event is an event which is *describable* in purely physical terms. Davidson goes on to explain what he means by an event being describable in mental terms:

> We may call those verbs mental that express propositional attitudes like believing, intending, desiring, hoping, knowing, perceiving, noticing, remembering, and so on. ...Let us call a description of the form 'the event that is *M*' or an open sentence of the form 'event *x* is *M*' a *mental description* or a *mental open sentence* if and only if the expression that replaces '*M*' contains at least one mental verb essentially. ...Now we may say that an event is mental if and only if it has a mental description, or ...if there is a mental open sentence true of that event alone. Physical events are those picked out by descriptions or open sentences that contain only the physical vocabulary essentially. (Davidson, 1970, p. 211, italics supplied)

But what is meant by 'mental verb' or 'mental predicate'? Looking back at an earlier quote, where Davidson states that what he means by 'mental event' is an event *describable* in mental terms, we can infer that mental terms are distinguished from physical terms in that the former somehow are characterized by intentionality, where the latter are not. More accurately, what this must mean is that intentionality is *applied, or allocated*, to an event when the mental term is used, i.e. an event has no intentional characteristics apart from those allocated to it by some mental term. Any other interpretation may lead to a dualism between, if not mind and matter directly, intentional and non-intentional events, which in turn may be reducible to the mind/matter issue. That is, we cannot say that the mental term *implies or assumes* the event *to be* intentional, nor may we be able to say that intentionality is *ascribed* to the event, in case the notions of implication, assumption and ascription imply the event already possesses a degree of intentionality (whereas other events do not): this leads us away from monism.

Be that as it may, there are nevertheless two questions which arise for Davidson. First, there is the question of whether a mental event is an event *described* in mental terms, or *describable* in mental terms. For instance, if 'an event describable in x terms' means 'an event which *it is possible* to describe in x terms', where 'x' stands for 'mental', 'physical', and 'biological', for example, then an event which is *described* in some way is of course *describable* in that way, but it also makes sense to say that an event which is describable in some way is not actually described in that way. That is, the question for Davidson is whether it is possible that there be some event which *could* be described in a certain way, but has not actually been so described because, for instance, we are not aware of the event occurring or we are not sure that our description is the right one, or whether an event describable in a certain way just means that the event is in fact described, or has been described correctly, in that way.

Davidson could claim that with regard to mental events the answer is simple. All events are physical; therefore a mental event is a physical event which either is, or could be, described by means of a mental predicate also. However, this does not answer the previous question concerning the relationship between one describable mental event and a described mental event. Is Davidson ruling out of court such statements as: 'This physical event x *could* be described as mental event y', where 'y' incorporates some mental predicate? Or is Davidson claiming that mental events deal with actual ascriptions of mental predicates to physical events, i.e. 'real' descriptions, rather than possible ones? There seems to be a difference between, say, a brain researcher saying: 'This pattern of physical activity *could* correspond to the mental state of pain', and the same brain researcher claiming: 'This pattern of physical activity *corresponds* to the mental state of pain.' In the former, the researcher is hypothesizing, not about the relationship between a finite class of observations and a general mental type, but between one particular observation and the ascription of one particular mental predicate. The hypothesis may be based on the simple fact that the brain which is being examined belongs to someone who is currently unconscious, for example. It is not at all clear what Davidson has to say on this matter.

The second question for Davidson is whether all he has done is just move dualism out of the world (i.e. events) into language (i.e. physical and mental predicates). The main reason why his metaphysical theory works at all may simply be that the problem has shifted away, from being a problem of the nature of the stuff that makes up the world, to the problem of how it is that language has two different types of predicate to start off with. When Davidson states that mental predicates *exhibit* intentionality, how is such exhibition performed or characterized, and why do certain predicates have the property of exhibiting intentionality and others not? One answer may be to state that, in the act of ascription, intentionality is exhibited, but Davidson does not say anything at all about who or what exhibits the intentionality, or how the intentionality is exhibited. For instance, if the person who makes the ascription (or allocation, or application) ascribes (allocates, applies) intentionality to an event, it is not clear that we have a mental *description* of an event: rather, we have a mental ascription (allocation, application) which may result in a description, for example, when the ascription (allocation, application) happens to be justified (given the interpretation that a description is a justified ascription). The relationship between ascription and description needs to be clarified by Davidson, and he also needs to answer the question as to why it is that certain language terms can be used in an intentionality-ascription way so that mental descriptions result, and others not. How did language come (logically) to possess these two types of predicate, given that there is only one type of event? What is the logical reason for there to be a mental description corollary to a physical description? How is it even possible, given anomalous monism, for there to be a difference in type between linguistic terms? Answers to these subquestions must of course not refer to events (physical or mental), otherwise circularity will arise.

This leads us on to some general questions concerning Davidson's approach. Why must science be characterized by the presence of 'physical laws' which know of no exception, and can such a claim ever be true? That is, Davidson may be starting from a metaphysically prescriptive base which can be tolerated as long as the resulting framework ties in with our experience of the world. If it does not, then we have no way of distinguishing a philosophically useful framework from an idealistic 'story'. How does science progress, and does the word 'progress' mean anything in a Davidsonian framework?

Davidson may well be able to provide satisfactory answers to these questions. What we have done is to point out that even in a carefully constructed philosophical framework, whilst some problems may indeed be satisfactorily explained, others pop up in unexpected places.

5.16 AI AND CONSCIOUSNESS

Let us return to the question which prompted our discussion of the views of the three contemporary philosophers above: 'Is it the case that solely in virtue of running a computer program of the appropriate sort a machine can be said to think, or understand, or have experiences?' So far, we have tackled this question as if it were a rephrasing of the general question, 'Can machines think, understand, or have experiences?' (i.e. 'Can machines be conscious?') and examined the views of three philosophers concerning the concepts of thinking, understanding and having experiences. We now examine the implications of their views with regard to the Argument from Consciousness. Also, for the sake of completeness, we shall try to explore the implications of their views for the Argument from Informality of Behaviour.

Given our exposition of Dennett's views, it is tempting to say that Dennett would answer the question in the positive. That is, an appropriately programmed computer could *be said* to think, understand and have experiences, *provided that* we understand this to mean that an intentional stance of some sort has been adopted towards that computer. The adoption of such a stance is not logically necessary: all that such a stance implies is that from a predictive and explanatory point of view (i.e. for the sake of simplicity) we are justified in the ascription of mental terms to programs and processes. The justification would then consist in part, as we saw earlier, of an appeal to the design and physical stances. The further question of whether a computer could do other than it is programmed to do (Argument from Informality of Behaviour) would not arise as such for Dennett, since this question depends on the entity under discussion being rational, where rationality is a normative concept, i.e. an entity's beliefs are those it ought to have given its biological needs and the means of satisfying them. Since we assume a computer to be rational for the sake of explanatory and predictive simplic-

ity, rather than for the sake of counterfactual analysis, the question concerns
the intentions of the (human) *programmer* or *designer* and not the program
or computer. So Dennett would probably answer the second question negatively. Dennett therefore represents a philosophical view which would not
rule out the possibility of statements involving mental terms being used with
regard to the behaviour of computers, provided that we acknowledge that
the computer does not *really* possess the mental states ascribed to it by the
terms.

Searle, however, would, and does, answer the question negatively. That
is, according to Searle, it *cannot* be the case that a computer, solely in virtue
of running a computer program, could think, understand or have experiences,
or even be said to think, understand or have experiences. For Searle, statements using mental terms made of computers are attempted descriptions
which fail significantly to be descriptions at all. Computers can only manipulate formal structures and therefore deal only with syntactic elements.
There is more to thinking, understanding and having experiences than these
syntactic elements. Therefore, computers cannot be said to think, understand or have experiences. The only entities which can think, understand
or have experiences are those which can grasp and manipulate the semantic aspects of mental states and processes, and this is possible only if those
entities have a brain which has sufficient causal power to produce minds
which grasp and manipulate such non-syntactic aspects of mental states and
processes. What it means for an entity to have a brain of sufficient causal
power requires analysis at the level of neurophysiology and biology as well as
of intentionality and semantics (which are biologically-caused phenomena).
Since programs are defined purely syntactically, it follows that computers
cannot think, understand or have experiences. Instead, the only entities
which can think, understand and have experiences, and can be said to think,
understand and have experiences, are those machines which have the causal
power of the brain. With regard to the question of whether a computer could
do other than it does (Argument from Informality of Behaviour), Searle's
answer would be negative, since the notion of an entity doing something
other than it does (in the sense of different behaviour or different mental
processes and states) requires a semantic or intentional analysis, and such
analysis would necessarily be beyond a computer manipulating a purely formal structure such as a program. Again, the only entities (machines) of
which it makes sense to ask this further question would be those which had
a sufficiently powerful brain, and computers cannot have such a brain since
computers manipulate only formal structures. Searle therefore represents

a philosophical view closest in spirit to the original Argument from Consciousness, with the twist that Searle further believes that we humans are essentially machines, albeit machines of a very particular type, namely, with brains of sufficient causal power to generate minds. The idea that there is something intrinsically human in the notion of doing something other than is the case may therefore be a notion to which Searle is not committed.

Davidson's views are more extreme in their implication. If Searle represents a view closest in spirit to the original Argument from Consciousness, Davidson essentially presents a modern version of it which, if true, destroys even Searle's position if Searle claims that biology and neurophysiology, as sciences, can help explain mental phenomena and mental processes. According to Davidson, there are, and can be, only correlations between physical events and mental events at the individual level, i.e. there can only be knowledge of the physical correlate to individual acts or movements, and there can only be knowledge of one mental description being correlated with a (suitable) physical description. There are, and can be, no (general and universal) *laws* which correlate the mental with the physical. This then means that it is not possible to *identify* mental phenomena with brain states at the level of anything other than individual events. Nor is it possible to conclude, from an understanding of the biological and neurophysiological workings of the brain, that an entity which possesses a brain has certain types of mental states or processes: all we have are statistical relationships between classes of events based on individual correlations, and statistical relationships are not laws and therefore cannot provide genuine knowledge. Davidson also uses the notion of supervenience, i.e. two mental events of the same type are different only because there is a physical (i.e. physically describable) difference between them. This does not mean, however, that there is, or must be, a physical difference between two mental events of two different types. Rather, we have no grounds for believing that there is any lawlike relationship between physical and mental events, since laws, by definition for Davidson, operate at the level of generality and universality and hence at the level of types. It therefore looks as if Davidson would certainly disagree with the view that solely in virtue of running a program of the right sort a computer can be said to think, understand or have experiences, since 'think', 'understand' and 'have experiences' are predicates which signify classes, or sorts, of mental phenomena for which there can be no physical descriptions related to them in a lawlike way. We probably also cannot write such a program even if wanted to, since presumably in order to write such a program we need to map, in a lawlike way, types of physical event with types of mental event, or at the very least relate types of mental event to other types of mental event, neither of which appears to be possible. The further question of whether a computer could do something other than it does (the Argument from Informality of Behaviour) with regard to mental states can only be answered if we had some principled way of distinguishing a mental event of one type from a mental event of another type, and in the absence of any laws relating physical differences with mental differences it is not even worth trying to start answering this question.

Davidson is expressing a radical view which threatens Searle's fundamental axiom that brains cause minds: brains can only cause minds if lawlike relationships exist between mental states and brain states, e.g. mental states are reduced to brain states. If no such laws exist, brains cannot cause minds, if that means that brain state types cause mind state types. All that can be said, according to Davidson, is that one particular brain state is correlated with one particular mental state, but that does not mean that in future (or in the past) the same brain state will cause (has caused) the same mental state. In fact, there probably cannot be any such thing as *the same* brain state, since there is almost certainly some physical difference (or, as Davidson puts it, some physically describable difference) between a brain state occurring at one time and what looks like the same brain state occurring at another time. Because of this physical difference, we may have two different mental events, and that is as far as we can go in our attempt to generalize from brain states to mental states. Davidson's views therefore question even the validity of Searle's own thesis that only machines of a certain type, namely, those which have the causal power of the brain, can think.

What we have done is to attempt to bring the Argument from Consciousness up-to-date and to present three different versions of it which represent a philosophical spectrum. (We have had to ignore a fourth, substantial (and varied) school of thought on the issue of the relationship between brain and mind, namely *functionalism*. Some of the papers in Biro and Shahan (1982) provide a good introduction to this subject.) One of our other tasks has been to show that any discussion concerning what it means for an entity (human or computer) to be a rule-follower, or for the behaviour of an entity to be determined or guided by rules, presupposes - in the context of the Argument from Informality of Behaviour - some philosophical stand on the relationship between mind and brain. Whichever stand is adopted, there will be implications of the relationship between mind and brain for the nature of the rules which an entity can or cannot follow, or for describing and explaining behaviour the nature of which can or cannot be subsumed under physical (scientific) laws.

The main aim in this chapter has been to show that when Turing first proposed the Argument from Consciousness as an objection, it was sufficient for him to provide, as we saw in Chapter 1, a simple answer along the lines that the Argument led to a solipsistic point of view, whereby anyone who seriously proposed this objection would have difficulty in justifying ascription of consciousness to other human beings, never mind machines. Turing's own proposal was for his Imitation Game to be used as a test for ascribing consciousness, but, as we have seen in this chapter (especially given the advances proposed by Dennett), this form of naive logical behaviourist response is not credible: he could not hope to escape with such an answer if he were to reply to the objection in the same way today. Progress in philosophy of mind has been substantial during the past three decades, to the extent that it could be argued that the Argument from Consciousness is the core objection that AI researchers and philosophers have to face.

This chapter has concerned itself with *whether* proposals exist for explaining the relationship between mind and consciousness, and if so *what form* the relationship takes. We concentrated on what is meant by 'mental events and processes' and the proposed relationships between mental events and processes, on the one hand, and consciousness on the other. We are now in a position to rephrase the original Argument from Consciousness objection as follows:

> What precisely is the relationship between the concepts of thinking, understanding and experiencing, on the one hand, and the concepts of mental events and processes on the other? Furthermore, what exactly is the relationship between mental events and processes, on the one hand, and consciousness, on the other? Finally, what are the implications of proposed relationships (first, between thinking, understanding, and experiencing on the one hand and mental events and processes on the other; and secondly between mental events and processes on the one hand and consciousness on the other) for the notion of "intelligent machine"?

This is a complex question, but nevertheless we claim that it is a modern rephrasing of the original Argument from Consciousness objection, given developments in philosophy of mind since 1950. We have only been able to present a restricted set of answers to these questions in this chapter:

the answers we have looked at should give a flavour of the sort of debate that needs to be conducted when tackling these questions. Turing's original answer to the objection, which was to say that an extreme version of this objection was simply that the only way to be certain that a machine thinks would be to *be* that machine and to feel oneself thinking, would not be considered to be adequate. What the above rephrasing shows is that the objection is in fact a complex one, and must be tackled head-on by any AI researcher who wishes to make claims about the mental life of machines.

Our next task is to examine *how* relationships between mind and brain can biologically and neurophysiologically exist at all. That is, we need to examine the underlying *mechanics* (not the logical mechanism) of proposed relationships between mind and *brain*. This leads us naturally to the next objection which Turing formulated (and the last which we shall examine in the two volumes), namely, the Argument from Continuity in the Nervous System.

References

Ayer, A. J. (1936) *Language, Truth and Logic*. Victor Gollancz. Reprinted by Penguin, 1971, from which the page reference is taken.

Biro, J. I. and Shahan, R. W. (eds.) (1982) *Mind, Brain, and Function*. Harvester Press.

Carr, B. (1987) *Metaphysics: An Introduction*. Macmillan Education.

Chomsky, N. (1976) *Reflections on Language*. Temple Smith.

Davidson, D. (1970) Mental events, in L. Foster and J. W. Swanson (eds.) *Experience and Theory*, The University of Massachusetts Press and Duckworth, 1970. Reprinted in D. Davidson, *Essays on Actions and Events*, Clarendon Press, 1980, from which the page references are taken.

Davidson, D. (1973) The material mind, in P. Suppes et al. (eds.), *Logic, Methodology and Philosophy of Science*, North Holland. Reprinted in J. Haugeland (ed.) *Mind Design*, MIT Press, 1981. The page references are to the reprinted version.

Davidson, D. (1978) Intending, in Y. Yovel (ed.) *Philosophy of History and Action*, Reidel and The Magnes Press. Reprinted in D. Davidson, *Essays on Actions and Events*, Clarendon Press, 1980, from which the page reference is taken.

Dennett, D. C. (1981) *Brainstorms*. Harvester Press.

Dennett, D. C. (1982) Making sense of ourselves, in J. I. Biro and R. W. Shahan (eds.) (1982).

Frankfurt, H. (1971) Freedom of the will and the concept of a person, *Journal of Philosophy*, LXVIII.

Griffiths, A. P. (1962/63) On belief, *Proceedings of the Aristotelian Society*, LXIII, 167-186.

Grice, H. P. (1957) Meaning, *Philosophical Review*, LXVI, 377-388.

Grice, H. P. (1968) Utterer's meaning, sentence meaning, and word-meaning, *Foundations of Language*, 4, 225-242.

Lycan, W. G. (1982) Psychological laws, in J. I. Biro and R. W. Shahan (eds.) (1982).

Mach, E. (1960) *The Science of Mechanics*. Open Court (translated by T. J. McCormick.

Quine, W. V. O. (1953) *From a Logical Point of View*. Harvard University Press. Second revised edition, Harper and Row, 1961, from which the page reference is taken.

Russell, B. (1914) On the nature of acquaintance, reprinted in R. C. Marsh (ed.) *Logic and Knowledge* (Essays of Russell 1901-1950), George Allen and Unwin, 1956, from which the page references are taken.

Searle, J. R. (1980) Minds, brains, and programs, *The Behavioral and Brain Sciences*, **3**, 417-424. Reprinted in J. Haugeland (ed.) (1981) *Mind Design*, MIT Press; and in D. R. Hofstadter and D. C. Dennett (eds.) (1981) *The Mind's I: Fantasies and Reflections on Self and Soul*, Penguin.

Searle, J. R. (1987) Minds and brains without programs, in C. Blakemore and S. Greenfield (eds.) *Mindwaves*, Blackwell.

Stich, S. P. (1982) Dennett on intentional systems, in J. I. Biro and R. W. Shahan (eds.) (1982).

Strawson, P. F. (1959) *Individuals*. Methuen.

Wirth, N. (1976) *Algorithms + Data Structures = Programs*. Prentice Hall.

Chapter 6

Neurocomputing

6.1 INTRODUCTION

The Argument from Continuity in the Nervous System is the objection that machines are discrete devices with discrete, identifiable states, whereas the nervous system is continuous. Turing's formulation of this objection to his Imitation Game was that, since it is not possible to simulate or mimic the behaviour of the nervous system with a discrete-state system, and since thought and intelligence are based on a continuous system, machines cannot think or be intelligent. Turing's own response was to say that the objection made no difference to his Imitation Game and the way it is played.

Turing's dismissive response was appropriate, given the way he formulated the objection in the first place, but we now wish to explore the more substantive points lying behind this objection and bring the objection up-to-date, as far as its relevance to artificial intelligence is concerned. First, there is the question of the relationship between continuous devices and systems, on the one hand, and, on the other, discrete devices and systems which are meant in some sense to be 'models' or simulations of their continuous counterparts. Ashby (1956) presents the following argument in defence of the idea of discrete modeling of continuous systems and devices (and thereby provides a more detailed answer to the Argument from Continuity in the Nervous System than that provided by Turing):

> The most fundamental concept in cybernetics is that of "difference", either that two things are recognizably different or that

> one thing has changed with time. ... Often a change occurs con-
> tinuously, that is, by infinitesimal steps, as when the earth moves
> through space, or a sunbather's skin darkens under exposure.
> The consideration of steps that are infinitesimal, however, raises
> a number of purely mathematical difficulties, so we shall avoid
> their consideration entirely. Instead, we shall assume in all cases
> that the changes occur by finite steps in time and that any dif-
> ference is also finite. We shall assume that the change occurs by
> a measurable jump, as the money in a bank account changes by
> at least a penny. Though this supposition may seem artificial in
> a world in which continuity is common, it has great advantages
> in [an introductory book on cybernetics] and is not as artificial
> as it seems. When the differences are finite, all the important
> questions ... can be decided by simple counting, so that it is
> easy to be quite sure whether we are right or not. Were we to
> consider continuous changes we would often have to compare in-
> finitesimal against infinitesimal, or to consider what we would
> have after adding together an infinite number of infinitesimals -
> questions by no means easy to answer. (Ashby, 1956, p. 9)

Having provided the fundamental assumption of cybernetics (and also of any
attempt to simulate continuous systems with discrete models, which would
include substantial areas of science and social science), Ashby then provides
a basic idea of what the mathematical techniques for such simulation would
look like:

> As a simple trick, the discrete can often be carried over into
> the continuous, in a way suitable for practical purposes, by mak-
> ing a graph of the discrete, with the values shown as separate
> points. It is then easy to see the form that the change will take if
> the points were to become infinitely numerous and close together.
> ... In fact, however, by keeping the discussion to the case of the
> finite difference we lose nothing. For having established with cer-
> tainty what happens when the differences have a particular size
> we can consider what happens when they are smaller. When this
> case is known with certainty we can consider what happens when
> they are smaller still. We can progress in this way, each step be-
> ing well established, until we perceive the trend; then we can say
> that what is the limit as the difference tends to zero. This, in
> fact, is the method that the mathematician always does use if he

> wants to be really sure of what happens when the changes are
> continuous. (Ashby, 1956, pp. 9-10)

Later, after introducing his notation for describing discrete transformations,
Ashby provides this further defence of the use of approximation techniques
and in so doing provides a certain philosophical view of natural systems:

> At this point it may be objected that most machines, whether
> man-made or natural, are smooth-working, while the transforma-
> tions that have been discussed so far [in Ashby's book] change
> by discrete jumps. These discrete transformations are, however,
> the best introduction to the subject. ...Their great advantage
> is their absolute freedom from subtlety and vagueness, for every
> one of their properties is unambiguously either present or absent.
> This simplicity makes possible a security of deduction that is es-
> sential if further developments are to be reliable. ...In any case
> the discrepancy is of no real importance. The discrete change
> has only to become small enough in its jump to approximate
> as closely as is desired to the continuous change. It must fur-
> ther be remembered that in natural phenomena the observations
> are almost invariably made at discrete intervals; the "continu-
> ity" ascribed to natural events has often been put there by the
> observer's imagination, not by actual observations at each of an
> infinite number of points. Thus the real truth is that *the natu-
> ral system is observed at discrete points*, and our transformation
> represents it at discrete points. There can, therefore, be no real
> incompatibility. (Ashby, 1956, p. 28, stress supplied)

We have quoted Ashby at length since it is important to understand some of
the basic assumptions that formulators of discrete models of natural systems
either take for granted or may themselves not be fully aware of. Ashby obviously felt the need, in 1956, to justify his approach (and that of cyberneti-
cians in general) in this way, and there is little doubt that such justifications
and defence are not questioned to any great extent by the majority of the
scientific community (and this would include the AI community). Another
reason for quoting Ashby is that we now have a way of replying in part to
Argument from Continuity in the Nervous System, namely, that mathematical techniques do exist for successfully simulating the continuous behaviour
of the nervous system.

However, there is a second part to the objection, overlooked by Turing, which is that *even if* such mathematical techniques can be successfully used for constructing models of the nervous system or machines which simulate the nervous system, that does not mean that machine intelligence and thought are possible. The further task for the model and simulation proposers is to demonstrate how it is possible for machine intelligence and thought to arise or emerge from, or be explained in terms of, the model or simulation of the nervous system. If the requirement for a demonstration is too strong, then at the very least the formulators of such models and simulations should be explicit in what they see to be the relationship between their models and simulations, on the one hand, and the concepts of intelligence and thought, on the other. In this way, some comparisons can be made between different models and simulations, as far as their relevance to AI is concerned. One of the tasks of this chapter is to examine, for AI concepts, the implications of such proposed relationships.

The chapter will start with a brief, historical survey of the development of an area now called *cognitive science*. This is important for appreciating a certain, fundamental, view in cognitive science which can, *very generally*, be called *computationalism*. We shall then outline the basic ideas of *connectionism* - a form of neurocomputing but by no means the only form. For example, the use of approximation techniques in cybernetics for modeling real neural systems can also, according to our general view, be called a form of neurocomputing. (We shall provide further justifications for distinguishing between neurocomputing and connectionism later in this chapter.) This will then lead us to a discussion of the differences between these two views and of attempts at reconciliation. Finally, we shall attempt to formulate contemporary versions of the Argument from Continuity in the Nervous System, from the point of view of neurocomputing and computationalism.

6.2   COGNITIVE SCIENCE

According to most historical accounts, there are two crucial dates in the development of the area we now call *Cognitive Science*: September 1948, and September 1956 (Gardner, 1985). In September 1948, a conference entitled 'Cerebral Mechanisms in Behavior' was held at the Californian Institute of Technology; because it was sponsored by the Hixon Fund, this conference is better known as the Hixon Symposium. It was during this conference that the first serious challenge to the then predominating paradigm in psychology - behaviourism - was issued. Speakers at this conference included John Von Neumann, who compared the electronic computer with the brain, Warren McCulloch, who discussed how the brain processed information, and Karl Lashley, who proposed various building blocks for the discipline that was later to become cognitive science. In addition, Warren McCulloch with Walter Pitts in 1943 had showed how the operations of a nerve cell and its connections with other nerve cells could be described in terms of the propositional calculus. Together, these contributions were generally in the area that we would now call *neurocomputing*.

In September 1956, a Symposium on Information Theory was held at the Massachusetts Institute of Technology (MIT). Several speakers who were later to grow in prominence gave presentations at this conference, including George Miller (who spoke about the limits of short term memory), Noam Chomsky (who argued for the advantages of a transformational grammar approach over the more limited information-theoretical approach provided by Claude Shannon), and Newell and Simon (who described their 'logic theory machine'). Taken together, these contributions, with their emphasis on the role of symbols and the processes required to manipulate these symbols so that explanations of internal cognitive processes and outward behaviour could be provided, were early ones in the area that we would now label computationalism. (Gardner (1985) provides a fuller historical survey.)

As a result of this symposium, as well as the earlier one, cognitive science as a discipline became internationally recognized. Among the various subdisciplines, which included computation theory, cybernetics, information theory, and linguistics, two particular themes began to emerge: the first was to place emphasis on the human mind as a type of *symbol manipulating and processing device*; the other was to place emphasis on the neurophysiological properties of the human brain. The former theme we have labeled 'computationalism' and the latter 'neurocomputing'.

During the first decade or so after 1956, these two themes of cognitive science - those of computationalism and neurocomputing - were researched into with vigour. Then in 1969 appeared Minsky and Papert's *Perceptrons* (Minsky and Papert, 1969), which popularly is believed to have pointed out the shortcomings of the neurocomputing approach to cognitive science. Their criticisms of neurocomputing carried weight because both authors had themselves been neurocomputing researchers, and when they concluded that in general a neurocomputing approach could not distinguish between the global and local components of an important class of problems (i.e. could not distinguish between those aspects of a solution to a problem which were peculiar to that problem alone, as opposed to those aspects of a solution to a problem which were generalizable to other problems of the same class), whereas a computationalist approach could make such distinctions, their views were widely respected. Financially as well academically, neurocomputing subsequently during the 1970s received little support in comparison to its computationalist counterpart.

It is interesting to quote at length Papert, who in 1988 gave the following retrospective view of the importance of, and background to, *Perceptrons* from the viewpoint of a neurocomputing researcher:

> Once upon a time two daughter sciences were born to the new science. ...One sister was natural, with features inherited from the study of the brain, from the way nature does things. The other was artificial, related from the beginning to the use of computers. Each of the sister sciences tried to build models of intelligence, but from different materials. The natural sister built models (called neural networks) out of mathematically purified neurones. The artificial sister built her models out of computer programs. ...In the first bloom of youth the two were equally successful and equally pursued by suitors from other fields of knowledge. They got on very well together. Their relationship changed in the early sixties when a new monarch appeared, one with the largest coffers ever seen in the kingdom of the sciences: Lord DARPA, the Defense Department's Advanced Research Projects Agency. The artificial sister grew jealous and was determined to keep for herself the access to Lord DARPA's research funds. The natural sister would have to be slain. ...The bloody work was attempted by two staunch followers of the artificial sister, Marvin Minsky and Seymour Papert, cast in the role of the huntsman sent to slay Snow White and bring back her heart as the proof of the deed. Their weapon was not a dagger but the mightier pen, from which came a book - *Perceptrons* - purporting to prove that neural nets could never fill the promise of building models of mind: *only computer programs could do this*. Victory seemed assured for the artificial sister. And indeed, for the next decade all the rewards of the kingdom came to her progeny, of which the family of expert systems did best in fame and fortune. (Papert, 1988, pp. 3-4, stress supplied)

Papert acknowledges that there was indeed some hostility in the energy behind the research reported in their book and some annoyance at the way that neural networks had developed, but nevertheless he still believes that the motivation was right:

> [P]art of our drive came, as we quite plainly acknowledged in our book, from the fact that funding and research energy were being dissipated on what still appears to me (since the story of new, powerful network mechanisms is seriously exaggerated) to be misleading attempts to use connectionist methods in practical applications. But most of the motivation for *Perceptrons* came from more fundamental concerns, many of which cut cleanly across the division between networkers and programmers. (Papert, 1988, pp. 4-5)

One of the subtasks of this chapter is to give substance to this particular claim, and this we shall do in the later sections. But first let us provide an introduction to the two 'daughter sciences': computationalism and neurocomputing.

6.3 COMPUTATIONALISM

Once cognitive science was launched in the 1950s, many researchers began to use information processing and computational concepts to describe and explain various cognitive phenomena. This application of the *computational metaphor* is most clearly described by Boden (1979), who states that the computational metaphor helped researchers (in particular, psychologists) generate and test hypotheses about the mind's contents and functions. (Comprehensive surveys and various examples of traditional information processing models, especially in the area of memory, are provided by a variety of authors, e.g. Winograd (1976) and Narayanan (1986)). The computational metaphor provides a philosophical motive to computationalism, or *computational theory of mind*. As Maloney (1988) points out, the philosophical assumption of computationalism is that the mind is a store of real, efficacious beliefs, desires and propositional attitudes generally. (A propositional attitude is, simply, an attitude towards an proposition. For example, in the sentence 'I wish to go home', the *proposition* is that the speaker goes home, and the *attitude* towards that proposition is a wish on the speaker's part.) A further assumption is that one's behaviour can be explained, to a large extent, by reference to one's propositional attitudes, in that variation of one's behaviour is somehow related to variation in one's propositional attitudes. From these assumptions, the questions that arise can be answered by an appeal to computationalism and representations:

> This leads to two questions. First, how is it that if behavior is driven by propositional attitudes, it is typically appropriate to the circumstances of its production? And second, if variation in behavior falls to variation in propositional attitudes, what accounts for variation among propositional attitudes? (Maloney, 1988, p. 55)

In sketching out answers to these two questions, Maloney provides a succinct overview of computationalism:

> Both questions are answered by the computational theory of mind. According to this proposal, propositional attitudes, beliefs in particular, are *representations*. An agent's (true) beliefs symbolize or represent her situation, including her external environment and internal states. As representations, beliefs can refer to, and predicate properties of, objects. When the object to which a belief refers itself exists and has the property ascribed to it by the belief, the belief is true. Should an agent's behavior result from true beliefs, the behavior has a fair chance of being appropriate to the agent's circumstances. This [is] since behavior is caused by belief in a surprising way. Beliefs so cause behavior that the cluster of beliefs implicated in causing a bit of behavior is, as a sequence of representations, a *derivation* of the behavior. ... Put differently, behavior is typically appropriate to an agent's situation because it is normally both the causal result, and inferential consequence, of true beliefs. Behavior, then, is a matter of inference .... (Maloney, 1988, p. 55, italics supplied in both cases)

As for the second question:

> If behavior is inferentially powered, then variation among propositional attitudes is nothing more than the sort of propagation displayed within inferences. Beliefs arise in the manner

> of theorems; they are the inferential consequences of prior beliefs.
> A sequence of beliefs may, as a physical configuration, cause a
> new belief to occur. And what insures that the internal effect
> of a sequence of beliefs is itself a belief is that the elements in
> its collective cause constitute a proof. The effect of such a se-
> quence, therefore, represents whatever the proof suffices to es-
> tablish. (Maloney, 1988, p. 56)

Whilst this serves as a starting point in our introduction to computationalism, we must remember that computationalists will have different interpretations of what a computational theory of mind consists of. For example,
computationalists may agree to a large extent that the mind is a sort of inferential system but disagree on the issue of what sort of inferential system
(logical versus non-logical); and they may agree that inferences operate on
representations but disagree with the idea that inferences are defined over
propositions or other structures encoded in a mental language within the
brain (propositional versus image-based representations). Also, pragmatic
cognitive scientists, especially those working in applied AI research, may not
be at all interested in the philosophical points outlined above; they may instead be concerned with more practical matters. For instance, Winograd and
Flores, in their critique of the *rationalistic*, logic-based tendencies in cognitive science (which is an example of computationalism, as we have described
it), provide the following overview of AI research:

> In general, artificial intelligence researchers make use of for-
> mal logical systems (such as predicate calculus) for which the
> available operations and their consequences are well understood.
> They set up correspondences between formulas in such a system
> and the things being represented in such a way that the opera-
> tions achieve the desired veridicality [i.e. results which are correct
> relative to the domain]. There is a great deal of argument as to
> the most important properties of such a formal system, but the
> assumptions that underlie all of the standard approaches can be
> summarized as follows:
>
> 1. There is a structure of formal symbols that can be manip-
>   ulated according to a precisely defined and well-understood
>   system of rules;
>
> 2. There is a mapping through which the relevant properties of
>   the domain can be represented by symbol structures. This

> mapping is systematic in that a community of programmers
> can agree as to what a given structure represents.
>
> 3. There are operations that manipulate the symbols in such a
>   way as to produce veridical results - to derive new structures
>   that represent the domain in such a way that the program-
>   mers would find them accurate representations. Programs
>   can be written that combine these operations to produce
>   desired results.
>
> (Winograd and Flores, 1986, p. 85)

Winograd and Flores therefore highlight the use of logic (specifically predicate calculus), the agreement that AI programmers can have in principle
on what objects a formal system represents, and the goal-directed aspect of
applied AI research in their characterization of 'programming as representation'. Despite such differences in goal and method, Maloney is probably
correct in his general overview of what holds AI and computationalism together:

> It is easy to see why computationalism goes hand in glove
> with Artificial Intelligence. For according to computationalism
> the mind is exactly like a programmable computer. Both are
> systems whose internal activities are traced in terms of compu-
> tationally characterized transformation. Both, then, essentially
> rely upon alterations of their theoretically relevant states occur-
> ring in accordance with certain principles insuring that their out-
> puts can be viewed as rational relative to assignment of content
> to their internal states. (Maloney, 1988, p. 56)

This section has introduced the important concept (from our point of view
as well as from the viewpoint of computationalism) of *representation*. According to computationalism, propositional attitudes and beliefs are, quite
simply, representations. Moreover, the contents of representations function
not only to separate internal states of the computer but also to serve as input
to transformations (inferences) the task of which is to enable the computer
to switch to another state. The behaviour of the computer can then be
described as a function of transformations on specific contents of representational states; the behaviour of the computer can also be described as being
caused by the computer switching states according to the contents of the
states being transformed to derive new states. The main idea that we have

to grasp here is that, for representations to have *content*, representations also have a *form* which can be used for deriving the content. Transformations on representations may therefore use either representational form, or representational content, or both, as a basis for input, and the transformations may then cause a switch of state. We shall see later how this aspect of representations is important for identifying one of the major disagreements between computationalists and neurocomputing researchers.

Kintsch (1984) provides the following, supportive statement on representations from the point of view of a computational psychologist:

> Formally, a representation can be considered as some function of a stimulus that encodes it internally. Performance is obtained by operating on the internal representation with another function, the output function. The problem is that both the representation itself and the encoding and output functions must be inferred from the observable stimuli and responses. Nevertheless, we like to infer internal representations because we believe that the scientifically interesting regularities reside at that level, rather than in the behavior itself. (Kintsch, 1984, p. 130)

Another, more contentious, aspect of computationalism is the appeal to *modules* and *encapsulated systems*, whereby the mind is seen as being organized, architecturally, into sub-units which are specialized in the cognitive tasks they perform. At a gross, *horizontal* level, we may have a module for natural language understanding and one for visual processing. At a finer level, the natural language understanding module may consist, *vertically*, of sub-modules which specialize in syntax recognition and semantics extraction: a module is vertically below another if the module above is dependent in some way on the module below. Typically, there would be an overall executive responsible for resolving conflicts which arise from the parallel execution of different modules. Modules may cooperate and compete with each other. Whilst there is much disagreement amongst computationalists as to what such modular organizations consist of, the forms of communication which are possible between different modules, and the precise role of the executive, there is general agreement as to the status and role of modules:

> Modules are, somehow, encapsulated. That is simply to say that the data structures available to a module are limited in size and are relatively immune to the influence of the information

> available to the system containing the module. And the modules
> may not tell their containing system all that they themselves
> know. (Maloney, 1988, p. 60)

Evidence cited on behalf of the modular hypothesis comes from Fodor (1983), where he provides an example of visual illusion: there appears to be a puddle ahead of us on the road on which we are driving during a hot day, but we know that this cannot be. Despite this, the puddle continues to appear until it disappears as we continue to drive towards it. According to Fodor and other proposers of modularity, the explanation for this is that our visual system module cannot but supply the illusory information to our executive. But our executive module, with access to other information (and perhaps other, reasoning modules) decides after evaluation that there cannot be such a puddle. Nevertheless, the executive module cannot 'switch off' the visual system module since the module is encapsulated, and therefore safe from direct control being imposed upon it by the executive module. Also, the visual system module does not have access to the same information that the executive module does and so cannot alter its own behaviour in the light of information available elsewhere in the system. Similar arguments could be applied to other, cognitively specialized tasks, therefore leading to the hypothesis that the mind is modular. However, we must not forget that this is a hypothesis not universally agreed upon even by computationalists. (See Haugeland (1985) for a critique of the modularity hypothesis.)

This is probably sufficient on computationalism, for the moment. We shall return to these central concepts once we describe the disagreements between computationalists and neurocomputing researchers. What we have tried to do is summarize the philosophical tradition which partners the information processing view of cognition, so that later discussions can take place within a philosophical context. We shall attempt wherever possible to distinguish the *methodological* differences between the two approaches from the differences in *content*, leaving the fundamentally important differences in methodology to be picked up for discussion in the next chapter.

6.4   THE REBIRTH OF NEUROCOMPUTING

Neurocomputing models (which include neural networks and connectionist networks) begin with a consideration of the brain, how it works and how it is organised. The model-builders then construct their memory theories.

For instance, the McCulloch-Pitts model of the nervous system, in which the brain is approximated to a set of binary elements (abstract neurons which are either on or off) can be used. The perceptron (originally developed by Rosenblatt (1962)) is a particular type of neuron and can be regarded as a threshold logic unit (TLU). The TLU has a number n of inputs, each associated with a real-valued weight that plays a role analogous to the 'synaptic strength' of inputs to a neuron. The total input to the TLU is an n-dimensional vector, a pattern of activity on its individual input lines. Each component of the input vector is multiplied by the weight associated with that input line and all these products are summed. The unit gives a value of 1 if this sum exceeds its threshold. Otherwise, it gives an output of 0. More formally, we can say that the output of a unit is the truth value of the expression:

$$\Sigma\,[f_i w_i] > \theta$$

where f_i is the activity on the ith input line and w_i is its weight, and θ is the threshold.

In the standard perceptron scheme each input to the TLU is the output of a feature detector that responds to the presence of some feature in an input array. Much work was done on perceptrons in the 1960s, the main task being to find a set of weights that would cause the perceptron to respond if and only if a pattern of a particular type were present in the input array. The search for an automatic procedure, known as the perceptron convergence procedure that would automatically adjust the existing weights of a TLU whenever those weights would cause the perceptron to give a wrong answer, was generally regarded as successful ((Nilsson, 1965), (Minsky and Papert, 1969)). However, it had severe limitations when used to deal with various classes of pattern recognition problems.

Neurocomputing models do not have to use perceptrons, however. Certainly, a necessary requirement for a neurocomputing researcher, when formulating a neural network, is that a type of neuron (node in the network) be constructed and various types of synaptic links (arcs) between neurons (nodes) be hypothesized: in this way, some physiological *basis* is provided for the resulting network or model. Different branches of neurocomputing can be loosely characterized by the type of neuron hypothesized (e.g. the amount of information a neuron can hold, the number and type of inputs possible to a neuron, and the type of output from a neuron), the type of link used to connect neurons (e.g. simple arithmetic values to signify synaptic strength, or more complex semantic information) as well as by the type of architecture (if any) used to organize the neurons into larger collections.

6.5 CONNECTIONISM

Let us now examine the basic tenets of one form of neurocomputing - *connectionism* - which, because of its increasing popularity, has made neurocomputing a respectable science once again in the eyes of many cognitive scientists. Connectionists reject the assumption that information (human or computer) is stored in a particular place. In their view, information is stored 'everywhere'. Distributed memories retrieve individual memory traces from complex memory traces in the same way that a filter extracts individual frequency components from a complex acoustic waveform (Rumelhart and Norman, 1981). The filter can respond to whatever frequency it is tuned for, no matter how complicated the source. As long as the individual memory traces are sufficiently different from one another there is no interaction among the stored traces. In these conditions, a distributed memory system can operate as a perfect storage and retrieval device. Storage is possible because each trace will be defined by its own pattern of activated memory elements. Links between activated elements will be formed at storage time. Retrieval is possible because at least a partial match of a search argument with a stored memory trace will be sufficient to evoke the original pattern, since memory elements are interconnected and activating one element will activate others: at most a total match will be required. The power of connectionist models resides in one memory trace interacting with others. Thus, the system can allow for similar items of information to interact with each other so that common aspects are reinforced (by an increase in the appropriate synaptic strengths) and differing aspects are cancelled out.

Another way to put this is to say that instead of having one internal element or unit responding when and only when its particular item occurs, we now have each element or unit responding to many of the possible input items. If only one item is presented at a time, it will be represented by the pattern of activity of the internal units even though no individual unit uniquely specifies the input item. Instead of a single unit or element causing particular effects on other internal representations or on motor output, the pattern of activity of many units causes those effects. It now becomes unnecessary to have a separate higher-level unit that detects the pattern of activity and causes the appropriate effects.

Another claim made by connectionists is that even though the computer operates with processing units capable of functioning in the order of 10s or 100s of nanoseconds (a nanosecond is a thousand millionth of a second), the brain consists of processing units that operate in the order of milliseconds (thousandths of a second). Yet the brain can perform within those milliseconds processing feats that cannot be emulated in hundreds of minutes of computer time. The conclusion is that the brain accomplishes this feat through the simultaneous operation of many processing units. So, executives and sequentially organized stages of processing are rejected, and a distributed processing system is substituted. Complex computations are assumed to be carried out through the concurrent action of an enormous number of independent processing units, each carrying out its own simple computations or reacting only to its own local set of inputs.

Connectionists argue for parallel processing on the grounds that we humans have the ability to recognize items uniquely when given only a partial description of it. The item often 'just comes to mind', with no awareness of any deliberate searching. Moreover, we can do this with no prior warning of the description to come. Connectionists argue that this ability is difficult to program on a Von Neumann, or typical computationalist, machine. Such a machine accesses items by addresses, and it is hard to discover the address of an item from an arbitrary subset of its contents. So the Von Neumann machine, which is based on the idea of a sequential central processor operating on the contents of a passive memory, is replaced by the idea of a large set of interconnected, relatively simple processors, which interact with one another in parallel via their own specific hardware connections. Changes in the content of memory are made by forming new connections or changing the strengths of old ones. This implies that the addressing mechanism is replaced by specific hardware connections. Items correspond to patterns of activity distributed over many simple hardware units, and the ability of an address to link one item to another is implemented by modifying the strengths of many different hardware connections in such a way that the pattern of activity corresponding to one item can cause the pattern corresponding to the other item. Thus, distributed representation appears to be a particularly appropriate method of coding for a highly parallel machine.

Connectionists present a wide variety of arguments and evidence to justify the use of such properties in their models, and so our brief description which follows of such arguments will not be complete. Some of these arguments are held in common with other forms of neurocomputing.

The *neurophysiological basis* is argued for on the grounds that memory can be 'shifted' from one part of the brain to another. It appears as if parts of the brain can be reprogrammed neurophysiologically. Much research evidence is available which appears to confirm this belief, and if memory models are to describe or explain memory adequately they must encompass the neurophysiological domain. Also, more and more research is being done on functional specialization within the cortex. Anderson and Hinton (1981) claim that it is possible to distinguish about 50 different cortical areas, one of which, Area 17, is called the 'primary visual cortex'. However, this does not mean that the cortex can be easily subdivided into areas corresponding to different functions. Rather, it appears that such sub-areas of the cortex are connected together in complex ways - in series, in parallel, and with potential loops. The point here is that a single cortical area containing many millions of neurons arranged and connected together will have significant implications for cognitive function. In addition, there appears to be considerable evidence to suggest that specified changes in synaptic connectivity store memory.

The arguments for *distribution* are more contentious, and, even if such arguments are accepted, there are at least two different ways in which distribution can be achieved. The more obvious one is to construct a distributed memory where each processor corresponds to a single node of the network. Then the arcs of the network can be represented by hardware links, such as wires between units, where the units essentially are neurons. The less obvious approach is to move up a level and say that each node of a network corresponds to a particular pattern of activity *over* a large number of units. According to this approach, a node now can be interpreted as representing a concept, but the node also represents a pattern of activity at a lower *microlevel*, at the level of neurons. The implication is that interactions between concepts (i.e. on the links) are actually generated by many (perhaps millions of) simultaneous interactions at the level of their microstructures.

Three arguments are usually quoted for *parallelism*. First, proposers of parallel models appeal to empirical evidence concerning the existence of highly parallel hardware in the brain, especially in relation to vision and motor skills. Marr (1976) argued that human vision depends on many processes operating in parallel and that such parallel operations have been found to exist in the brain. Also, many neurophysiologists now accept that there is clear evidence of parallelism (and a degree of distribution) in the mammalian neocortex.

Secondly, various theoretical arguments can be proposed to demonstrate that a parallel architecture, at least at the bottom microlevel, offers a much richer and more satisfactory model of cognitive processes, such as those found in memory, than a purely sequential architecture. The implication here is that although we can simulate such parallel models on a Von Neumann machine and at a certain level of description, this does not mean that the Von Neumann concept is applicable at lower levels. It can also be argued that in certain areas, such as computer vision, a parallel architecture is more successful than a sequential architecture. That is, whilst for certain tasks, such as chess-playing and problem-solving, the sequential mode of operation corresponds closely to observations of how humans on the surface tackle these problems and also to verbal reports from those involved in the task, the connectionist claim is that there are unconscious processes which demand the use of a parallel architecture.

And thirdly, there is the '100-step program constraint' first highlighted by Feldman (1985) and summarized by Rumelhart, Hinton and McClelland (1986) as follows:

[T]he operations in our models can be characterized as "neurally inspired". We wish to replace the "computer metaphor" as a model of the mind with the "brain metaphor" as model of mind. This leads us to a number of considerations which further inform and constrain our model building efforts. Perhaps the most crucial of these is time. Neurons are remarkably slow relative to components in modern computers. Neurons operate in the time scale of milliseconds whereas computer components operate in the time scale of nanoseconds - a factor of 10^6 faster. This means that human processes that take on the order of a second or less can involve only a hundred or so time steps. Since most of the processes we have studied - perception, memory retrieval, speech processing, sentence comprehension, and the like - take about a second or so, it makes sense to impose what Feldman (1985) calls the "100-step program" constraint. That is, we seek explanations for these mental phenomena which do not require more than about a hundred elementary sequential operations. Given that the processes we seek to characterize are often quite complex and may involve consideration of large numbers of simultaneous constraints, our algorithms *must* involve considerable parallelism. Thus, although a serial computer could be created out of the kinds of components represented by our units,

> such an implementation would surely violate the 100-step pro-
> gram constraint for any but the simplest processes. (Rumelhart,
> Hinton and McClelland, 1986, p. 75, stress supplied)

It is because of these basic tenets and justifications that 'connectionism' is synonymous with the phrase *parallel distributed processing (PDP)* (PDP).

6.6 INHERITING PROPERTIES

It may be useful at this point to look at a form of distributed representation introduced by Hinton (1981), since it leads on to some points we wish to discuss later in this chapter. Briefly, Hinton's proposal allows a node to represent or correspond to a particular pattern of activity over a large number of lower units. Thus, Hinton's proposal is for an 'abstract' type of representation in that nodes (names) can stand for particular distributed patterns of activity at a lower, microstructure level. This allows Hinton to demonstrate how simple neural networks may one day perform highly 'intelligent' tasks.

Before we examine Hinton's proposal, we should say a few words on *property inheritance*. Suppose we are told that Clyde is an elephant. From this one simple fact, we immediately know a lot about Clyde which has not been explicitly mentioned. For instance, we know that Clyde is probably grey, has four legs, would not be a good pet for someone living in a basement flat, and so on. We would find it difficult to believe that all this knowledge about Clyde is stored explicitly with our recently acquired fact. Rather it appears that we have general knowledge about elephants. When we are told that Clyde is an elephant, this general knowledge is accessed by us and the general information about elephants is made available.

The importance of this example lies in the implications it has for AI. If an AI system is to serve as a model for human knowledge retrieval and storage, it must exhibit comparable speed and flexibility. We can answer almost immediately what colour Clyde is, or whether he would be a good pet for a flat, once we are given the information that Clyde is an elephant. That is, humans with brains built from elements that are very slow by computer standards are able to answer such questions very quickly and with none of the apparent mental effort that one feels when, say, adding up a column of figures.

The property inheritance problem in AI consists of finding a suitable way to represent a token (such as 'Clyde') and a type (such as 'elephant') so that the facts or properties associated with the type are inherited by the token. Two methods have traditionally been used.

(i) Duplicate all the information associated with the type and store it with the token. This approach is obviously space-consuming, and if new knowledge is acquired about the type, it must be added to all the tokens that exist.

(ii) Use a pointer which allows a token to pick up its type so that, whenever a question arises about a token which cannot be answered using the information stored at the token, the type can be inspected. We then have the idea of token-type relationships that hold between adjacent levels of property inheritance trees. Every time a question is asked which cannot be answered at that level the node's 'parent' or super-ordinate type is examined. If the question still cannot be answered at that level, then the node's super-superordinate type is examined, and so on.

The second method can be implemented using local representations in a parallel machine that needs specific hard-wired connections between the representations of types and tokens in order to allow property inheritance (Fahlman's NETL system (Fahlman, 1979)). However, Hinton adopts a different approach, in that he codes type names and token names in such a way that they have certain patterns in common at a microlevel. Any effects that are caused by the pattern for the type will automatically transfer to the patterns for the tokens (unless explicitly overridden). So property inheritance becomes automatic.

For instance, if we present the system with the following three facts, symbolically encoded:

> **has-legs (Ernie four)**
>
> **has-legs (elephant four)**
>
> **has-legs (person two)**

and ask it to recall

> **has-legs (elephant ?)**
>
> **has-legs (person ?)**

units	units	symbol
000000	000000	-
111000	000000	elephant
000111	000000	person
111000	000111	Ernie
111000	111000	Clyde
000111	101010	Scott
000111	010101	Bill

Figure 6.1

there would be no problem in retrieving the explicitly mentioned facts. Through simple pattern matching, the question marks are 'instantiated' with respect to the values **four** and **two**, respectively. But Hinton's method of distributed, as opposed to symbolic, representation is such that if the following query were input:

has-legs (Clyde ?)

the system would respond with **four** even though there has been no explicit linking of **Clyde** with **elephant** at the observed level. Also, the query

has-legs (Bill ?)

would receive the answer **two**.

The reason for this is apparent if we examine the distributed coding of these items (*Figure 6.1*), where 'patterns of activity' are used to represent the various objects. The states of the first six units code the type of object (elephant or person). The remaining six units are used to code a particular token. The similarity between the patterns for a type and a token cause them to have similar effects, which then causes the appropriate generalization. So, the pattern for **Clyde** contains the pattern for **elephant**, and the effects of this pattern are inherited by **Clyde**. Similarly, the pattern for **Bill** contains the pattern for **person**.

Hinton believes this form of distributed representation by-passes the property inheritance problem because the distributed representation of a type is made to be a constituent of the distributed representation for each token of that type. (Critics just see his 'solution' as a clever sleight of hand, since it depends on the way the items are originally coded when presented to the system and the coding has to be done by a human operator. This criticism ignores the fact that even for computationalists some degree of 'hand-coding', i.e. some degree of human involvement, is required.)

6.7 BASIC CONNECTIONIST PRINCIPLES

It is time to examine in greater detail some of the basic principles and mechanisms involved in the resurgent connectionist, or PDP, approach. Rumelhart, Hinton and McClelland (1986) provide the following summary of a general framework for PDP:

> a set of processing units
>
> a state of activation
>
> an output function for each unit
>
> a pattern of connectivity among units
>
> a propagation rule for propagating patterns of activities through the network of connectivities
>
> an activation rule for combining the inputs impinging on a unit with the current state of that unit to produce a new level of activation for the unit
>
> a learning rule whereby patterns of connectivity are modified by experience
>
> an environment within which the system must operate

We shall work through these eight points in order.

First, *processing units* can represent microfeatures, letters, words and concepts:

> [T]his is to be contrasted to a *one-unit-one-concept* representational system in which single units represent entire concepts or other large meaningful entities .... There is no executive or overseer. These are only relatively simple units, each doing its own

> relatively simple job. A unit's job is simply to receive input from
> its neighbors and, as a function of the inputs it receives, to com-
> pute an output value which it sends to its neighbors. (Rumelhart,
> Hinton and McClelland, 1986, p. 47, stress supplied)

There are three types of units: input, output, and *hidden*. Hidden units are
purely internal to the system and are used to collect activations from the
input units and to disperse activations to the output units. A network with
only input and output units is called a *single layer* network, and a network
with input, output, and one set of hidden units is called a *two-layer* network.
Multi-layer networks would consist of more than one layer of hidden units.

PDP networks can be hierarchically organized *bottom-up*, *top-down*, or
interactively. In a bottom-up organization, units at one level cannot affect
the activity of units at a level lower than that level. In a top-down organization, units at one level cannot affect the activity of units at a higher
level. In an interactive organization, there can be both bottom-up and top-
down connections. In a *restricted* interactive organization, units can only be
connected with units at an adjacent level.

Rumelhart, Hinton and McClelland stress that hierarchical structure by
itself adds no extra computational power over a single layer structure in
which input is connected directly to output: the presence of levels in fact
adds restrictions to the free flow of information across the network. However,

> ...a "one-step" system consisting of only input and output
> units and no communication between them in which there is no
> opportunity for feedback or for hidden units is less powerful than
> systems with hidden units and with feedback. (Rumelhart, Hin-
> ton and McClelland, 1986, p. 60)

Second, a description of a network consisting of n units at a certain time
point t is achieved by means of a vector a of n real numbers at time t.
$a(t)$ stands for the *pattern of activation* over the set of units at a particular
time-point t. The notation $a_i(t)$ stands for activation of unit u_i at time t.

Activation values can be continuous or discrete, and, if continuous, bounded or unbounded. If discrete, they may be binary (e.g. 0,1) or restricted to
a finite range (e.g. -1, 0, 1).

Third, associated with each unit u_i there is an *output function*, $f_i(a_i(t))$,
which maps the current state of activation of that unit, i.e. $a_i(t)$, to an output

(a)

units	u_1	u_2	u_3	u_4	u_5
u_1	0	0	0	+2	-3
u_2	0	0	0	-5	+1
u_3	0	0	0	+1	+4
u_4	0	0	0	0	0
u_5	0	0	0	0	0

(b)

units	u_1	u_2	u_3	u_4	u_5
u_1	0	0	0	+2	-3
u_2	0	0	0	-5	+1
u_3	0	0	0	+1	+4
u_4	-5	-2	-1	0	0
u_5	+1	-6	+3	0	0

Figure 6.2

signal $o_i(t)$ which is sent to its neighbours. Hence, $o_i(t) = f_i(a_i(t))$. The current set of output values is represented by the vector, $o(t)$. Typically, f is some sort of threshold function so that a unit has no effect on its neighbors unless the threshold is exceeded by the unit's activation value.

Fourth, a *pattern of connectivity* describes how the units are connected together, and an instance of this pattern at any one moment describes the values between interconnected units. For example, imagine that we had three input units and two output units, $u_1 \cdots u_5$. The *weight matrix* of *Figure 6.2 (a)* describes the pattern of connectivity as well as the strength of the connections between input and output units, assuming that the output units cannot affect the input units. The rows represent input units and the columns the output units. Input u_1 is connected to output u_4 with strength +2 and to output u_5 with strength -3.

The reason why a matrix is useful for portraying connectivity patterns is that if feedback from the output units to the input units is required other parts of the matrix can be used for describing the feedback weights. For example, given the matrix in *Figure 6.2 (b)*, output u_4 feeds back -5, -2 and -1 to inputs u_1, u_2, and u_3, respectively. In order to distinguish non-connectedness from zero value strengths, we could stipulate that all connections had to be either greater than or less than zero. Zero entries therefore denote non-connections.

Such a weight matrix is usually signified by W, in which entry w_{ij} represents the strength of the connection from unit i to unit j[1]. There could be more than one type of connection for a network, depending on the nature of the rule, or rules, of propagation. In this case, we use W_i to denote the set of connectivity matrices, where each i signifies one type of connectivity. For instance, we could use one matrix to describe all the excitatory links, and another matrix to describe all the inhibitory links.

Fifth, a *rule of propagation* takes the output vector, $o(t)$, which represents the output values of the units at one moment t and combines it with the connectivity matrix (or matrices, if the rule is a complex one) to produce a *net input* for each type of input into a unit. The notation net_{ij} signifies the net input of type i (i.e. for each W_i) to unit u_j. If there is only one type of connectivity, i.e. only one W, we can drop the first subscript: net_j. Using vector notation, we can say that $net_i(t)$ represents the net input vector for inputs of type i. A common propagation rule is one which simply *sums*, using weights, all the inputs of a certain type to a unit.

Sixth, once we have the net inputs to each unit, an *activation rule* will use these inputs to that unit to derive a new level of activation for that unit. We now need a function F which takes the current pattern of activation $a(t)$ and the vector net_j (if there is only one type of connection) to produce a new state of activation. Usually, F is a threshold function, so that the net input must exceed some value before affecting the current activation value of a unit as well as take the current activation value into account.If there is only one type of connectivity (net), we can write: $a(t+1) = F(a(t), net(t))$. That is, the state of activation of the network for each unit at time $t+1$ is the result of applying the function F to two arguments: the state of activation for each unit at time t, and the net input vector net for each unit at time t.

F is therefore the activation rule, and the nature of F will determine the nature of the PDP model. For instance, if a PDP network uses a *linear* activation rule, the model is called *linear*; similarly with *semi-linear*, *quasi-linear*, and so on. In a linear model, activation values are real and have no limits:

---

[1] In connectionist literature, w_{ij} is usually interpreted as signifying the strength and sense of the connection from unit j to unit i.

The output function, $f(a_i)$, in the linear model is just equal to the activation level a_i. Typically, linear models consist of two sets of units: a set of *input* units and a set of *output* units .... In general, any unit in the input layer may connect to any unit in the output layer. All connections in a linear model are of the same type. Thus, only a single connectivity matrix is required. (Rumelhart, Hinton and McClelland, 1986, pp. 61-62, italics supplied)

So, there is no feedback in a linear model, nor are there any hidden units between input and output. However, simple *error correction* can be incorporated in a linear model, as we shall see shortly.

Seventh, patterns of connectivity need to be modified whilst the network *learns* how to pair input with output. There are three ways this modification can take place:

> new connections can be added (e.g. a zero entry in the connection matrix, which signifies a non-connection between two units, is replaced with a non-zero entry);
>
> existing connections can be pruned (e.g. a non-zero entry in the connection matrix is replaced with zero to signify that the connection between two units has been broken); and
>
> the existing connection between two units is strengthened or weakened.

Rumelhart, Hinton and McClelland agree that more work needs to be done on *learning rules* which add and prune connections; by far the most popular type of learning rule modifies the strengths between existing connections. This form of learning generally uses some variation of the *Hebbian* learning rule (Hebb, 1949), which essentially states that if unit u_j receives an input from another unit u_i, then if they are both highly active the weight w_{ij} should be increased. We shall provide an example of such a rule soon.

And eighth, the success or failure of a connectionist network in learning how to associate input with output depends on the way the input patterns are represented and presented to the network, i.e. on the *environment*. If a connectionist network can learn to associate input patterns with output patterns only because of a particular order of presentation of input patterns, this restricts the power of such networks. If a PDP network does not learn,

	source	target
	0 0 1	0
	0 1 0	0
(a)	0 1 1	1
	1 0 0	0
	1 0 1	1
	1 1 0	0
	1 1 1	1

units	u_1	u_2	u_3	u_4
u_1	0	0	0	0.2
u_2	0	0	0	0.4
u_3	0	0	0	0.6
u_4	0	0	0	0

(b)

Figure 6.3

for instance, and we know that learning success is dependent on presentation order, we may not be able to decide whether the network failed because of the order or because of some deeper reason irrespective of the order of presentation, e.g. the form of representation is not adequate, the problem is too complex for the type of learning, propagation and activation rules involved, or the connection matrix is not adequately set up. For this reason, it is normal to specify the environment in such a way that order of presentation is not important, i.e. a random order should be used, and to choose a representation of the patterns which optimizes the chances of the network succeeding in learning.

Let us provide a couple of examples of connectionist networks. Imagine we have four units - three input and one output, where all three inputs are connected to the output. Imagine we want the network to learn to map seven source patterns onto one of two target values (*Figure 6.3 (a)*). The *learning procedure* consists of presenting the source patterns - the sequence of three bits (0s and 1s) in the 'source' column of *Figure 6.3 (a)* - to the three input units (u_1, u_2, u_3) of the network (one bit per unit), observing what the output value is at u_4, comparing the actual output value at the output unit with the *target* output value (as given by the single bit under the 'target' column of *Figure 6.3 (a)*), and changing the value of the link between the input units and the output unit appropriately.

Let us imagine that when the network is created weights between input and output units are assigned randomly (*Figure 6.3 (b)*), such that u_1, u_2 and u_3 are connected to u_4 with weights 0.2, 0.4 and 0.6, respectively. Let us assume for the sake of exposition that the minimum value of a connection is 0, and the maximum is 1; this means that we do not have a strictly linear model as such, but one that is bounded. Also, let us assume that the output unit will respond with 1 if its value is greater than or equal to 0.5, 0 otherwise. The threshold, θ, is therefore 0.5.

Since there is no feedback, these are the only connections in our network. Whilst working through this example, we shall use a vector $[x_1, x_2, x_3]$ to describe the current weights as given in the fourth column of the matrix above, as well as the input values to each of the three inputs. We can now abbreviate our connection matrix to the *connection vector* $[0.2, 0.4, 0.6]$ after random assignment of values, and $[0, 0, 1]$ represents the first pattern.

Our rule of activation and propagation rule are quite simple. They are very similar to that used in a *perceptron* network:

1. Weights are only changed on a given connection when the input unit associated with that connection is 1.

2. If the actual output value of a unit is the same as the target value, make no change.

3. If the output unit responds 1 when the target is 0, decrease the weight of the connection by 0.1.

4. If the output unit responds 0 when the target is 1, increase the weight of the connection by 0.1.

Let us now work through the example.

(a) First, $[0, 0, 1]$ is presented.

(b) Each element of this vector is multiplied by the corresponding current weight in the connection vector, i.e. 0 times 0.2, 0 times 0.4, and 1 times 0.6, to derive another vector called the *output vector*, signified by **o**. In the above case, **o** equals $[0, 0, 0.6]$. In linear algebra terms, **o** is the *inner product* of the input and connection vectors.

iv	ccv	ov	sum	t	ncv
$[0,0,1]$	$[0.2,0.4,0.6]$	$[0,0,0.6]$	0.6	0	$[0.2,0.4,0.5]$
$[0,1,0]$	$[0.2,0.4,0.5]$	$[0,0.4,0]$	0.4	0	no change
$[0,1,1]$	$[0.2,0.4,0.5]$	$[0,0.4,0.5]$	0.9	1	no change
$[1,0,0]$	$[0.2,0.4,0.5]$	$[0.2,0,0]$	0.2	0	no change
$[1,0,1]$	$[0.2,0.4,0.5]$	$[0.2,0,0.5]$	0.7	1	no change
$[1,1,0]$	$[0.2,0.4,0.5]$	$[0.2,0.4,0]$	0.6	0	$[0.1,0.3,0.5]$
$[1,1,1]$	$[0.1,0.3,0.5]$	$[0.1,0.3,0.5]$	0.9	1	no change

Table 6.1

(c) Next, we *sum* the elements of **o**. If the sum is greater than or equal to our θ, i.e. 0.5, the actual output value on the single output unit is 1. Since 0.6 is greater than 0.5, the actual output is 1.

(d) We compare the actual output value with the target output value, which is 0 for this pattern. We then need to perform some error correction. According to our simple rules, we only change the weights of connections which have an active input value. In the case of this particular input pattern, it is the third unit's value which now needs to be changed. Since a 0 was the target and a 1 was output, we *decrease* the strength of the connection between u_3 and u_4 by 0.1, to give us the new connection vector $[0.2,0.4,0.5]$.

(e) We repeat the above procedure for all the other patterns.

So, for instance, working through the next pattern: $[0,1,0]$ with $[0.2,0.4,0.5]$ gives $[0,0.4,0]$; since the sum, 0.4, is not greater than or equal to the threshold 0.5, the actual output value is 0, which is the same as the target value. No connections need to be changed at this point.

We can represent what happens to the patterns by means of a table (*Table 6.1*) where *iv* stands for 'input vector', *ccv* stands for 'current connection vector', *ov* stands for 'output vector', *sum* stands for the sum of the elements in *ov*, *t* stands for 'target', and *ncv* stands for 'new connection vector' which becomes the *ccv* for the next pattern.

Note how the pattern $[1,1,0]$ caused the two connections to be decreased in value. Of course, we have not finished yet. After the last pattern, we have concluded just one *cycle*. We go back to the first pattern and present them

iv	*ccv*	*ov*	*sum*	*t*	*ncv*
$[0,0,1]$	$[0.1,0.3,0.5]$	$[0,0,0.5]$	0.5	0	$[0.1,0.3,0.4]$
$[0,1,0]$	$[0.1,0.3,0.4]$	$[0,0.3,0]$	0.3	0	no change
$[0,1,1]$	$[0.1,0.3,0.4]$	$[0,0.3,0.4]$	0.7	1	no change
$[1,0,0]$	$[0.1,0.3,0.4]$	$[0.1,0,0]$	0.1	0	no change
$[1,0,1]$	$[0.1,0.3,0.4]$	$[0.1,0,0.4]$	0.5	1	no change
$[1,1,0]$	$[0.1,0.3,0.4]$	$[0.1,0.3,0]$	0.4	0	no change
$[1,1,1]$	$[0.1,0.3,0.4]$	$[0.1,0.3,0.4]$	0.8	1	no change

Table 6.2

iv	*ccv*	*ov*	*sum*	*t*	*ncv*
$[0,0,1]$	$[0.1,0.3,0.4]$	$[0,0,0.4]$	0.4	0	no change
$[0,1,0]$	$[0.1,0.3,0.4]$	$[0,0.3,0]$	0.3	0	no change
$[0,1,1]$	$[0.1,0.3,0.4]$	$[0,0.3,0.4]$	0.7	1	no change
$[1,0,0]$	$[0.1,0.3,0.4]$	$[0.1,0,0]$	0.1	0	no change
$[1,0,1]$	$[0.1,0.3,0.4]$	$[0.1,0,0.4]$	0.5	1	no change
$[1,1,0]$	$[0.1,0.3,0.4]$	$[0.1,0.3,0]$	0.4	0	no change
$[1,1,1]$	$[0.1,0.3,0.4]$	$[0.1,0.3,0.4]$	0.8	1	no change

Table 6.3

all over again, but this time using the last derived *ccv*. We repeat these cycles until no more changes to the connection vector are made during one cycle. Details of the second and third cycles are provided in *Tables 6.2* and *6.3*, respectively.

Our simple pseudo-linear model settles down after three cycles and is reproducing the appropriate output for all the input patterns. The full connection matrix after the third cycle is presented in *Figure 6.4*.

There are several points which arise out of this simple example. (Connectionist experiments are typically much more complex than this - see the models described in McClelland, Rumelhart and the PDP Research Group (1986).) First, the weights finally arrived at may not be the only set of weights which allows the network to produce the right responses. For example, if we had started with random assignments $[0.6,0.4,0.2]$, i.e. a reversal of the original weights, the final connection vector, this time after four cycles,

units	u_1	u_2	u_3	u_4
u_1	0	0	0	0.1
u_2	0	0	0	0.3
u_3	0	0	0	0.4
u_4	0	0	0	0

Figure 6.4

would have been $[0.2, 0.2, 0.3]$.

Secondly, the number of cycles required for other simple networks which use three input units and one output depends not only on the initial assignment of weights but also on the order of presentation of the learning patterns, the number of learning patterns, and the increment and decrement value used when changing weights.

Thirdly, all we have done is *trained* the network by presenting examples and using the target values as a way of tuning the network to provide the desired results. Most of the important work in PDP research depends on what happens *after* a network is tuned. For example, how well does a tuned network respond to patterns it has not been trained on? Training is usually just the first step in connectionist work, and the *testing* stage, whereby the network is exposed to patterns which are similar in some way to the *training set*, is often the more important part.

Let us suppose that the patterns we presented in our example are meant to represent the truthtable of the propositional form: *(p or q) and r*. That is, the input vector $[0, 1, 1]$ stands for p being false (**0**) and q and r being true (**1**). The output (target) values of **0** and **1** stand for the propositional form being false and true, respectively, given actual truth values of the propositions. In one sense, we can say that the network has 'learned' how to combine truth values according to this propositional form in such a way as to provide a correct result, but the test for a network having learned would be if at least one assignment of truth values had been kept out of the training set and used as a test for the network, i.e. how would the network respond to the previously unseen pattern of truth assignments, once it had settled its own connections on the learning set? In our case above, we could point out that one particular assignment of truth values *had* been kept to one side, namely, the pattern $[0, 0, 0]$, but it would not be desirable to use such a pattern here

source	target
0 0 0	0
0 0 1	1
0 1 0	1
0 1 1	0
1 0 0	1
1 0 1	0
1 1 0	0
1 1 1	1

Figure 6.5

for testing: by the very nature of the activation and propagation rule we used, the output vector would consist of zeros, hence the sum would be 0, which is the desired result.

Let us now provide an example of a simple, pseudo-linear network which does not settle down. Again, we have three inputs and one output (*Figure 6.5*). We shall provide an interpretation of the patterns only after presenting the results. Let us assume an initial random assignment of values [0.6, 0.4, 0.2]. We again assume a threshold of 0.5 or greater for a response of 1 at the output unit. At the end of each of the first three cycles, the connection vector looks like this:

$$first \quad [0.4, 0.3, 0.1]$$
$$second \quad [0.3, 0.2, 0]$$
$$third \quad [0.3, 0.3, 0.1]$$

Details of the fourth cycle are presented in *Table 6.4*.

At the end of the fourth cycle the connection vector is the same as at the beginning of the cycle, and subsequent cycles will repeat this pattern. Therefore, the network has not managed to stabilize to an appropriate set of weights for this particular problem: to count the number of 1s in the input pattern and return 1 if there is an *odd* number of 1s, 0 otherwise.

There are several ways of interpreting this looping process, and it may be useful to spell them out to give an indication of some of the major issues that arise in neurocomputing. Before we do that, let us first highlight the differences between perceptrons, as described by Rosenblatt, and the type of processing unit adopted in our connectionist examples.

iv	ccv	ov	sum	t	ncv
$[0,0,0]$	$[0.3,0.3,0.1]$	$[0,0,0]$	0	0	no change
$[0,0,1]$	$[0.3,0.3,0.1]$	$[0,0,0.1]$	0.1	1	$[0.3,0.3,0.2]$
$[0,1,0]$	$[0.3,0.3,0.2]$	$[0,0.3,0]$	0.3	1	$[0.3,0.4,0.2]$
$[0,1,1]$	$[0.3,0.4,0.2]$	$[0,0.4,0.2]$	0.6	0	$[0.3,0.3,0.1]$
$[1,0,0]$	$[0.3,0.3,0.1]$	$[0.3,0,0]$	0.3	1	$[0.4,0.3,0.1]$
$[1,0,1]$	$[0.4,0.3,0.1]$	$[0.4,0,0.1]$	0.5	0	$[0.3,0.3,0]$
$[1,1,0]$	$[0.3,0.3,0]$	$[0.3,0.3,0]$	0.6	0	$[0.2,0.2,0]$
$[1,1,1]$	$[0.2,0.2,0]$	$[0.2,0.2,0]$	0.4	1	$[0.3,0,3,0,1]$

Table 6.4

The perceptron, as developed by Rosenblatt (1962), could have one of
three values, not two as in our simplified networks. The formulae for working
out the output value of a perceptron response unit, u_j, are as follows. First,
compute a weighted sum, s_j, of the inputs to that unit:

$$s_j = \Sigma_i w_{ij} x_i$$

where x_i is the ith input to the unit and w_{ij} is the weight for the ith input
to the jth unit. Secondly, the output, o_j, for u_j is determined by comparing
the sum with a threshold:

$$o_j = \left\{ \begin{array}{ll} +1 & \text{if } s_j > \theta; \\ -1 & \text{if } s_j < -\theta; \\ 0 & \text{otherwise} \end{array} \right\}$$

(Note that the threshold θ is used in both its positive and negative form for
calculating the output value.) Learning takes place by adjusting the values
of weights on the inputs to the perceptrons according to a certain difference
Δ (Delta):

$$\Delta w_{ij} = \left\{ \begin{array}{ll} 0 & \text{if the output is correct;} \\ +\,x_i & \text{if the output is } -1 \text{ and should be } +1; \\ -\,x_i & \text{if the output is } +1 \text{ and should be } -1 \end{array} \right\}$$

where $+\,x_i$ and $-\,x_i$ signify that something is to be added or subtracted,
respectively, to the ith input. The perceptron convergence rule stated that

if a perceptron *could* learn to classify a set of patterns, it would do so within a finite number of iterations of the above rule.

Let us now try to summarize the implications of the failure of our last example network to stabilize. If one interpretation of the lack of convergence is that our model is not sufficiently powerful to cope with the task, there are several ways of proceeding.

(a) We can change the nature of the activation rule to include a more complex way of deriving the output vector. For instance, instead of taking just the product of input value and connection weight and summing, we may want to attach different ways of combining input values and weights, and more complex ways of summing.

(b) The propagation rule can be changed. For example, instead of increasing and decrementing weights by a fixed amount, a more complex incrementing and decrementing process could be used. Also, instead of altering the weights *during* a cycle, a different procedure which uses the connection matrix at the start of the cycle but does not alter that matrix's weights until *after* all the weight changes have been identified for the patterns could be tried. At the end of a cycle the connection matrix is updated for the next cycle. One minor problem to overcome with such an approach, as we saw above, concerns how to distinguish between a network which has stabilized (i.e. requires no modification during a cycle) from one which loops within a cycle.

(c) The learning rule itself can be modified to take into account repeated presentations of the same patterns. For instance, we could include a bias factor of some sort which pushes the network along a certain path once a trend has been established, using some measure of trends.

(d) The environment can be changed either so that the patterns are presented in a different order, if it can be shown that ordering is important to the success of failure of learning, or so that a new form of representation of the patterns makes ordering unimportant. (If the representations can be presented in any order for learning to succeed, the representations are said to be *orthogonal*.)

(e) The pattern of connectivity could be changed to cater for more complex network configurations, including layers of hidden units, feedback, interactive processing, and so on.

(f) Some evaluation of the *theoretical* nature of the problem should be carried out to identify classes of problems which types of neural networks cannot handle before further effort is expended on modifying the network.

Our task so far has been to provide an introduction to one form of neurocomputing, namely, connectionism, so that some idea is provided as to the activities and concerns of neurocomputing researchers. We now need to go beyond the introduction and examine some of the claims made not just for connectionism but also for neurocomputing in general. The best way of doing this is to look at ways connectionists reply to their critics: some of these replies will be relevant to connectionists only, while others will provide a more general defence of neurocomputing as an alternative approach to computationalism.

Rumelhart, Hinton and McClelland (1986), and Rumelhart and McClelland (1986) provide a defence of connectionism against a variety of attacks, and this is where we shall start our discussion on the implications of neurocomputing. Overall, there are seven main issues discusses by these authors. They are:

that PDP models are too weak;

that PDP models are not cognitive;

that PDP models are at the wrong level of analysis;

the issues of reductionism and emergent properties;

that not enough is known from neuroscience to seriously constrain cognitive theories;

that PDP models lack neural realism;

the issue of nativism versus empiricism; and

the issue of conscious knowledge and explicit reasoning.

The issue of PDP models being the wrong level of analysis we shall leave, as much as we can, until the next chapter, since this is a fundamental methodological objection. Let us work through the other issues one by one.

6.8 ARE PDP MODELS TOO WEAK?

Very roughly, Minsky and Papert (1969) claimed to identify various classes of problems which, although easily and well handled by conventional processing methods, could not be handled by neural networks. They based their conclusions on results from neural models which used similar propagation and activation rules to the ones that we have used in our examples, but with a slightly more complex learning rule (a measure of the *distance* or *difference* (called *Delta*) between actual output activation and target output activation was used - see our earlier example of a *Delta* rule). But, essentially, a restricted form of single layer, non-feedback, linear model which is similar to the perceptron model was used in their experiment, and the results of these experiments provided the basis for their conclusions. So it is not surprising to find neurocomputing researchers disagreeing with their conclusions, not on the basis of fact but on the basis that Minsky and Papert did not adequately examine some of the alternatives to the simple model:

> [E]ven though multilayer linear threshold models [as discussed in their book] are potentially much more powerful ...it was the limitations on what perceptrons could possibly learn that led to Minsky and Papert's (1969) pessimistic evaluation of the perceptron. Unfortunately, that evaluation has incorrectly tainted more interesting and powerful networks of linear threshold and other nonlinear units .... [T]he limitations of the one-step perceptrons in no way apply to the more complex networks. (Rumelhart, Hinton and McClelland, 1986, p. 65)

This is an argument rejected by Minsky and Papert (1988):

> Certainly, some chapters [of the first edition of *Perceptrons* (Minsky and Papert, 1969)] prove that various important predicates have perceptron coefficients that grow unmanageably large. But many chapters show that other predicates can be surprisingly tractable. It is no more apt to describe our mathematical theorems as pessimistic than it would to say the same about deducing the conservation of momentum from the laws of mechanics. (Minsky and Papert, 1988, pp. 248-249)

Minsky and Papert (1988) then go on to clarify their original criticisms. First, they stress that they were concerned with the issue of *complexity*.

Although a neural network may work successfully for small problems, there was, and they claim still is, a lack of understanding of how much complexity would be involved if these neural networks were scaled up to deal with larger examples of the same type of problem. There appeared to be no rule or principle which would allow programmers to be able to estimate the complexity attached to a particular domain or problem. From the point of view of a *scientist*, this is an unsatisfactory state of affairs, since there is no method of estimating how learning mechanisms in neural networks differ from, or offer advantages over, exhaustive, brute-force methods.

Secondly, while the claim concerning the perceptron convergence theorem seemed impressive, that does not mean that the convergence theorem is interesting or important, since nothing is being said about efficiency. That is, there are many procedures which, by means of an exhaustive search, also guarantee to find a solution of some sort as long as the problem is represented appropriately, but such brute-force procedures are not usually considered interesting or important for a learning theory. However, this is not to deny the *appeal* of the convergence theorem: from an intuitive point of view it seems to fit in quite well with our understanding of what happens in biological nervous systems, and from a mathematical point of view it is relatively simple.

Thirdly, even accepting the intuitive appeal of neural networks, there is the question of *managing* networks where different parts of the network, because of the idea of distributed representation, do different things:

> This is why we maintain that the scientific future of connectionism is tied not to the search for some single, universal scheme to solve all problems at once but to the evolution of a many-faceted technology of "brain design" that encompasses good technical theories about the analysis of learning procedures, of useful architectures, and of organizational principles to use when assembling those components into larger systems. (Minsky and Papert, 1988, p. 274)

And finally, and perhaps most surprisingly, they offer to 'make peace' between *connectionists* and *symbolists* i.e. between neurocomputing researchers and computationalists. We shall return to their peace proposal later.

Other problems in this area of PDP models being too weak concern *stimulus equivalence* and *recursion*. With regard to the former, the problem that connectionists have to address is how

> ...[a]n *A* is an *A* is an *A*, no matter where on the retina
> it appears or how large it is or how it is oriented; and people
> can, in general, recognize patterns rather well despite various
> transformations. It has always seemed elegant and natural to
> imagine that an *A*, no matter where it is presented, is normalized
> and then processed for recognition using stored knowledge of the
> appearance of the letter .... (Rumelhart and McClelland, 1986,
> p. 113, italics supplied)

Rumelhart and McClelland admit that whilst some PDP models do not address this point, it is nevertheless possible for PDP models to deal with stimulus equivalence. They describe some work by Hinton (1981), where he differentiates between the lowest level feature detectors, called *retinocentric* features, i.e. feature detectors for features as they appear to the retina, and *canonical* feature units, which correspond to the corrected, or normalized, versions of the retinocentric features. It is the canonical feature units which send excitatory or inhibitory signals to the level of the letters, which are of course normalized. In between the retinocentric feature detectors and canonical units sits a set of *mapping units* which provide *dynamically programmable connections* from the retinocentric feature detectors to the canonical units. There are a variety of mapping unit set types, depending on the amount of rotation that has to be applied to the retinocentric features in order to normalize them (e.g. turn 90 degrees clockwise, turn 90 degrees anti-clockwise, turn upside-down, and so on). Once the degree, or amount, of rotation has been decided, one particular mapping unit set will be activated which will then apply the right amount of rotation to subsequent retinocentric features (see Rumelhart and McClelland, 1986, pp. 114-117). Rumelhart and McClelland make the following claims:

> Hinton's mapping scheme allows us to make two points. First,
> that parallel distributed processing is in fact compatible with
> normalization ...; and, second, that a PDP implementation of a
> normalization mechanism can actually produce a computational
> advantage by allowing what would otherwise be a painful, slow,
> serial search to be carried out in a single settling of a parallel
> network. In general, Hinton's mapping system illustrates that
> PDP mechanisms are not restricted to fixed computations but
> are quite clearly capable of modulation and control by signals
> arising from other parts of an integrated processing system; and
> that they can, when necessary, be used to implement a serial

> process, in which each of several patterns is considered, one at a
> time. (Rumelhart and McClelland, 1986, p. 117)

With regard to recursion, and the use of recursion to add computational
power to their networks, Rumelhart and McClelland are dismissive:

> We have not dwelt on PDP implementations of Turing ma-
> chines and recursive processing engines because we do not agree
> with those who would argue that such capacities are of the ess-
> ence of human computation. As anyone who has ever attempted
> to process sentences like "The man the boy the girl hit kissed
> moved" can attest, our ability to process even moderate degrees
> of center-embedded structure is grossly impaired relative to that
> of [recursively defined mechanisms]. And yet, the human ability
> to use semantic and pragmatic contextual information to facil-
> itate comprehension far exceeds that of any existing sentence
> processing machine we know of. (Rumelhart and McClelland,
> 1986, p. 119)

For Rumelhart and McClelland, what is needed instead is a language parser
built from

> ...the kind of mechanism which facilitates the simultaneous
> consideration of large umbers of mutual and interdependent con-
> straints. The challenge is to show how those processes that oth-
> ers have chosen to explain in terms of recursive mechanisms can
> be better explained by the kinds of processes natural for PDP
> networks. (Rumelhart and McClelland, 1986, p. 119)

As we shall shortly see, Fodor and Pylyshyn (1988) have something to say
about this dismissive attitude towards recursion.

6.9 ARE PDP MODELS COGNITIVE?

It is worth quoting Rumelhart and McClelland's description of this objection
in its entirety, since it is this point more than any other which has provoked
the strongest response by opponents of connectionism. If the opponents of
connectionism are correct in their response, then the scope of neurocomputing in general may be severely constrained in its cognitive (psychological)
explanatory power.

> A ... claim that some people have made is that our models
> appear to share much in common with behaviorist accounts of
> behavior. While they do involve simple mechanisms of learning,
> there is a crucial difference between our models and the rad-
> ical behaviorism of Skinner and his followers. In our models,
> we are explicitly concerned with the problem of internal repre-
> sentation and mental processes, whereas the radical behaviorist
> explicitly denies the scientific utility and even the validity of the
> consideration of these constructs. The training of hidden units is
> ... the construction of internal representations. The models de-
> scribed throughout the book [(Rumelhart, McClelland and the
> PDP Research Group, 1986)] all concern internal representations.
> In this sense, our models must be seen as completely antithetical
> to the radical behaviorist program and strongly committed to
> the study of representation and process. (Rumelhart and Mc-
> Clelland, 1986, p. 121)

Whilst this is a strong statement by Rumelhart and McClelland, it also
presents a target for critics. That is, if it can be shown that connectionism
is another form of associationism, then even Rumelhart and McClelland
will be forced to admit that connectionism may have little to say about
cognitive concepts and processes. Fodor and Pylyshyn identify this point as
the crucial one in their attack on connectionism, and it is worth looking at
their criticisms in some detail.

In their paper, Fodor and Pylyshyn (1988) make a number of points concerning connectionism and its cognitive implications. They point out that
connectionism appears to provide an alternative way of looking at cognitive architecture. Traditional cognitive science (i.e. computationalism), or
'Classical cognitive science', as the authors call it (abbreviated hereafter to
'classicism'), uses the notions of Turing Machines and Von Neumann machines insofar as the idea of symbol manipulation is used for describing cognitive processes. Connectionism, on the other hand, involves using a large
number of interconnected units. Whilst Fodor and Pylyshyn accept that
connectionism has provided unexpected results and that many researchers
are tempted by connectionism, both for practical purposes (that is, the inherent and surprising power of a network of simple, interconnected units)
and by the appearance of neural plausibility (that is, the human brain also
appears to consist of a vast network of simple, interconnected units), their
task is to evaluate the claim that connectionism offers something new over

classicism. The core of their argument that connectionism does not offer anything new is based on a detailed examination of mental processes and mental representations.

Fodor and Pylyshyn introduce the terms 'Representationalism' and 'Eliminativism' when discussing some preliminary methodological questions about levels of explanation:

> Representationalists hold that postulating representational (or 'intentional' or 'semantic') states is essential to a theory of cognition; according to Representationalists, there are states of the mind which function to encode states of the world. Eliminativists, by contrast, think that psychological theories can dispense with such semantic notions as representation. According to Eliminativists the appropriate vocabulary for psychological theorizing is neurological or, perhaps, behavioral, or perhaps syntactic; in any event, not a vocabulary that characterizes mental states in terms of what they represent. (Fodor and Pylyshyn, 1988, p. 7)

After providing this radical division, Fodor and Pylyshyn claim that connectionists are *on the representationalist side* of this divide and refer to some connectionist literature (written by Rumelhart and McClelland, and Feldman and Ballard) to justify their claim:

> As Rumelhart & McClelland [(Rumelhart and McClelland, 1986)] say, PDPs "are explicitly concerned with the problem of internal representation (p 121)". Correspondingly, the specification of what the states of a network *represent* is an essential part of a Connectionist model. Consider, for example, the well-known Connectionist account of the bistability of the Necker cube [(Feldman and Ballard, 1982)]. "Simple units representing the visual features of the two alternatives are arranged in competing coalitions with inhibitory ...links between rival features and positive links within each coalition ...The result is a network that has two dominant stable states ..." Notice that, in this as in all other Connectionist models, the commitment to mental representation is explicit: the label of a node is taken to express the representational content of the state that the device is in when the node is excited, and there are nodes corresponding to monadic and rela-

> tional properties of the reversible cube when it is seen in one way
> or another. (Fodor and Pylyshyn, 1988, p. 7, stress supplied)

Hence, say Fodor and Pylyshyn, classicism and connectionism *are both representational*. That is, any level of a cognitive architecture at which states of the system are taken to encode properties of the world counts as a *cognitive* level. This means that if connectionists wish to propose a connectionist theory as a theory of cognitive architecture,

> ...[they] have to show that the processes which operate on
> *the representational states* of an organism are those which are
> specified by a Connectionist architecture. (Fodor and Pylyshyn,
> 1988, p. 10, stress supplied)

That is, whilst accepting that connectionism may well provide a suitable way of describing non-psychological (or non-cognitive) states of an organism, and may even provide an implementation model for classical theories, that is of no use, as far as cognitive science is concerned. Instead, if connectionists truly want their theories to be representational, then the burden of proof is on them to show how the processes involved in their theory tie up with psychological, or cognitive, processes of an organism. If they could not,

> ...that would leave open the question whether the mind is
> [a connectionist network] *at the psychological level*. (Fodor and
> Pylyshyn, 1988, p. 10, stress supplied)

Fodor and Pylyshyn believe that the main disagreement between researchers adopting a classicist approach and connectionists centres around precisely the attempts made by connectionists to tie up their processes with psychological ones. Since both sets of researchers are representationalist, at some stage semantic content must be assigned to something:

> Classicists assign semantic content to *expressions* - i.e. to the
> sorts of things that get written on the tapes of Turing machines
> and stored at addresses in Von Neumann machines. (Fodor and
> Pylyshyn, 1988, p. 12, stress supplied)

Connectionists, however,

> ... assign semantic content to "nodes" (that is, to units or aggregates of unit ...) - i.e. to the sorts of things that are typically labelled in Connectionist diagrams. (Fodor and Pylyshyn, 1988, p. 12)

The main disagreement between the two sets of researchers centres around the nature of the primitive relations which hold among these content-bearing entities. Fodor and Pylyshyn state that 'causal connectedness' is the only primitive relation among nodes. That is, nodes in a network (i.e. the primitives) are linked (related) to each other by excitatory and inhibitory flows; one node can cause another node to go up or down in value, and that is the only primitive relation. Classicists, on the other hand, accept not only causal relations as primitives but also structural relations, of which *constituency* is paradigmatic. Fodor and Pylyshyn argue that this disagreement leads to two architectural differences between connectionist and classical cognitive theories:

(a) Classicists postulate, and are committed to, symbolic structures, or complex mental representations (a 'language of thought') which have syntactic and semantic structure (i.e. a combinatorial syntax and semantics).

(b) Classicists also accept that the principles by which mental states are transformed, or by which an input selects the corresponding output, are defined over structural properties of mental representations. That is, because mental representations have structure (see (a) above), mental representations can be manipulated, or transformed, by rules or operations which are triggered by the form, and not the content, of those representations. Fodor and Pylyshyn use the phrase 'structure sensitivity of processes' to describe this notion.

For instance, the formula [**A and B**] $\rightarrow$ **C** is syntactically well-formed because it adheres to the syntactic principles of the propositional calculus, namely, three atomic symbols **A**, **B**, and **C**, connected by $\rightarrow$, with bracketing signifying that **A** and **B** are to be conjoined by **and**. The underlying form of this formula is **p**$\rightarrow$**q**. The operation, or rule, of Modus Ponens states that if **p**$\rightarrow$**q** occurs, and if **p** also occurs, then, irrespective of how structurally simple or complex **p** happens to be, **q** can be derived. The application of this operation is determined by the form of the representation, and not the content, i.e. not on the basis of what **A**, **B** and **C** stand for.

Fodor and Pylyshyn make two claims for classicism. First:

> We take [(a) and (b) above] as the claims that define Classical models, and we take these claims quite literally; they constrain the physical realizations of symbol structures. In particular, the symbol structures in a Classical model are assumed to correspond to real physical structures in the brain and the *combinatorial structure* of a representation is supposed to have a counterpart in structural relations among physical properties of the brain. For example, the relation 'part of', which holds between a relatively simple symbol and a more complex one, is assumed to correspond to some physical relation among brain states .... (Fodor and Pylyshyn, 1988, p. 13, stress supplied)

Secondly,

> ...Classical theory is committed not only to there being a system of physically instantiated symbols, but also to the claim that the physical properties onto which the structure of the symbols is mapped *are the very properties that cause the system to behave as it does*. In other words the physical counterparts of the symbols, and their structural properties, *cause* the system's behaviour. (Fodor and Pylyshyn, 1988, p. 14, stress supplied)

Fodor and Pylyshyn then present a simple example to demonstrate a weakness, concerning the role of labels, in connectionist theory (*Figure 6.6 (a) and (b)*). The connectionist interpretation of *Figure 6.6 (a)* is that drawing an inference from **A & B** to **A** corresponds to an excitation at node 2 being caused by an excitation at node 1. A classical interpretation is that whenever a formula with the form **p & q** appears, then **p** by itself can be derived. **A & B** conforms structurally to **p & q**, hence **A** can be derived.

Fodor and Pylyshyn point out that, if the diagram in *Figure 6.6 (a)* represents a connection machine, the labels **A & B**, **A**, and **B** play no part: the operation of the machine is unaffected by changing the labels (*Figure 6.6 (b)*), since node 2 is still excited by activation at node 1. That is,

> ...the node labels in a Connection machine are not part of the causal structure of the machine. (Fodor and Pylyshyn, 1988, p. 16)

(a)

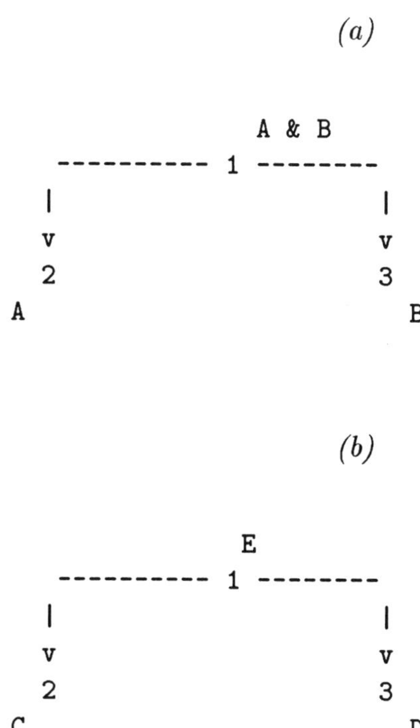

(b)

Figure 6.6

Fodor and Pylyshyn then go on to claim:

> [B]y contrast, the state transitions of Classical machines are causally determined *by the structure - including the constituent structure - of the symbol arrays that the machines transform*: change the symbols and the system behaves quite differently. ...So, although the Connectionist's labels and the Classicist's data structures both constitute languages, only the latter language constitutes a medium of computation .... (Fodor and Pylyshyn, 1988, p. 17, stress supplied)

Fodor and Pylyshyn then examine the notion that a connectionist representation does indeed have structure. Connectionists claim that mental representations are distributed, in that

> ...commonsense concepts (CHAIR, JOHN, CUP, etc.) are "distributed" over galaxies of lower level units which themselves have representational content. (Fodor and Pylyshyn, 1988, p. 19)

For instance, the concept BACHELOR might be though to correspond to a 'vector in space of features' that includes $+ human$, $+ male$, $- married$, $+ adult$. It is then tempting to think that, for example, $+ human$ is a constituent of BACHELOR. However, Fodor and Pylyshyn claim that this is very unlike **Mary** being a constituent of the expression **John loves Mary**. In the latter case, called 'real constituency', **Mary** literally appears in the expression **John loves Mary**, whereas in the former case we are expressing a definition; that is, we are defining BACHELOR in terms of primitive expressions:

> It really is very important not to confuse the semantic distinction between primitive expressions and defined expressions with the syntactic distinction between atomic symbols and complex symbols. (Fodor and Pylyshyn, 1988, p. 22)

That is, connectionists cannot adequately describe the important syntactic, or formal, relationship between atomic and complex symbols. If the connectionist replies that **John loves Mary** can be represented by a feature vector or set, such as {+**John** − **subject**; +**loves**; +**Mary** − **object**}, and that the classical distinction between complex symbols and atomic symbols can be

```
            actor            object
    John <--------- loves -------> Mary
```

Figure 6.7

replaced by the distinction between feature sets and their subsets, then this too will not work since there are various subsets, such as {+**John** − **subject**; +**Mary** − **object**}, which

> ...do not, of course, correspond to constituents of the complex symbol "John loves Mary". (Fodor and Pylyshyn, 1988, p. 23)

That is, Fodor and Pylyshyn claim that 'real constituency', as they have described it, just cannot be adequately described in a connectionist framework. Since real constituency embodies the basic and important principle of a primitive syntactically belonging to a larger complex, connectionism just cannot handle this important representationalist feature. If that is the case, then semantic structure also cannot be catered for, since one of the main features of a representation is that semantic structure of the expressions is dependent on the (syntactic) form of the expression.

Fodor and Pylyshyn claim that one of the reasons why this lack of syntactic and semantic structure has been overlooked or ignored may be because connectionist graphs look like ordinary graphs. But whereas graph notation can be used to describe or express the internal structure of a representation by means of arcs and nodes (*Figure 6.7*), such an interpretation is inappropriate for graphs of connectionist networks. Fodor and Pylyshyn go on to say:

> Connectionist graphs are not structural descriptions of mental representations; they're specifications of causal relations. All that a Connectionist can mean by a graph of the form $X \longrightarrow Y$ is: *states of node X causally affect states of node Y*. In particular, the graph can't mean X *is a constituent of* Y or X *is*

> *grammatically related to Y* etc., since these sorts of relations are,
> in general, not defined for the kinds of mental representations
> that Connectionists recognize. ...Another way to put this is
> that links in Connectionist diagrams are not generalized point-
> ers that can be made to take on different functional significance
> *by an independent interpreter*, but are confined to meaning some-
> thing like "sends activation to". The intended interpretation of
> the links as causal connections is intrinsic to the theory. If you
> ignore this point, you are likely to take Connectionism to offer
> a much richer notion of mental representation than it actually
> does. (Fodor and Pylyshyn, 1988, pp. 18-19, stress supplied)

Later, Fodor and Pylyshyn put these points differently, this time stressing
the lack of structure in connectionist representations:

> There are ... two questions that you need to answer to specify
> the content of a mental state: "Which concepts are 'active'" and
> "Which of the active concepts are in construction with which oth-
> ers?" Identifying mental states with sets of active nodes provides
> resources to answer the first of these questions but not the second.
> That's why the version of network theory that acknowledges sets
> of atomic representations but no complex representations fails,
> in indefinitely many cases, to distinguish mental states that are
> in fact distinct. (Fodor and Pylyshyn, 1988, p. 27)

Fodor and Pylyshyn then go on to claim that the notion of mental process is accounted for differently by classicists and connectionists. Classicists
postulate three distinct levels of organisation: a physical level, a semantic
level, and a syntactic level. At the physical level, symbols are mapped onto
physical states that cause the system to behave in a certain way. At the
syntactic level, symbols are combined structurally to form more complex
representations. At the semantic level, the meaning of a representation is
a function of the meaning of its syntactic parts. Operations, such as inference, are structure-sensitive in that, given a representation such as $\mathbf{p}$ & $\mathbf{q}$,
$\mathbf{p}$ can be derived syntactically. The inference is, of course, truth-preserving
(i.e. semantically correct). Mental operations, according to classicists, are
structure-sensitive in that the logical, or syntactic, form of mental representations is used to define the starting point and end result of mental operations. Such a notion is, however, unavailable to orthodox connectionists
since this notion - that the form of mental representations can be used to

define the range and domain of mental operations - presupposes that there are nonatomic mental representations. Connectionism cannot account for nonatomic mental representations. Instead, connectionism must account for, say, inference by using processes that are not structure-sensitive but frequency-sensitive:

> If a Connectionist learning machine converges on a state where it is prepared to infer A from A&B (i.e. to a state in which when the 'A&B' node is excited, it tends to settle into a state in which the 'A' node is excited) the convergence will typically be caused by statistical properties of the machine's training experience: e.g. by correlation between firing of the 'A&B' node and firing of the 'A' node, or by correlations of the firing of both with some feedback signal. Like traditional Associationism, Connectionism treats learning as basically a sort of statistical modelling. (Fodor and Pylyshyn, 1988, p. 31)

From this, Fodor and Pylyshyn go on to conclude that connectionist theories are, contrary to Rumelhart and McClelland's claims, *associationalist*, in that, for traditional associationism,

> ... the probability that one Idea will elicit another is sensitive to the strength of the association between them .... And the strength of this association is in turn sensitive to the extent to which the Ideas have previously been correlated. (Fodor and Pylyshyn, 1988, p. 32)

That is, in a connectionist model one idea leads to another, not on the basis of the structure of the first idea and its formal relationship to the second idea, but on the basis of how frequently the first idea is associated with the second. According to Fodor and Pylyshyn, connectionism therefore has little to say on structural relationships.

Fodor and Pylyshyn then go on to examine the 'productivity argument', which essentially is based on the Chomskyan notion of generative capacity (Chomsky, 1965). Fodor and Pylyshyn agree with Chomsky that, from a finite vocabulary of symbols and rules, an infinite number of linguistic expressions can, in principle, be generated because at least one of the rules is recursive. Fodor and Pylyshyn adopt this stance with respect to mental representations. One of the reasons why classical theories can cater for the notion of productivity is that there is a distinction, on Von Neumann lines, between memory and program. The rules (program) are finite and fixed, and it is memory that is affected as the rules (some of which are recursive) are applied. Connectionist cognitive architectures, claim Fodor and Pylyshyn, cannot, by their very nature, support an expandable memory, so they cannot support productive cognitive capacities. This leads to connectionists being forced to deny that recursion is an important, cognitive capacity. Fodor and Pylyshyn point out that for Rumelhart and McClelland any independent evidence that demonstrates that some cognitive capacities are recursive is sufficient for connectionism to be rejected in favour of classicism, as far as cognitive modeling is concerned.

Rather than pursue this point in their paper, Fodor and Pylyshyn are content to argue for *systematicity* of cognitive representation. If systematicity is demonstrated, that provides as good a reason for postulating combinatorial structure in mental representation as the productivity of cognition does. Fodor and Pylyshyn then describe what they mean by systematicity:

> What we mean when we say that linguistic capacities are *systematic* is that the ability to produce/understand some sentences is *intrinsically* connected to the ability to produce/understand certain others. (Fodor and Pylyshyn, 1988, p. 37, stress supplied)

After producing some example sentences which are claimed to demonstrate a systematic linguistic capacity, e.g.

> ...no speaker understands the form of words 'John loves the girl' except as he also understands the form of words 'the girl loves John' (Fodor and Pylyshyn, 1988, p. 39),

Fodor and Pylyshyn claim that thought is systematic also:

> [J]ust as you don't find people who can understand the sentence 'John loves the girl' but not the sentence 'the girl loves John', so too you don't find people who can *think the thought* that John loves the girl but can't think the thought that the girl loves John. ...But now if the ability to think that John loves the girl is intrinsically connected to the ability to think that the girl loves John, that fact will somehow have to be explained.

> For a Representationalist (which, as we have seen, Connection-
> ists are), the explanation is obvious: ...just as the systematicity
> of language shows that there must be some structural relations
> between the sentence 'John loves the girl' and the sentence 'the
> girl loves John', so the systematicity of thought shows that there
> must be structural relations between the mental representation
> that corresponds to the thought that John loves the girl and the
> mental representation that corresponds to the thought that the
> girl loves John; namely, the two mental representations, like the
> two sentences, *must be made of the same parts.* But if this expla-
> nation is right (and there doesn't seem to be any other on offer),
> then mental representations have an internal structure and there
> is a language of thought. So the architecture of the mind is not
> a Connectionist network. (Fodor and Pylyshyn, 1988, pp. 39-40,
> stress supplied)

Fodor and Pylyshyn adopt exactly the same line or argument to show that
representations are compositional. The principle of compositionality is described thus:

> [I]nsofar as a language is systematic, a lexical item must make
> approximately the same semantic contribution to each expression
> in which it occurs. It is, for example, only insofar as the 'the',
> 'girl', 'loves', and 'John' make the same semantic contribution to
> 'John loves the girl' that they make to 'the girl loves John' that
> understanding the one sentence implies understanding the other.
> (Fodor and Pylyshyn, 1988, p. 42)

Systematicity depends on compositionality, so to the extent that a natural
language is systematic it must be compositional also.

Having argued for compositionality of language, Fodor and Pylyshyn
extrapolate the argument to thought:

> Sentences are used to express thoughts; so if the ability to use
> some sentences is connected with the ability to use certain other,
> semantically related sentences, then the ability to think some
> thoughts must be correspondingly connected with the ability to
> think certain other, semantically related thoughts. (Fodor and
> Pylyshyn, 1988, p. 44)

The point that Fodor and Pylyshyn wish to make here is that connectionism has nothing to say on these matters:

> It's certainly true that compositionality is not generally a feature of Connectionist representations. Connectionists can't acknowledge the facts of compositionality because they are committed to mental representations that don't have combinatorial structure. But to give up on compositionality ... [leads] ... to the rejection of Connectionist networks as cognitive models. (Fodor and Pylyshyn, 1988, p. 45)

A related point here concerns the role of *rules* and their status in cognitive (both classical and connectionist) models. Rumelhart and McClelland argue that PDP models have shown how it is possible to account for behaviour which had previously been attributed to the application of specific rules of grammar or rules of thought. They claim that the apparent application of rules could easily *emerge* from the interactions among many simple processing units rather than from the application of any higher level rules. They go on to say:

> Some have viewed our argument against explicit rules as an argument against the cognitive approach to psychology. We do not agree. We believe that we are studying the *mechanisms* of cognition. The application of a rule ... is neither more nor less cognitive than the activation of our units. The real character of cognitive science is the attempt to explain mental phenomena through an understanding of the mechanisms which underlie those phenomena. (Rumelhart and McClelland, 1986, p. 120, stress supplied)

So, it is not as if rules of compositionality, for instance, are derived or learned from expressions which are structured according to those rules; rather, according to connectionists, these rules, and others, emerge as a result of interactions amongst a large number of units which have as their task the processing of expressions. These rules may therefore not be logically related to the expressions but represent abstractions, at a symbolic level, of the way a connectionist network is operating. Such abstract descriptions may well perform a useful role in describing various emergent properties of the network, but that does not mean that the organism in which the network is located has used these rules in the processing of the expressions.

Also, connectionists can argue that classical approaches, by using rules, adopt an all-or-nothing approach to cognitive tasks: either a rule is applicable because, say, certain conditions are satisfied, or it is not. A connectionist approach, by doing away with explicit rules, adopts a different line. First, there is continuous variation in the degree of applicability of different principles, where many different constraints are brought to bear on a problem simultaneously and the outcome is a combined effect of all the different factors. Secondly, cognitive processes are never rigidly determined or precisely replicable, as would be implied by the classicist's use of rigid, deterministic rules. And, thirdly, cognition displays 'graceful degradation': a person will not give up just because a rule fails. Connectionists therefore propose, in opposition to classicists, a system where graceful degradation is displayed by means of prototypes and degrees of pattern matching, and not by the success or failure of explicit rules.

Fodor and Pylyshyn reply that the distinction between rule-implicitness and rule-explicitness is an empirical one and should not be confused with the classicism versus connectionism issue, since classicists themselves disagree on the implicitness or otherwise of rules. In some cases,

> ...Classical machines can be *rule implicit* with respect to their programs, and the mechanism of their state transitions is entirely subcomputational (i.e. subsymbolic). (Fodor and Pylyshyn, 1988, p. 60, stress supplied)

However, Fodor and Pylyshyn admit that although rules in classical models can vary in their explicitness, data structures cannot: objects that are manipulated by rules, no matter what level of explicitness the rules take, must be explicitly represented:

> A [Universal Turing Machine] is "rule explicit" about the machine it is simulating (in the sense that it has an explicit representation of that machine which is sufficient to specify its behaviour uniquely). Yet the target machine can perfectly well be "rule-implicit" with respect to the rules that govern *its* behavior. (Fodor and Pylyshyn, 1988, p.61, stress supplied)

Fodor and Pylyshyn continue their attack on connectionism by pointing out that connectionist models and classical models may well be both rule-implicit; what is fundamentally different is that connectionist networks do not have explicit *representations* (data structures), whereas classical models do. Since the debate is about representationalism, the explicitness or implicitness of the rules (algorithms) is not important. Classical models have the property of being representationalist because their representations are explicit (these representations also possess certain defining properties of what it is be a representation), whereas connectionist 'representations' not only are not explicit but also do not possess any of the major characteristics one would identify of representations.

Fodor and Pylyshyn also turn the argument around and say that, whereas classicism cannot be attacked by showing that certain processes are rule-implicit, connectionism can be attacked by showing that a cognitive process is rule-explicit: since connectionism rejects logico/syntactic capacities that are required to encode rules, any rule-explicit cognitive process would embarrass connectionists. Fodor and Pylyshyn point to empirical work in linguistics and mathematical learning theory, where structures are described, taught and learnt by means of explicit rules (for instance, in teaching the grammar of a language, or in demonstrating the derivations of theorems in a formal system).

Although Fodor and Pylyshyn concentrate their attack on connectionism, there is little doubt that if their charges against connectionism stick then neurocomputing, as a viable, alternative scientific strategy in cognitive science, will be discredited as being associationalist and non-representational in character. If connectionism is non-representational, then the only alternative, given Fodor and Pylyshyn's divide between representationalism and eliminativism as valid scientific strategies in cognitive science, appears to be for connectionism to claim that it is eliminativist. That is, Fodor and Pylyshyn believe that, by showing that connectionism is not representational, they have forced connectionists into the eliminativist camp, where by implication connectionism must accept the position of rejecting psychological theories in favour of neurophysiological, or behavioural, explanations: psychological concepts, according to eliminativists, can be eliminated altogether, since such concepts can be reduced to, or are nothing more than, neurophysiological, or behavioural, concepts, in that whatever can be explained psychologically can be (better) explained neurophysiologically or behaviourally. This accusation of connectionism, and more generally neurocomputing, being *reductionist* in nature is the topic of the next section, and there we shall also see how connectionists attack the computationalist view of representations.

6.10 REDUCTIONISM

Rumelhart and McClelland next tackle the objection that connectionism is essentially reductionist, that connectionists want to reduce all psychology to neurophysiology and finally physics. In such a reductionist program, even though each stage in the reduction will require its own language of description appropriate at that level, connectionists appear to deny the essence of what is cognitive by reducing it to connections between units, rather than adopting a more psychology-relevant language in their explanations.

Rumelhart and McClelland answer this objection by stating that they classify themselves not as reductionists but as *interactionalists* . That is, they try to understand the essence of cognition as *a property emerging from* the interactions of connected units:

> We certainly believe in emergent phenomena in the sense of phenomena which could never be understood or predicted by a study of the lower level elements in isolation. These phenomena are functions of the particular kinds of groupings of the elementary units. In general, a new vocabulary is useful to talk about aggregate phenomena rather than the characteristics of isolated phenomena .... Knowing about [the elementary units] tells us little about the structure of the [grouping], but we can't *understand* the structure of the higher level [groupings] without knowing a good deal about [elementary units] and how they function. This is the sense of emergence we are comfortable with. We believe that it is entirely consistent with the PDP view of cognition. (Rumelhart and McClelland, 1986, p. 128, stress supplied)

That is, Rumelhart and McClelland deny the primitive/complex relationship proposed by Fodor and Pylyshyn, where knowledge of primitives and of the way such primitives combine to form larger units (syntactically and semantically) is wholly predictable of the larger unit, in some linear sense. Rumelhart and McClelland are not convinced that complex structures in psychology work in this linear sense:

> As we learn more about a topic and as we look at it in more and more detail we are going to be forced to consider more and more how it might emerge (in the above sense) from the *interactions* among its constituents. Interaction is the key word

here. *Emergent properties occur whenever we have nonlinear interactions.* In these cases the principles of interaction themselves must be formulated and the real theory at the higher level is ... a theory of interactions of elements from a theory one level lower. (Rumelhart and McClelland, 1986, p. 129, stress supplied in the first case and added in the second)

6.11   NEUROSCIENCE AND COGNITION

The objection here, according to Rumelhart and McClelland, is that, while many cognitive scientists accept that there will eventually be an understanding of the relationships between cognitive phenomena and brain functioning, it is better to proceed in a top-down manner so that we have explanations of cognition at the top level which are independent of any discoveries we make of the way the brain functions. This is because the brain appears to be such a powerful computational device that our current knowledge of the brain places few constraints on what is theoretically possible at the cognitive level. Also, with top-level cognitive theories in place, PDP researchers can be guided in their bottom-up approach.

Rumelhart and McClelland, whilst agreeing in general with the sentiments expressed in the objection, do not agree that current knowledge from neuroscience provides no guidance to those interested in the functioning of the *mind*. In making this point, they also provide a clear statement as to why connectionism is one form of neurocomputing, and not the only form:

> [W]e have, by and large, not focused on *neural modeling* (i.e., the modeling of neurons), but rather we have focused on *neurally inspired* modeling of cognitive processes. Our models have not depended strongly on the details of brain structure or on issues that are very controversial in neuroscience. ...We have found that top-down considerations revolving about a need to postulate parallel, cooperative computational models ...have meshed nicely with a number of more bottom-up considerations of brain style processing. (Rumelhart and McClelland, 1986, p. 130, stress supplied)

That is, connectionism is concerned with neurally-*inspired*, or neurally-*derived* models, rather than neurally-*based* ones. Rumelhart and McClelland then describe ten characteristics which feature in their PDP models and which help to distinguish connectionism from other forms of neurocomputing as well as provide a basis for distinguishing neurocomputing from computationalism:

(i) neurons are slow (as exemplified in the 100-step constraint of Feldman, as described earlier), which leads to the conclusion that *massive parallelism* is required;

(ii) there is a very large number of neurons, hence aspects of brain-style modeling require large numbers of processing units;

(iii) neurons receive inputs from a large number of other neurons, where one or a small number of action potentials received are not enough to generate an action potential, which leads to the conclusion that human computation involves a kind of statistical process in which decisions are the product of cooperative action of many somewhat independent processing units;

(iv) learning involves modifying connections, which leads to the conclusion that knowledge is in the connections rather than in the units themselves;

(v) neurons communicate by sending activation or inhibition through connections, not symbol-passing, which leads to the conclusion that the role and function of symbols must emerge from this subsymbolic level of processing;

(vi) connections in the brain appear to have a clear geometric and topological structure, such as mappings between nearby regions of the brain, symmetry of connections between region to another, and activation connections *between* systems but inhibitory connections *within* a region; such structural properties of the brain are often reflected in PDP models;

(vii) information is continuously available, rather than (as with a standard approach) output occurring in stages with sometimes no output being available at all;

(viii) connectionist models exhibit graceful degradation under conditions of damage and information overload, where a region's performance may be increasingly affected as more and more units are destroyed but no critical point exists at which the system breaks down: this is to be contrasted with the classical idea of one instruction of a large computer program not working, which then leads to a complete system crash;

(ix) there is distributed, not central, control, i.e. there is no central executive in charge of the general flow of processing; and

(x) relaxation is the dominant mode of computation, where the primary mode of computation in the brain is best understood as a kind of relaxation system which *settles into* a solution rather than *calculates* a solution.

Fodor and Pylyshyn attack some, but not all, of these characteristics in their critique. With regard to the first - speed - they look again at the 100-step constraint, i.e. in the time that it takes for a human to, say, recognise a word or picture, only a hundred or so instructions can be carried out if one assumes a serial program and given the speed with which neurons fire. Connectionists argue that since simple cognitive tasks may require millions of instructions, the brain must operate differently from serial computers, i.e. the brain must be organised in a massively parallel way. Fodor and Pylyshyn point out that this confuses architecture with implementation. A conventional computer, such as a VAX, runs many serial programs quite happily in parallel and at great speed:

> Operating on symbols can even involve "massively parallel" organizations; they might indeed imply new architectures, but they are all *Classical* in our sense, since they all share the Classical conception of computation as symbol-processing. ...The point here is that an argument for a network of parallel computers is not in and of itself either an argument against a Classical architecture or an argument for a Connectionist architecture. (Fodor and Pylyshyn, 1988, p. 56, stress supplied)

6.12 PDP MODELS AND NEURAL REALISM

Rumelhart and McClelland then describe a variety of ways in which their own brand of *brain-style* modeling differs from the facts of neuroscience. For example, whilst PDP models generally assume that a unit can have both excitatory and inhibitory connections, it seems clear from brain research evidence that most cortical units are *either* excitatory *or* inhibitory, but not both. Rumelhart and McClelland claim that their PDP models fall in between the levels of the 'macrostructure of cognition' on the one hand, and the details of neurophysiology on the other - a level they call 'microstructure of cognition'. Models built at this intermediate level will be approximations, and scientific progress is achieved by making the right approximations and the right simplifications.

Rumelhart and McClelland also admit that microstructure models currently do not include all the facts of neuroscience, one of which is mean firing rates (a point raised by Searle - see the last chapter). However, they suggest that while mean firing rates may well be important so are 'spikes' - sudden surges of signal energy - and that these may be computationally significant also. Another fact of neuroscience is that chemicals can affect brain processing, but this too has not been seriously examined by PDP researchers. Yet another fact of neuroscience, apparently, is that there are *hundreds* of different kinds of neurons, rather than the two types - excitatory and inhibitory - currently adopted in PDP models.

Justifying the exclusion of neuroscience facts which can later be included as PDP models become more complex is very different from justifying the inclusion of 'facts' which appear to have no neuroscience basis, as Rumelhart and McClelland admit. Their defence is that mechanisms chosen in order to fulfil various functional purposes in a model but which cannot be justified on the basis of current facts can be hypothesized to exist but are currently not recognized:

> In that sense our work could be considered as a source of hypotheses for neuroscience. It is also possible that we are correct about the computations that are performed, but that they are performed by a different kind of neural mechanism than our formulations seem at first glance to suggest. If this is the case, it merely suggests that the most obvious mapping of our models into neural structures is incorrect. (Rumelhart and McClelland, 1986, pp. 138-138)

Rumelhart and McClelland explicitly reject the view that connectionism is implementational, i.e., that connectionist models somehow are just physical implementations of symbol systems in neural hardware. According to Rumelhart and McClelland, connectionist models cannot be implementations because, quite simply, connectionist models are themselves abstractions, and embody hypotheses, of what takes place in the brain. The implementation of connectionist models will therefore be one level removed from the design and construction of connectionist models, since it is in the act of implementation (physical realization on neural hardware of some sort) that a variety of decisions will have to be taken on how best to implement the abstractions and hypotheses contained in the connectionist model on the hardware available.

We are in danger of opening up discussion on fundamental methodological issues here - the province of the next chapter. Instead, we can note what Fodor and Pylyshyn have to say on this matter of brain style modeling. Fodor and Pylyshyn claim that some connectionists, contrary to Rumelhart and McClelland's views, *do* believe they are attempting to build brain models based on neural properties, whereas others, such as Smolensky, believe they are providing mathematical models which can be given either a neural or psychological interpretation. In either case, Fodor and Pylyshyn ask whether anything is gained by providing models when the proposers fail to state *exactly how* the models are mapped onto the brain. That is, assuming that various biological facts are included in connectionist models, such as neurological connections and threshold properties, in what way are these facts relevant to *inferring* the nature of a cognitive architecture? According to Fodor and Pylyshyn, very little is gained at this intermediate level of microstructure. For example, assuming that neural systems *are* networks that transmit activation which results in some state change, this does not necessarily mean that higher level processes, such as reasoning, consist of the spread of activation among representations. Fodor and Pylyshyn therefore question the role of this intermediate level between cognitive architecture - or the macrostructure of cognition - on the one hand, and the level of the brain on the other, if researchers working at this intermediate microlevel provide no rules for inferring the macrostructure from the microstructure.

6.13 NATIVISM VERSUS EMPIRICISM

Rumelhart and McClelland accept that perceptron-like models have historically been linked to the empiricist school of thought concerning what is and what is not innate to a child when it is born. That is, PDP models appear to support the empiricist view that, apart from some basic principles, there is nothing in the child's mind at birth and that subsequent learning emerges from a *tabula rasa* (or 'blank slate') as the child is exposed to the world and learns through experience. However, Rumelhart and McClelland claim that PDP models are 'agnostic' about the issue of innate versus learned knowledge. PDP models can be interpreted along radical nativism lines as well as radical empirical lines.

For instance, a radical nativist could argue that the behaviour of an organism was entirely determined by a preset (i.e. genetically determined at birth) pattern of interconnections among the units, with some units preset to be input units and others output units. Such a system can perform *any* of the possible behaviours that such a system of units and interconnections is capable of, and the question of why an organism did actually perform one actual behaviour could be answered empirically. A radical empiricist, on the other hand, would argue that there are no *a priori* limits on how the network of interconnections could be constituted, and that any pattern of interconnections is possible. The actual set of interconnections chosen is the pattern of experience the system receives, and the organism could eventually settle on a set of interconnections which were maximally adaptive, given its exposure to the environment.

Rumelhart and McClelland stress that while they are neutral on the nativism versus empiricism issue connectionism provides a new perspective on the debate:

> Suppose, for the sake of argument, that we have an organism whose initial state is wholly determined genetically. Suppose further that all of the connections were modifiable so that whatever the start state, any pattern of interconnections could emerge through interaction of the organism with its environment. In such a system as this we have, it seems to us, the benefits of both nativism and empiricism. (Rumelhart and McClelland, 1986, p. 140)

That is, whilst part of a network may well be prewired to carry out a certain task, if that task is not relevant in the organism's environment then that part of the network can be used for some other purpose.

6.14 KNOWLEDGE AND REASONING

Rumelhart and McClelland accept that even researchers sympathetic to PDP models may feel that something is missing from a connectionist account of cognitive processes, namely, an account of how behaviour is guided by explicit, conscious knowledge, how we reason from what we know to new conclusions based on that knowledge, and how we sequentially traverse a problem space in order to find a solution. As Rumelhart and McClelland put it:

> Can parallel distributed processing have anything to say about these explicit, introspectively accessible, temporally extended acts of thinking? Some have suggested that the answer is no - that PDP models may be fine as accounts for perception, motor control, and other *low-level* phenomena, but that they are simply unable to account for the higher level mental processing of the kind involved in reasoning, problem-solving, and other higher level aspects of thought. (Rumelhart and McClelland, 1986, p. 144, stress supplied)

Rumelhart and McClelland reply that they are convinced that PDP models are equally applicable to these higher level processes, but that more complex PDP models, where there is interaction between several networks, are required. They point out that PDP models have already been developed for such higher level cognitive processes as language acquisition, sequential thought, and problem solving.

As a way of bringing this discussion to a close, it is worth quoting at length Fodor and Pylyshyn's concluding remarks on connectionism and, by implication, on neurocomputing in general:

> [O]nce one admits that there really are cognitive-level principles distinct from the (putative) architectural principles that Connectionism articulates, there seems to be little left to argue about. Clearly it is pointless to ask whether one should or shouldn't do cognitive science by studying "the interaction of lower levels" as opposed to studying processes at the cognitive level since we surely do *both* .... We have, in short, no objection at all to networks as potential implementation models, nor do we suppose that any of the arguments we've given are incompatible with this proposal. The trouble is, however, that if Connectionists do want their models to be construed in this way, then they will have to radically alter their practice. For, it seems utterly clear that most of the Connectionist models that have actually

been proposed must be construed as theories of cognition, not as theories of implementation. This follows from the fact that it is intrinsic to these theories to ascribe representational content to the units ... that they postulate. And ... a theory of the relations among representational states is ipso facto a theory at the level of cognition, not at the level of implementation. It has been the burden of our argument that when construed as a cognitive theory, rather than as an implementation theory, Connectionism appears to have fatal limitations. The problem with Connectionist models is that all the reasons for thinking that they might be true are reasons for thinking that they couldn't be *psychology*. (Fodor and Pylyshyn, 1988, p. 66, stress supplied)

Summing up, Fodor and Pylyshyn claim that there are four ways that connectionists (and hence neurocomputing researchers) can proceed. First, they can argue that mental representations are indeed unstructured, in which case they must tackle productivity and systematicity. Secondly, they can adopt structured mental representations but insist upon an associationist account of the nature of mental processes. This not only is a retreat to an empiricist's view of the mind with all the implications that such a view carries for concepts such as cause, time, language and reasoning (i.e. such concepts can only be learned through experience and not because of any innate knowledge we possess) but also rejects structure-sensitivity of operations. The result of such a retreat is that connectionism returns to the state that psychology was in before the cognitive science revolution. Thirdly, they can accept that connectionism is an implementation theory, in which case a lot of material must be rewritten. And, fourthly, they can give up the idea that networks offer a reasonable basis for modeling cognitive processes in general, i.e. they can weaken connectionism to such an extent that connectionist models are useful only for drawing statistical inferences, and nothing more. In this case, connectionism retreats to the position of offering statistical models of learning which, since 1957 (Chomsky, 1957), are widely acknowledged as extremely limited in their applicability.

6.15 AI AND NEUROCOMPUTING

Our task in this concluding section is to identify ways in which the disagreements between computationalists (classicists) and neurocomputing researchers can be reconciled, especially with respect to AI. We shall have to refer some of the more important methodological points, especially concerning neurocomputing as implementational, until the next chapter. However, that will not stop us from making some general points concerning the relationship between computationalism and neurocomputing. We shall also offer a modern version (or, more accurately, more modern version*s*, of the Argument from Continuity in the Nervous System.

Let us look first at the precise disagreement between computationalists and connectionists on the matter of representations. There are two main issues involved here: that a connectionist 'representation' cannot be tied up with a suitable level of cognitive architecture, and that a connectionist 'representation' does not contain, as primitives, the types of construct one would expect in a representation. We shall return to the first of these issues in the next chapter. Let us concentrate on the second.

According to Fodor and Pylyshyn, connectionism has 'causal connectedness' as the only primitive relation among nodes, i.e. only excitatory and inhibitory links between nodes are allowed. Classicists allow not just causal relations but also structural relations, of which constituency is paradigmatic. This in turn leads to two architectural differences. First, classicists are committed to symbolic structures that have syntactic and semantic structure and, secondly, classical mental representations are manipulated by structure-sensitive processes.

However, these differences are not so apparent once we examine more carefully the notion of cause, which Fodor and Pylyshyn claim is the only primitive relation amongst nodes in a connectionist model. As we saw in Chapter 1 in the first volume, 'cause' can be unpacked in logical terms. Specifically, the concept of something causing another can be rephrased in the terms of the propositional calculus. That is, *X is causally necessary for Y* can be unpacked, logically, as *If not-X then not-Y*, or *If Y then X*. Also, *X is causally sufficient for Y* can be unpacked, logically, as *If X then Y (de facto)*, or *If not-Y then not-X*. This means that it is possible to *reason* about connectionist processes and architectures, provided that the causal links are translated into propositional logic terms. Once the translation has been achieved, we have a description of the connectionist network which can be manipulated and given meaning to in the same way as other descriptions in the propositional logic. In addition, it is possible to interpret the logical description as a *representation*, thereby overcoming one of the major criticisms that Fodor and Pylyshyn level against connectionism, as long as the representation is taken to be one of the connectionist network in abstract terms. Actual propositions could replace nodes to determine whether the network still works consistently for different propositions. Moreover, the network as a whole can be checked for logical consistency, given the translations into logical propositions. The gulf between connectionists and classicists may not be so wide, after all.

Although classicists may counter-argue that connectionists are not explicit in their assumptions concerning causality, neither are Fodor and Pylyshyn. If causality can be unpacked in terms which Fodor and Pylyshyn accept as including a combinatorial syntax and semantics, as well as structure-sensitivity, the main disagreement is not about the primitive relations but the level of theory description, i.e. how far down does one need to go before an adequate foundation is laid for a theory? Fodor and Pylyshyn may justifiably claim that classical representations explicitly go deeper, or further, than connectionist ones, but that is a different claim from the one they wish to make, namely, that connectionist representations have fewer primitive relations than classical ones. If they want to make this criticism stick, their task should be to demonstrate that causal connections cannot in principle be translated into logical formulae.

Fodor and Pylyshyn may well be right on this point, but further conceptual analysis is required on their part. For instance, they could examine how inhibition (rather than excitation, as in our examples above) can be unpacked in logical terms: if they find that inhibition cannot be unpacked logically, that would give them good grounds for claiming that links cannot all be 'represented' in classical terms.

The next major point concerns the notion of mental processes. In classical representations, Fodor and Pylyshyn claim, the syntax of a formula encodes its meaning. Namely, the meaning of a formula is somehow a function of the meaning of the individual syntactic elements. Fodor and Pylyshyn claim that languages having this property encode those aspects of the meaning of a formula that determine its role in inference, i.e. truth-preserving transformations. But a criticism that can be levelled at classicism here is that it is quite possible to have a different view of semantics, and thereby of the notion of explanation. For instance, in computer science, there is a view of semantics known as operational semantics, which can be described as follows:

Concentrating on the program as a function mapping inputs

> ...into ...results ...leads to operational ...semantics. Operational semantics imagines the program running on an abstract machine. This machine may be quite unlike any real computer, either low-level, simple and easy to analyse, or high level with an easy translation from the programming language. The machine and translation must be specified. Such a definition is most useful to a compiler writer if the abstract machine is close to real hardware. (Allison, 1986, p. 2)

If classicists argue that in the specification of an abstract machine and a translation the syntax at least of the formulae in the source language is used to map onto formulae in the target language, and that therefore the formulae in the target language are the semantic representations of formulae in the source language, exactly the same response can be proposed by connectionists, i.e. that 'translating' classical representations into connectionist ones is to give some meaning to the classical representations. Classical representations can then be imagined to run on abstract machines called connection machines. Specifying the (abstract) behaviour of these (abstract) machines then provides the semantic interpretation of classical representations. If Fodor and Pylyshyn want to rule out this possibility, it is up to them to come up with examples of classical representations which in principle cannot be translated into connectionist representations. Again, this is not to claim that such examples cannot be found, only that Fodor and Pylyshyn need to do some more work if they are to make their criticisms stick. After all, adopting an operational semantics standpoint, connectionists could claim that their approach provides, *from a computational point of view*, not just a better, i.e. more acceptable and effective, way of specifying the semantics of symbolic structures, but also perhaps the *only* way of interpreting symbolic structures computationally.

This takes us on to the comment concerning implementation. Fodor and Pylyshyn claim that they have no objection to the view that connectionist theories are implementation theories. They are happy to view connectionism as a theory of how cognition is neurally implemented:

> If Connectionism is considered simply as a theory of how cognition is neurally implemented, it may constrain cognitive models no more than theories in biophysics, biochemistry, or, for that matter, quantum mechanics do. ...The point is that 'implements' is transitive, and it goes all the way down. (Fodor and

Pylyshyn, 1988, p.68)

This may well be true, but given our previous comments it is clear that a translation is not an implementation. That is, if classical representations can be translated into connectionist ones which are imagined to run on an abstract machine, it is the running (imagined or otherwise) which gives rise to the implementation (imagined or otherwise), not the translation itself. If connectionists want to argue that their representations could in some sense be regarded as translations and not implementations of classical representations, and that it is these translations that are cognitively valid, Fodor and Pylyshyn must adopt a different line. They could

(a) deny that connectionist translations are possible, by providing examples of classical representations which are in principle untranslatable (as previously described); or

(b) accept that connectionist 'translations' are possible, but argue that such translations are really implementations (in which case they deny any other semantic model apart from their own); or

(c) argue that classical representations are at a higher level than connectionist translations, because the translation process can only be one way, i.e. it is not possible to translate from connectionist representations to classical ones and therefore 'translates' in this case is transitive, just like 'implements'.

It is not at all clear, after a thorough reading of their critique, which of these strategies Fodor and Pylyshyn would adopt. If they were to adopt (c), they would have to be careful that they did not come up with an inconsistent critique: for much of the paper they deny that connectionist representations have any syntactic or semantic structure, yet c) would involve them accepting connectionist representations as somehow meaningful.

The point of the above comments is that computationalism need not have a monopoly on the notion of representation, nor are all the questions concerning the role of representations answered. That should not detract from the relevance and appropriateness of Fodor and Pylyshyn's criticisms, provided that they are relevant and appropriate. If, however, some of the criticisms are not, then far from demonstrating the weaknesses in connectionist 'representations' Fodor and Pylyshyn may end up highlighting the weaknesses in the computationalist approach and thereby providing even further motivation for a search for alternative, neurally-inspired or neurally-based paradigms.

Let us tie up one loose strand and look at Minsky and Papert's solution to the 'war', as they see it, between connectionists and computationalists. Having admitted that one of their main criticisms against neural network research was that it was difficult, if not impossible, to determine the complexity involved in scaling up the problem from a toy one to a real world one, they make the following claim:

> But now we propose a somewhat shocking alternative: Perhaps the scale of the toy problem is that on which, in physiological actuality, much of the functioning of intelligence operates. Accepting this thesis leads into a way of thinking very different from that of the connectionist movement. We have used the phrase "society of mind" to refer to the idea that mind is made up of a large number of components, or "agents," each of which would operate on the scale of what, if taken in isolation, would be little more than a toy problem. [See Minsky (1987) and Papert (1982).] (Minsky and Papert, 1988, pp. 226- 267)

The idea of a society of mind consisting of agents is, essentially, a version of the modularity hypothesis we introduced earlier, with the characteristic that modules, instead of necessarily being horizontally and vertically organized, are independent units each of which performs a trivial task. Such modules are called agents, and agents can be triggered by other agents or by incoming data. These agents can be active concurrently, which leads to the idea of cooperating or competing concurrent processes. For Minsky and Papert, the question is not whether connectionism offers the right level of description for processes: on that point, they have no disagreement with connectionists. Rather, the point is *how* neurocomputing can be represented as the operation of *societies of networks*. That is, if toy connectionist systems cannot be scaled up, because it is not clear how the mechanisms for such scaling up would work, nor whether such scaling up is possible for certain classes of problems, then the only alternative is for connectionists to describe the way simple neural nets are organized into effective large systems:

> The power of the brain stems not from any single, fixed, universal principle. Instead it comes from the evolution (in both the individual sense and the Darwinian sense) of a variety of ways to

> develop new mechanisms and to adapt older ones to perform new
> functions. Instead of seeking a way to get around that need for
> diversity, we have come to try to develop "society of mind" theo-
> ries that will recognize and exploit the idea that brains are based
> on many different kinds of interacting mechanisms. (Minsky and
> Papert, 1988, pp. 268-269)

Minsky and Papert accept the intuitive appeal of connectionism, but also
remind computationalists, and neurocomputing researchers, that in addition
to the idea of module encapsulation there is another intuitive concept - *insulation* - which also needs explaining. Insulation is the concept that processes,
whilst cooperating with each other over a particular task by breaking that
task down into subtasks which are then tackled individually by subprocesses,
must nevertheless *keep the subtasks apart*. In other words, Minsky and Papert remind researchers that even with neural network systems there must
be *network* or *system managers*.

In response to the question as to where these managers come from, Minsky and Papert claim that the easiest way of answering is to assume that
the managers are agents genetically programmed to make new connections
at predetermined times. However, that does not detract, they claim, from
their view that

> ...the scientific future of connectionism is tied not to the
> search for some single, universal scheme to solve all problems
> at once but to the evolution of a many-faceted technology of
> "brain design" that encompasses good technical theories about
> the analysis of learning procedures, of useful architectures, and
> of organizational principles to use when assembling those com-
> ponents into larger systems. (Minsky and Papert, 1988, p. 274)

Minsky and Papert then outline what their peace solution is. If different
neural networks perform, in cooperation, different tasks, and if those tasks
have somehow to be insulated from each other, then the role of *symbols*
becomes interesting. That is, assuming that symbols are represented in a
distributed form within a subnetwork, one of the questions which arise is
how two subnetworks performing, in cooperation, two different tasks can
represent the information they process in the same way. A related, and just
as important, question is how two subnetworks performing two completely
separate and independent tasks (i.e. tasks not related in any way) are to

be *prevented* from making connections to each other. Minsky and Papert's answer is through seriality:

> Perhaps the only ultimate escape from the limitations of internal interactions is to evolve towards organizations in which each network affects others primarily through the use of *serial* operations and specialized short-term-memory [i.e. symbolic] systems, for although seriality is relatively slow, its use makes it possible to produce and control interactions between activities that occur at different and separate places and times. (Minsky and Papert, 1988, p. 277, stress supplied)

For Minsky and Papert, one of the ways the differences can be reconciled is that neurocomputing, whilst biologically, psychologically and empirically appealing, nevertheless needs computationalism in order to provide organizational principles and mechanisms concerning the connectivity and insularity of individual networks which cooperate or not on related and unrelated tasks.

Despite what one thinks of the details of Minsky and Papert's proposal for reconciliation, there is no doubt that they have identified *one* basis on which it is possible to explore the prospects of reconciliation, namely, the basis of modularity. If both computationalists and connectionists agree that the mind is modular, at some common level of explanation and to some agreed degree, then it may indeed be possible to explore, as a first step towards reconciliation, a form of modular organization which would allow both computationalists and connectionists to contribute jointly. (This is essentially the proposal of Bechtel (1988).) *Another* basis for reconciliation could arise out of the forms of representation used by computationalists and connectionists: if, as we pointed out earlier, connectionist representations could be identified with 'equivalent' computationalist representation translations, and vice versa, where the term 'equivalent' has to be unpacked in some way (probably with regard to the equivalence of connectionist network types with certain automata types), this may also provide a way forward.

In conclusion, let us provide modern versions of the Argument from Continuity in the Nervous System. There are essentially two interpretations of this objection, given the developments in neurocomputing since the appearance of the objection in 1950. The first interpretation is provided from a neurocomputing point of view, irrespective of the precise details of which form of neurocomputing is involved, and goes like this:

> *Argument from Continuity in the Nervous System₁*: An understanding
> of mental and psychological concepts is not possible, and explanations
> of such concepts cannot be adequately provided or evaluated, unless, or
> until, the underlying models and simulations of the nervous system on
> top of which such concepts can be posited are *brain-like*, *brain-derived*,
> or *brain-based*.

This is to interpret the Argument as an attack, by neurocomputing researchers, against computationalism. The task of neurocomputing research
is then to demonstrate how it is possible for neural networks to give rise to
explanations of mental and psychological concepts. Proposers of this version
of the Argument from Continuity in the Nervous System would believe that
neurocomputing offers not just an alternative paradigm for cognitive science,
and AI, research but also the only paradigm. The task of computationalists is then to state how their 'classical' theories can be neurally derived or
neurally based. This version of the Argument therefore requires computationalist theories, if they are to have plausibility as theories of the mind, to
be neurally plausible also.

Whilst this may seem to be a strong interpretation of the neurocomputing approach, it may nevertheless be possible for certain neurocomputing
researchers to argue for this interpretation. Attacks such as those by Fodor
and Pylyshyn can now be interpreted as modern counterarguments to this
interpretation.

The second version of the original objection, and one close in spirit to
the original, runs something like this:

> *Argument from Continuity in the Nervous System₂*: Even if a variety
> of techniques can be successfully used for constructing models of the
> nervous system or machines which simulate the nervous system, that
> does not mean that machine intelligence and thought are possible.

This interpretation can be held by both computationalists and by those theorists who believe that mental and psychological concepts cannot be explained
by either the neurocomputing or computationalist approach. Computationalists might argue that neurocomputing is at the wrong level of analysis and
therefore cannot provide adequate explanations of mental and psychological
phenomena; anti-AI theorists might argue, more generally, that any attempt
to explain mental and psychological phenomena, by both computationalists
and neurocomputing researchers, is doomed to failure: the former because

computationalism assumes that human mental and psychological phenomena can be explained by an appeal to the mind as a sort of information processing device, and this is a false hypothesis; and the latter because neurocomputing assumes that mental and psychological events and processes just are, or can be reduced to, or can be derived from, brain events and processes, and this too is false (because, for instance, the brain and the mind cannot be lawfully or scientifically related).

Our next task is to examine, from an AI point of view, the computationalist interpretation outlined above of the Argument from Continuity in the Nervous System, namely, that neurocomputing is at the wrong level of analysis. This will necessitate an examination of what AI researchers are trying to do, and in the process we shall tidy up the various loose strands of this chapter.

References

Allison, L. (1986) *A Practical Introduction to Denotational Semantics*. Cambridge University Press.

Anderson, J. A. and Hinton, G. E. (1981) Models of information processing in the brain, in J. A. Anderson and G. E. Hinton (eds.) *Parallel Models of Associative Memory*, Lawrence Erlbaum.

Ashby, W. R. (1956) *An Introduction to Cybernetics*. Chapman and Hall. Republished by Methuen and Co. in 1964; the page references are taken from the 1976 reprint.

Bechtel, W. (1988) Connectionism and rules and representation systems: are they compatible?, *Philosophical Psychology*, 1, 1, pp. 5-16.

Boden, M. (1979) The computational metaphor in psychology, in N. Bolton (ed.) *Philosophical Problems in Psychology*, Methuen.

Chomsky, N. (1957) *Syntactic Structures*. Mouton.

Chomsky, N. (1965) *Aspects of the Theory of Syntax*. MIT Press.

Fahlman, S. E. (1979) *A System for Representing and Using Real-World Knowledge*. MIT Press.

Feldman, J. A. (1985) Connectionist models and their applications: Introduction, *Cognitive Science*, 9, 1-2.

Feldman, J. A. and Ballard, D. H. (1982) Connectionist models and their properties, *Cognitive Science*, 6, pp. 205-254.

Fodor, J. A. (1983) *Modularity of Mind*. Bradford Books/MIT Press.

Fodor, J. A. and Pylyshyn, Z. W. (1988) Connectionism and cognitive architecture: A critical analysis, *Cognition*, Volume 28. Reprinted in S. Pinker and J. Mehler (eds.) *Connectionism and Symbols*, MIT Press, 1988, from which the page references are taken.

Gardner, H. (1985) *The Mind's New Science*. Basic Books.

Haugeland, J. (1985) *Artificial Intelligence: The Very Idea*. MIT Press.

Hebb, D. O. (1949) *The Organization of Behaviour*. Wiley.

Hinton, G. E. (1981) A parallel computation that assigns canonical object-based frames of reference, *Proceedings of the 7th International Joint Conference on Artificial Intelligence (IJCAI)*.

Kintsch, W. (1984) Approaches to the study of the psychology of language, in T G. Bever, J. M. Carroll and L. A. Miller (eds.) *Talking Minds: the Study of Language in Cognitive Science*, MIT Press.

McClelland, J. L., Rumelhart, D. E., and the PDP Research Group (eds.) (1986) *Parallel Distributed Processing: Explorations in the Microstructure of Cognition. Volume 2: Psychological and Biological Models*. Bradford Books/MIT Press.

Maloney, J. C. (1988) In praise of narrow minds: the frame problem, in J. H. Fetzer (ed.) *Aspects of Artificial Intelligence*, Kluwer Academic Publishers.

Marr, D. (1976) Early processing of visual information, *Philosophical Transactions of the Royal Society*, Series B, 1976, 275, pp. 483-524.

Minsky, M. (1987) *The Society of Minds*. Simon and Schuster.

Minsky, M. and Papert, S. (1969) *Perceptrons: An Introduction to Computational Geometry*. MIT Press.

Minsky, M. and Papert, S. (1988) *Perceptrons: Expanded Edition*. MIT Press.

Narayanan, A. (1986) Memory models of man and machine, in M. Yazdani (ed.) *Artificial Intelligence: Principles and Applications*, Chapman and Hall.

Nilsson, N. J. (1965) *Learning Machines*. McGraw-Hill.

Papert, S. (1982) *Mindstorms*. Basic Books.

Papert, S. (1988) One AI or many?, in S. R. Graubard (ed.) *The Artificial Intelligence Debate: False Starts, Real Foundations*, MIT Press.

Rosenblatt, T. (1962) *Principles of Neurodynamics*. Spartan.

Rumelhart, D. E., Hinton, G. E. and McClelland, J. L. (1986) A general framework for parallel distributed processing, in D. E. Rumelhart, J. L. McClelland and the PDP Research Group (1986).

Rumelhart, D. E. and McClelland, J. L. (1986) PDP models and general issues in cognitive science, in Rumelhart, McClelland and the PDP Research Group (1986).

Rumelhart, D. E., McClelland, J. L. and the PDP Research Group (eds.) (1986) *Parallel Distributed Processing: Explorations in the Microstructure of Cognition. Volume 1: Foundations*. Bradford Books/MIT Press.

Rumelhart, D. E. and Norman, D. A. (1981) A comparison of models, in J. A. Anderson and G. E. Hinton (eds.) *Parallel Models of Associative Memory*, Lawrence Erlbaum.

Winograd, T. (1976) Computer memories: A metaphor for memory organisation, in C. N. Cofer (ed.) *The Structure of Human Memory*, Freeman.

Winograd, T. and Flores, F. (1986) *Understanding Computers and Cognition*. Ablex. Reprinted by Addison Wesley in 1987, from which the page reference is taken.

Chapter 7

AI and methodology

7.1   INTRODUCTION

There is remarkably little consensus on the part of AI researchers as to what
exactly they do when they carry out AI research. The historically interesting,
but now unpopular, view that AI

> ...is the science of making machines do things that would
> require intelligence if done by men (Minsky, 1968, p. v)

was considered the least controversial (see (Boden, 1977, p. 4)) simply because it was the most general: it left open the crucial question as to which
activities did require intelligence, and why. Here is a more modern view:

> [AI] is the study of mental faculties through the use of com-
> putational models. (Charniak and McDermott, 1985, p. 6)

Note the 'science' in Minsky's quote has been replaced by 'study', and that
the word 'model' has been introduced.

Some authors and commentators do not provide their own views on what
it is that they are doing when they carry out AI research. For instance, they
assume that the reader already has knowledge of what AI is or can be introduced to what AI is by reading about it. For instance, O'Shea and Eisenstadt
(1984) put together a collection of papers on AI which describe the various
programming languages ('tools') available, practices used ('techniques') and

systems ('applications') implemented. That is, the book describes the technology rather than the theory of AI.

Others openly state that they do not consider that it is important to say exactly what AI is:

> I don't think it matters at all whether or not AI is a discipline or where its boundaries might be. (Feldman, 1985, p. 376)

Many commentators believe that AI cuts across many disciplines:

> [AI] is inherently multi-disciplinary, and the more AI is applied the more disciplines will be involved. There is a central use of AI/Cognitive Science which is the systematic study of actual and possible intelligent systems. (Sloman, 1985, p. 377)

> AI, broadly conceived, is just too large to be a single discipline - mainly because intelligent perception and behaviour touch so many aspects of computer science, control theory, and signal processing theory. (Nilsson, 1985, p. 376)

Bobrow and Hayes (1985), the editors of the responses they received to a questionnaire, sum up the part of the questionnaire dealing with AI methodology as follows:

> The distinction between on the one hand AI as a science, essentially part of Cognitive Science, with its focus being theories of intelligence; and on the other hand AI as a technology, part of Computer Science, with its focus being on the design of systems, ran through several responses. (Bobrow and Hayes, 1985, p. 380)

The aim of this chapter is to explore the implications of AI being a science, or study, on the one hand, and AI being a technology, on the other. This will then provide the basis for a more detailed examination of how AI can be placed on sound, methodological ground. We shall introduce the views of three philosophers of science (Hempel, Popper and (briefly) Kuhn) in order to provide some understanding of what a science, in some people's eyes, should consist of methodologically. We shall then examine one particular methodological framework - that provided by Marr - which has much relevance for AI. This will lead us on to examine two proposals (by Peacocke

dad	child
John	Ken
John	Betty
John	Mary
Ken	Myself
Ken	Albert

Table 7.1

and by Rumelhart and McClelland) for extensions to Marr's framework. We shall briefly discuss the possibility of methodological reconciliation between computationalists and neurocomputing researchers before finally rephrasing Turing's Imitation Game in a more modern way - one which stresses the methodological stances available to AI researchers in their pursuit of 'the intelligent machine'.

7.2   THE NEED FOR A METHODOLOGY OF AI

Suppose I am sitting in my armchair one evening and for some reason I start thinking about memory. I become fascinated by the question: 'How exactly do I remember things?' After a lot of thought, I come up with the following scheme.

In my memory there are many items of information collected into 'tables'. For instance, *Table 7.1* shows part of a table that contains all the information I have on who is the father of whom. My father is Ken, and Ken's father is John. *Table 7.2* shows part of a table that contains all the information I have on who is the mother of whom. I call the first table **father** and the second **mother**. Whenever I am given information on who is the father or mother of whom, I store the information in one of these tables.

In addition to the above two tables, I have other tables which contain information on each of the people whose names occur in the **father** and **mother** tables. For instance, there may be tables called **is male** and **is female**, parts of which are provided in *Table 7.3*. I now say that I remember an item if, after a search of a table, an item is found. For instance, if I am

mum	*child*
Betty	Simon
Betty	Mary
Mary	Clare
Joan	Myself
Glynis	Ken
Jan	John

Table 7.2

is male	is female
John	Betty
Ken	Mary
Albert	Clare
Simon	Joan
	Glynis
	Jan

Table 7.3

asked 'Who is the father of Betty?', a search is made through the **father** table until **Betty** is found in the second column of the table, and then the name occurring as the first item in that same row, i.e. **John**, is returned. So, if I am asked 'Who is the daughter of Betty?', I might respond: 'Well, actually, Mary is, and Simon is her son.' In the latter case, a search is made of the **mother** table and **Mary**, who is a child of Betty, is found. Then, since being a daughter involves being female, the **is female** table would be searched to check that Mary is female, which she is, so her name is returned. The additional information that Simon is a son of Betty is also returned, perhaps signifying a half-successful search (i.e. Simon is a child of Betty but, being male, cannot be a daughter).

I now need to provide some mechanism for allowing new information to be entered into tables not previously existing. That is, let us suppose that I am not happy with the thought of a great number of these tables in my memory system and instead think that it is more elegant if tables of information could be created only when needed and then thrown away. So, I hypothesise that tables can be created to store new information not previously categorised. For instance, I know that the mother of a mother of a child is a grandmother of that child. This can be expressed as a rule for storing information in a new table called **grandmother**. I supply the notation as follows:

$$\textbf{grandmother(X)} \leftarrow \textbf{mother(X,Y) and mother(Y,Z)}$$

which is to be interpreted as 'An unnamed individual X is a grandmother if X is the mother of an unnamed individual Y and if Y is the mother of an unnamed individual Z.' If I work through the previously supplied part of the **mother** table, putting names to the unnamed individuals consistently, I find that only Betty being a grandmother is justified. This is because the value of **mother (X,Y)** can be instantiated with respect to the row of the **mother** table which has Betty being the mother of Mary, and also the value of **mother (Y,Z)** can be instantiated with respect to the row of the **mother** table which has Mary being the mother of Clare. So, **X** equals **Betty**, **Y** equals **Mary** and **Z** equals **Clare**. (Notice that the two **Y**s on the right-hand side of the **grandmother** rule are instantiated with respect to the same symbol, **Mary**.)

I can supply more rules for storing and creating information on other types of blood relationships. For instance,

Ken	Betty
Myself	Albert
Albert	Myself

Table 7.4

brother(X,Y) ← father(Z,X) and father(Z,Y) and is male(X)

which can be interpreted as 'An unnamed individual signified by **X** is the brother of an unnamed individual signified by **Y** if some unnamed individual signified by **Z** in the father of the individuals signified by **X** and **Y** and if the individual signified by **X** is male.' If I work through this rule using the above tables, I find I obtain a new **brother** table *Table 7.4*. The last two rows, although they seem to duplicate each other, provide the important information that not only is my brother Albert but also Albert's brother is myself. (Betty's brother could be Martin but Martin's brother is not Betty. There will, of course, be several ways to formulate a certain blood relationship which can take these factors into account.)

So, my answer to the question 'How exactly do I remember things?' is that my mind contains a lot of information stored away in relevant tables. I remember an item of information by searching through the tables. I can also construct new tables of information only when required, and to do this I hypothesise rules for such table construction. These rules are expressed in a '**B if A**' format. Although the examples I have given concern blood-relations, there is no reason to believe that this tabular approach could not be generalised to other information domains.

Some very interesting questions arise at this stage.

1. At what point does the above scheme, which is supposed to answer the question 'How exactly do I remember things?', become a theory? Could it be that all I have to do is change the word 'I' in the question to 'people', thereby removing the question from the personal domain, and then I shall have a theory? What is a theory?

2. Does the above scheme have any psychological relevance? If it does, is it solely because I used a psychological term 'remember' in the original question and I now claim that the above scheme is an answer to that

question? If it does not, what else must be done to the above scheme to give it psychological relevance? Do I need to add extra memory concepts to my question, such as 'forget'? Or do I need to construct the scheme in some well-defined way which is accepted as being 'the psychological way'? Is it the case that I need to outline certain implications that follow from my scheme which can be empirically tested?

3. Does the above scheme have any AI relevance? If it does, is it solely because an affirmative answer may have been given to 2. first? Or is it because the scheme has computational relevance in that a computer program could conceivably be written to run the scheme on a computer, on the basis of which we can then say that the computer 'remembers'? If it does not have AI relevance, is it because a negative answer may have been given to 2. first? Or is it because the scheme has no more computational relevance than, say, a space-invaders type arcade-game: clever programming but not an intelligent program? What is AI programming? Come to that, what is AI?

4. Is it possible to ask these questions in the order given? Is it possible to provide answers which are clear and distinct? What would count as an answer, and how do I know whether the answers are correct?

A lot of questions have been raised here. The main point is that all four sets of questions can, very generally, be called *methodological* questions. That is, these questions are asking whether there exists a system, or body, of *methods*, i.e. special procedures or techniques, which can be used in a principled way to provide consistent, and coherent, answers to these questions.

Let me pursue my hypothetical memory scheme a bit further, since it is not at all obvious at this stage that the scheme is a theory, has psychological relevance, or has AI relevance.

Here is the first elaboration. I hypothesise the following:

(a) Tables are searched in a strictly sequential fashion, i.e. from the top to the bottom;

(b) there is an executive which breaks up the original query (in natural language) into an internal representation which can be described by my rule notation;

(c) there is an executive which co-ordinates the search for information in the tables;

(d) there is an executive which returns a response in natural language;

(e) the executive can only deal with one row of one table at a time.

Some implications of this elaboration are as follows. An item near the bottom of a table should take longer to retrieve than an item near the top of the table. For instance, given the previous **father** table and assuming one unit of time for each examination of a row, then the query 'Who is Ken's father?' should take one unit of time and the query 'Who is Albert's father?' should take five units of time to answer. I can hypothesize further that rows are ordered so that most commonly accessed rows are placed at the top. So perhaps the row which contains the information that Ken is my father should, strictly speaking, go towards the top or be at the top but may be further down the table if I am not asked frequently for my father's name. Another hypothesis is that a computer program can be written which has as a part an executive which calls various subroutines to break down a query into an internal representation, execute a search, and formulate a response.

Does my scheme have psychological relevance or AI relevance yet? If previously the answer was 'No' to either or both questions and if now the response is 'Yes' to either or both, then it must be because of this elaboration.

Another question that arises is: 'Does my scheme seem plausible?' That is, is it the case that my scheme is a plausible description or explanation of human memory? Perhaps plausibility depends on the results obtained from experimentation and program construction, so I shall have to wait for the results first.

The second elaboration runs like this. I hypothesise the following:

(a) tables are not searched in strictly sequential fashion; instead, within a table, there is a separate processor for each row, and the task of each processor is to store the information in that row and to wait for a query. If a query requires some part or all of the information that is stored on a processor, the processor responds, otherwise it keeps quiet.

Hypotheses (b), (c) and (d) remain the same as before.

(e) the executive does not need to execute a sequential search. Rather, it feeds the query to all processors in the table at the same time and then waits for the response.

Some implications of this elaboration are as follows. It now no longer matters whereabouts in a table an item is, as far as search time is concerned. Instead, I now hypothesize that an item in a table that is further away from the point of search than an item in a table nearer the point of search will take longer to retrieve. So tables frequently accessed are searched first.

Another implication is that my system architecture now needs some expansion, as far as table search is concerned. A 'table' will now consist of a sequence of processors, each with one item of information. The query is fed to all processors in parallel, and the response from each processor is monitored. The computer system may have either a hardware implementation of these tables (usually called 'content addressable memory') or a software simulation of the hardware.

Does my scheme have psychological or AI relevance yet? Is it plausible?

The next elaboration will consist of allowing a parallel search of all tables at the same time. I hypothesize the following:

(a) a query is now fed to all tables at the same time, and within each table a parallel search takes place.

Hypotheses (b), (c), and (d) remain the same as before.

(e) the executive executes a parallel, distributed search on all tables.

One implication of this elaboration is that search time now no longer depends on the location of a table. I might now wish to introduce complexity of the search argument as a basis for predicting search time. Another implication is that I shall have to re-assess my architecture and either provide the necessary hardware support or simulate the hardware in the software.

The same questions as before can be asked about psychological relevance, AI relevance, and plausibility. Notice that 'plausibility' now no longer concerns just psychological plausibility but also neural plausibility. That is, is my system an adequate model for the neural processes involved in memory?

The final elaboration I shall mention concerns the rejection of the executive. Now there is no central executive to coordinate the breaking down of a query, the search, and the reformulation of a response. Rather, a query is automatically fed into a query analyser that feeds the information it gleans from the query as the query enters the system either to tables directly or onto a common data-pool which is available to every table. Tables put information back onto the data-pool and the response formulator formulates a response as it picks up information from the pool. The tables, in effect, now compete amongst themselves as to which table is to have its response accepted.

No doubt, further elaborations along neurocomputing lines can be made. But the point of these elaborations is to demonstrate the difficulty that arises when attempting to distinguish between a fanciful and speculative idea on the one hand and a factual and explanatory theory on the other. Matters are complicated when different disciplines and sciences have their own distinguishing criteria. The relationship between AI and cognitive psychology is strong. Does that mean that AI theories must conform to the same methodological rigour as psychology theories? If not, then a clear methodology must be provided for constructing and testing AI theories, otherwise AI might end up being a completely speculative subject, more akin to science fiction than science.

It may be useful at this point to look at some established, but contrasting, methodologies as supplied by three philosophers of science: Hempel, Popper and Kuhn. All three methodologies have their supporters and critics, but they provide frameworks for evaluating the degree to which the 'armchair' memory model above is scientific.

7.3   SCIENCE ACCORDING TO HEMPEL

Hempel's (1966) view on the philosophy of science starts with some basic observations, among which are the following. The different branches of scientific inquiry can be divided into two major groups: the empirical and the non-empirical. Statements in the former must be checked against the facts of our experience by experimentation, observation, surveys, and so on. Propositions in the latter (e.g. logical and mathematical propositions) are proved without essential reference to empirical findings. Hempel wishes to discuss how scientific knowledge is arrived at, supported and changed, how empirical science explains empirical facts, and what explanation actually consists of.

Given these basic observations, five major claims are made by Hempel. *First*, it is sometimes thought that scientific inquiry consists of inductive inference, from antecedently collected data to appropriate general principles. By 'inductive inference' is meant the step from statements describing particular events to a statement of universal form. Hempel discusses the four stages that an inductive scientist would consider to make up an ideal scientific inquiry:

(a) observation and recording of all facts;

(b) analysis and classification of these facts;

(c) inductive derivation of generalizations from them; and

(d) further testing of the generalizations.

Hempel calls this 'the narrow inductivist conception of scientific inquiry' and claims that it is untenable because:

> if we have to wait for *all* the facts to be collected our scientific investigation would never get off the ground, as there are an infinite number of facts;
>
> even if we stipulate that all relevant facts should be collected, we can ask: 'Relevant to what?', i.e. we have, as yet, not specified the problem to which the facts are relevant; and
>
> even if we have specified a problem, we have no hypotheses to guide us in our search for 'relevant' facts, i.e. facts are relevant or irrelevant only in reference to a given hypothesis, not to a given problem.

Hempel claims that the transition from data to theory requires creative imagination, not mechanical rules of induction, or even deduction. Scientific hypotheses and theories are not derived from observed facts but invented to account for them. These 'happy guesses' require ingenuity and imagination, though whether they are accepted into science or not depends on whether they pass critical scrutiny, which includes, in particular, the checking of suitable test implications by careful observation or experiment. The interests of scientific objectivity are safeguarded by the demand for an objective validation of such conjectures. So, for Hempel, scientific knowledge is arrived at by inventing hypotheses as tentative answers to a problem under study, and then subjecting these to empirical test.

Second, concerning the testing of a hypothesis, Hempel states that the test implications of a hypothesis are normally of a conditional character: they tell us that under certain specified test conditions an outcome of a certain kind will occur. In other words, test implications are of the form: 'If conditions of the kind C are realized, then an event of kind E will occur.'

Sometimes we need to add auxiliary hypotheses or assumptions to our original hypothesis, in which case the general scheme looks like this: 'If both H (the hypothesis) and A (the auxiliary hypotheses) are true, so is I (our test implication).' So if our test implication now happens to turn out to be false, we know that both H and A cannot both be true, i.e. at least one of them must be false. So H need not be rejected straight away because I happens to be false. In principle, it would always be possible to retain H even in the face of seriously adverse test results - provided that we are willing to make sufficiently radical and burdensome revisions in our auxiliary hypotheses. But we may start introducing *ad hoc* hypotheses - hypotheses made solely to protect and save a hypothesis seriously threatened by adverse evidence. There is no precise criterion for *ad hoc* hypotheses, though two relevant considerations should be kept in mind:

> is the hypothesis proposed just for the purpose of saving some current conception against adverse evidence, or does it also account for other phenomena?

> if more and more hypotheses have to be added to reconcile a certain basic conception, the resulting total system will become so complex that it has to give way when a simple alternative conception is proposed.

For Hempel, no statement or set of statements **T** can be significantly proposed as a scientific hypothesis or theory unless it is amenable to objective empirical test, at least 'in principle'. We must be able to derive from **T** certain test implications of the form 'If C then E', although the test conditions C need not be technologically realizable at the time when **T** is propounded or contemplated as long as the hypothesis is testable in principle. If a statement or set of statements is not even testable in principle, i.e. has no test implications at all, then it cannot significantly be proposed or entertained as a scientific hypothesis or theory. This is because no conceivable empirical finding can then accord or conflict with it.

Third, according to Hempel the *confirmation* of a hypothesis will normally be regarded as increasing with the number of favourable test findings, although generally speaking the increase in confirmation effected by one new favourable instance will become smaller as the number of previously established favourable instances grows. Moreover, it is desirable that a hypothesis should be confirmed by 'new' evidence - by facts that were not known or not taken into account when the hypothesis was formulated. 'Simplicity' of theories is difficult to define, but Hempel makes the general remark that any criterion of simplicity must be objective, i.e. it must not have reference to intuitive appeal or the ease with which a hypothesis is remembered or understood.

Fourth, Hempel gives two basic requirements for scientific explanation:

> the requirement of explanatory relevance: the explanatory information adduced from an explanatory theory affords good grounds for believing that the phenomenon to be explained did, or does, occur under the specified circumstances; and

> the requirement of testability: the statements constituting a scientific explanation must be capable of empirical test.

These two requirements are interrelated: a proposed explanation that meets the requirement of relevance also meets the requirement of testability.

And *fifth*, according to Hempel theories are introduced when previous study of a class of phenomena has revealed a system of uniformities that can be expressed in the form of empirical laws. The formulation of a theory requires two sorts of principles: 'internal principles' and 'bridge principles'. Internal principles characterize the basic entities and processes invoked by the theory and the laws to which they are assumed to conform. Bridge principles, on the other hand, indicate how the processes envisaged by the theory are related to empirical phenomena with which we are already acquainted and which the theory may then explain and predict. Internal principles therefore characterize the 'inside' of a theory, and bridge principles provide the contact between the theory and the phenomena it is said to explain (i.e. the empirical world). Bridge principles may be said to connect certain theoretically assumed entities that cannot be directly observed or measured with more or less directly observable or measurable aspects of physical systems, even though bridge principles do not always connect 'theoretical unobservables' with 'experimental observables'. They may instead connect the unobservable 'theoretical' entities with the subject matter or phenomena to be explained, even though these phenomena need not be 'directly' observable or measurable; they may well be characterized in terms of previously established theories, and their observation and measurement may presuppose the principles of those theories. Without bridge principles, however, a theory and its internal principles would have no explanatory power and would be incapable of test, since the derivation of test implications from the internal principles of the theory requires further premises that establish connections between the theoretical concepts of the theory and concepts already understood and outside the theory; and this is accomplished by appropriate bridge principles.

Overall, Hempel's basic assumption about a scientific theory is that it must not only satisfy the conditions of testability-in-principle and explanatory import but also deepen our understanding by:

> providing a systematically unified account of quite diverse phenomena;

> showing that previously formulated empirical laws do not hold strictly and unexceptionally but only approximately and within a certain limited range of application; and

> predicting and explaining phenomena that were not known when the theory was first formulated.

In summary, Hempel argues that scientific knowledge is arrived at by inventing hypotheses as tentative answers to a problem under study and then subjecting these hypotheses to empirical test. These hypotheses should be at least testable in principle if current technology cannot provide the tools for such testing. The confirmation of a hypothesis will normally be regarded as increasing with the number of favourable test findings. The hypotheses should not be saying something about phenomena that are in principle unobservable or unmeasurable, according to Hempel. However, Hempel also allows 'bridge principles' to link the hypotheses or theory with observable or measurable aspects of physical systems. (For instance, a theory in psychology may well use unobservable theoretical constructs, such as 'ego', 'superego' and 'id'; the purpose of bridge principles would then be to link these theoretical constructs with experimental observables indirectly, either by invoking previously established (i.e. tested) theories or by predicting what sort of physical behaviour would be manifest.) These predictions can then be tested and, if the predictions turn out not to be accurate, modified. There will usually be a limit to the amount of prediction modification in the face of adverse evidence. Scientists usually recognise when *ad hoc* modifications to a theory have reached a limit by realising that the theory has become so complex that an alternative, simpler theory should be sought. Hempel also argues that a scientific theory deepens our understanding by predicting and explaining phenomena that were not known when the theory was first formulated.

7.4 SCIENCE ACCORDING TO POPPER

Let us turn our attention to another philosopher of science, Karl Popper. Popper (1959) attacks the view that empirical sciences can be characterized by the fact that they use 'inductive methods'. An inference is usually called 'inductive' if it passes from singular statements, or 'particular' statements (e.g. 'This swan is white') to universal statements, such as hypotheses or theories ('All swans are white'). Popper's view is that:

> from a logical point of view it is far from obvious that we are justified in inferring universal statements from singular ones;

> it would be difficult to establish the truth of universal statements, as any account of experience can only be a singular statement and not a universal one; and

> to support such a view of empirical sciences, scientists would have to establish a 'principle of induction' with which they could put inductive inferences into a logically acceptable form.

With regard to the last point, Popper argues that such a principle cannot be a purely logical truth, like a tautology or analytical statement, since all inductive inferences would then have to be regarded as purely logical or tautological transformations, just like inferences in deductive logic, which is clearly not the case. And if the principle is a synthetic, or empirical, statement, we can ask why the principle should be accepted at all.

Popper believes that the difficulties inherent in the doctrine that inductive inferences are 'probable inferences', i.e. can attain some degree of 'reliability' or 'probability', are likewise insurmountable. His own proposal has no dependence on either inductive logic or probable inferences and is called 'the theory of the deductive method of testing'. He writes that scientists do not wait passively for repetitions and regularities in the world about them but instead actively impose regularities upon the world, discover similarities in the world, and interpret these in terms of invented laws. Instead of waiting for premises and drawing conclusions from them, scientists 'jump' to conclusions straight away:

> This was a theory of trial and error - of conjectures and refutations. It made it possible to understand why our attempts to force interpretations upon the world were logically prior to the

> observation of similarities. Since there were logical reasons be-
> hind this procedure, I thought that it would apply in the field of
> science also; that scientific theories were not the digest of obser-
> vations, but that they were inventions - conjectures boldly put
> forward for trial, to be eliminated if they clashed with observa-
> tions; with observations which were rarely accidental but as a
> rule undertaken with the definite intention of testing a theory by
> obtaining, if possible, a decisive refutation. (Popper, 1965, p. 46)

Popper conceives of the task of the logic of knowledge as consisting solely in
investigating the methods employed in those systematic tests to which every
new idea must be subjected if it is to be seriously entertained as a scientific
hypothesis. There are five lines along which the testing of a theory can be
carried out after conclusions are deductively drawn from the theory:

> there is the logical comparison of the conclusions among themselves,
> by means of which the internal consistency of the theory is tested;

> there is the investigation of the logical form of the theory, with the
> object of determining whether it has the character of an empirical or
> scientific theory, or whether it is, for instance, tautological;

> there is the comparison with other theories, chiefly with the aim of
> determining whether the theory would constitute a scientific advance
> should it survive various tests;

> there is the testing of the theory by way of empirical applications of
> the conclusions which can be derived from it, i.e. that is, we form
> predictions that are easily testable or applicable; and

> if the results of practical experiments show the predictions to be veri-
> fied, we say that the theory has, for the time being, passed its test, but
> if the predictions are falsified, then the theory from which they were
> drawn is also falsified.

For Popper, there are three requirements which an empirical theoretical system will have to satisfy. First, the theory must be synthetic so that it may
represent a non-contradictory, i.e. a possible, world. Secondly, the theory
must not be metaphysical, i.e. it must represent a world of possible experience. And thirdly, the theory must be a system distinguished in some way
from other such system as the one which represents our world of experience.

This is done by submitting the theory to tests and observing whether the theory has stood up to these tests.

To distinguish an empirical theory from a metaphysical one, Popper uses as his criterion of demarcation the notion of 'falsifiability'. He requires of a scientific system not that it should be capable of being singled out once and for all in a positive sense (verified) but that its logical form should be such that it can be singled out, by means of empirical tests, in a negative sense, i.e. it must be possible for an empirical scientific system to be refuted by experience. Thus, a theory not refutable by any conceivable event is non-scientific, and every genuine test of a theory is an attempt to falsify it, or to refute it:

> Testability is falsifiability, but there are degrees of testability: some theories are more testable... than others. (Popper, 1965, p. 46)

Popper stresses that he is not attempting to overthrow or annihilate metaphysics. Moreover, his criterion is one of *demarcation*, not one of *meaning*, as many philosophers (e.g. Ayer (1936), p. 51, Footnote) had wrongly interpreted. The criterion of falsifiability draws a line 'inside' meaningful language and not between meaningful and meaningless language.

He dismisses the criticism that, since we can always change definitions or add extra *ad hoc* hypotheses, it will never be possible conclusively to falsify a system. He proposes that the empirical method should be characterised as a method which excludes precisely these ways of evading falsification. The empirical method is characterised by the fact that it exposes the system to be tested to falsification in every conceivable way.

Finally, rules governing methodology are regarded by Popper as conventions, or simple agreements among scientists; they have no stronger claim to scientific status than that.

In summary, Popper (1972), like Hempel, also argues that a scientific theory should be tested by empirical application of the conclusions that are deductively drawn from it. That is, predictions are formed which are easily testable or applicable. If the results of practical experiments show the predictions to be verified, we say that the theory, for the time being, passed its test. But if the predictions are falsified, then the theory from which they were drawn is also falsified. This gives rise to the notion of 'falsifiability': a scientific theory is not required to be capable of being singled out once and for all in a positive sense (verified); rather, its form should be such that it can be singled out, by means of empirical tests, in a negative sense. Thus, according to Popper, it must be possible for a scientific theory to be refuted by experience. If a theory is not falsifiable, it is metaphysical, i.e. it is not saying anything about the physical world at all.

7.5   COMPARING HEMPEL AND POPPER

Let us return at this stage to my memory model. If I wanted to argue that my armchair theory is a scientific or psychological theory within the 'Hempelian' framework, I should have to demonstrate that:

(a) a hypothesis has been invented as a tentative answer to a problem and will be subjected to empirical testing;

(b) the hypothesis has implications which are testable 'in principle' (for example, longer search time for rows further down a table), even though, technologically speaking, such testing may not be feasible in the near future;

(c) the hypothesis is relatively simple compared to other psychological theories of memory;

(d) the hypothesis has powerful explanatory power; and

(e) there exist internal and bridge principles which characterize the internal processes of the hypothesis and relate these processes to well-established and well-understood concepts in other theories.

If I wanted to argue that my armchair theory is a scientific or psychological theory within the 'Popperian' framework, I should have to demonstrate that:

(a) the hypothesis is an invention which will will be rejected if it does not agree with observations;

(b) the hypothesis is internally consistent, is an advance over other theories of memory, and will be rejected if its implications are falsified; and

(c) the hypothesis is not metaphysical or unfalsifiable in principle, and it represents a possible world.

The question as to whether my armchair theory is really a theory, whether it is scientific, or psychological, or metaphysical, or speculative, or a piece of AI, may now actually have answers, or at least the established views of Hempel and Popper, contrasting as they are, should provide pointers to where such answers can be found. Of course, this does not mean that Hempel's views and Popper's views are the only views concerning methodology, or that there is no room for a more radical view of theories of AI and psychology. For example, we have ignored the views of many other philosophers, particularly Kuhn and Marr, to whom we shall return shortly.

However, the views of Hempel and Popper are usually regarded as being at two ends of what might be called 'the traditional methodological spectrum'. They disagree sharply on what the status of a theory should be whilst tests are taking place. Hempel's views are the more orthodox: a scientific theory is true if confirmatory evidence is found for it. Modification of the theory is allowed to take into account any hiccups in the evidence, although such modifications usually have a limit set by the increased and undesirable complexity of the theory. The task of the scientist is to confirm the theory. For Popper, on the other hand, a scientific theory is characterised by the possibility that a single negative piece of evidence will refute it. The task of the scientist is to refute the theory, and the scientist should try any number of ways to falsify the theory. *Ad hoc* modifications of the theory are not allowed by Popper.

What is remarkable about these two opposing methodologies is the agreement they both share concerning the construction of a theory in the first place, and the requirement for a scientific theory to have some 'cash value' in the real world. That is, they both attack a view of science which may be called 'the narrow inductivist conception of scientific enquiry', which essentially holds that a scientist first collects data through observation and then generalises from these observed facts to a theory. Hempel claims that scientific theories are not derived from observed facts but invented by the scientist to account for them. Popper (1959) believes that scientists do not wait passively for repetitions and regularities but instead actively impose regularities upon the world by inventing theories - conjectures - that are to be eliminated - refuted - if they clash with observations. Both philosophers therefore agree that the role of a scientist is much more active and inventive than the role assumed by the narrow inductivist approach. Also, they both agree that the theory must have some applicability in the real world. Conclusions and predictions are derived from the theory and these must be subjected to empirical testing. The results of the tests will then have further implications for the theory.

We can use these two extreme views in an attempt to locate AI methodology somewhere on the spectrum in between, as a way of starting our discussion on AI methodology.

7.6   SCIENCE ACCORDING TO KUHN

Let us look briefly at another popular view of science, originally articulated by Kuhn (1970). For Kuhn, scientific methodology centres around the notion of *paradigm*, which denotes a set of 'achievements' which are

> ...sufficiently unprecedented to attract an enduring group of adherents away from competing models of scientific activity (Kuhn, 1970, p. 10)

and

> ...sufficiently open-ended to leave all sorts of problems for the redefined group of practitioners to resolve. (Kuhn, 1970, p. 10)

Kuhn goes on to say:

> By choosing [the term 'paradigm'], I mean to suggest that some accepted examples of actual scientific practice - examples which include law, theory, application, and instrumentation together - provide models from which spring particular coherent traditions of scientific research. These are the traditions which the historian describes under such rubrics as 'Ptolemaic astronomy' (or 'Copernican'), 'Aristotelian dynamics' (or 'Newtonian'), 'corpuscular optics' (or 'wave optics'), and so on. The study of paradigms, including many that are far more specialized than those named illustratively above, is what mainly prepares the student for membership in the particular scientific community with which he will later practice. (Kuhn, 1970, pp. 10-11)

For Kuhn,

> ... transformations of ... paradigms ... are scientific revolutions, and the successive transition from one paradigm to another via revolution is the usual development pattern of mature science. (Kuhn, 1970, p. 12)

Interesting as Kuhn's ideas are, it is debatable as to whether AI has reached a point where there is widespread acceptance of an 'AI paradigm'. In fact, the search for some methodology of AI can be interpreted as a search for precisely the sort of paradigm that Kuhn argues for and which caters for 'usual' scientific development by means of paradigm transition. The argument presented so far in this chapter is that, without a *first* paradigm, it is impossible for there to be others. It is also impossible to characterize not just transition in AI but also improvement and progress. Yet if those AI researchers who believe that they are carrying out a scientific activity adopt a 'wait-and-see' attitude, both Hempel and Popper provide powerful arguments as to why such an inductive approach will not work.

This supports our argument that the search for a methodology for AI is not an idle one. Even if the proposed methodology is not ideal or correct, it can at least form the first approximation (or paradigm, to use Kuhn's terminology) from which subsequent ones can be derived. AI researchers who believe in the science of their subject must, at some stage, confront this problem, and the rest of this chapter will provide some indication of the complexity of the problem as well as ways in which the problem can be tackled.

7.7 IMPLEMENTABILITY

Given the above views, AI appears to occupy a highly ambiguous position if it is claimed that it is a science, or a study, of mental faculties through the use of computational models , where by 'model' is meant nothing more than some program implementation of a theory. For instance, Cendrowska and Bramer claim:

> A particular feature of AI programs is that they are generally written to illustrate a particular theory, and if judged successful it is this theory that will be featured in published accounts. (Cendrowska and Bramer, 1984, p. 454)

Hayes (1984) also adopts a criterion of success based on program implementability:

> AI's criterion is not experimental corroboration, but implementability. An acceptable explanation of a piece of behaviour must be, in the last analysis, a program which can actually be implemented and run. And such an explanation is a good explanation just to the extent that the program, when run, does indeed exhibit the behaviour which was to be explained. (Hayes, 1984, p. 158)

It can be argued that the criterion of implementability is vacuous at the level of the Church-Turing Thesis. There are many different versions of the Thesis, but Hofstadter's version (1979) is the most appropriate here:

> Mental processes of any sort can be simulated by a computer program whose underlying language is of a power equal to [a language] in which all partial recursive functions can be programmed. (Hofstadter, 1979, p. 578)

This essentially states that any mental process can be described by an algorithm which can be executed on a computer. It is called a 'thesis' because it cannot be proved to be the case; nevertheless, no evidence has arisen to the contrary. So as long as the AI researcher takes care to construct theories which can be written down as a sequence of algorithmic or computational steps, these theories can be implemented.

However, the vacuity of the implementability criterion becomes apparent when one realizes that in AI research the fundamental assumption is that computational concepts can be used to describe the workings of the human mind. (See, for instance, our comments concerning the computational metaphor in the previous chapter.) An AI researcher will therefore use the concepts of computational theory to construct AI theories. But this leads to the conclusion that all AI theories will then necessarily be *implementable* on a computer, if the researcher has specified the problem and its solution in computational terms or used computational concepts in such a specification. It then follows that implementability *per se* leads to a self-perpetuating methodology: an AI theory is necessarily implementable, therefore implementability as a criterion is vacuous.

The authors of the above quotations may want to make the further claim that the *results* of the computer program should exhibit the behaviour or produce the results that are predicted of it. Let us briefly examine how such predictions can be made.

One way to make predictions is for a human to work through the algorithm (theory) by hand and produce a set of results for a certain input. But then all the implementation will show is whether the human's working through of the algorithm (theory) is correct. The use of a computer in this way may be useful for checking a human's ability to work logically through a set of instructions, but there would then be no justification for claiming that the results had an empirical validity over and above this simple checking exercise. The computer results are correct if they match the results of a human working through the same algorithm, and computer results can sometimes show that the human is wrong in his or her calculations. But this only gives us an indication of how closely matched human and computer performance of the same algorithm are, and says nothing about how accurate or relevant a description of human mental capability the theory (algorithm) itself is.

Another way to make predictions is for the human, once an AI theory has been constructed, to specify what he or she would like to see the program do. This method therefore does not rely on a human working through the algorithm (theory); rather, this method allows an AI researcher to use the program as a tool for testing and sharpening his or her own theories. In other words, a form of weak AI, in the Searlian sense (see Chapters 2 and 5), is being appealed to. One suspects that this is really the point the authors of the above quotations wish to make. But what happens if the results produced by the program are not the expected or predicted results? It is a well known fact in computer science that programs never work the first time. Just how much modification and fine-tuning of the program - and the theory - is allowed?

Hempel (1966) argues that *ad hoc* modifications to a theory are limited by the increased complexity of the theory, and that after a certain threshold level of complexity is exceeded scientists would naturally and logically pursue simpler alternative theories. Popper argues (1959) that no *ad hoc* modifications of any sort should be allowed to a theory. If it does not work for one instance, the whole theory should be discarded. Popper's view may appear too strict for AI researchers (and computer scientists!), who would naturally believe that any computer program requires time to debug and test before being used for serious applications. But Hempel's views could be of use here to those AI researchers who believe in the implementability - and also weak AI - criterion. Perhaps the main requirement for AI researchers is some criterion of program complexity which would allow them to judge just how complicated their programs are becoming as modifications, kludges and fine-tuning take place. Certainly, without such a criterion, there is a great danger that AI programs end up being highly complex and inconsistent in their theory as well as in their behaviour, simply because AI researchers continually modify their programs so that the desired and expected results are produced. So, if an AI program is or embodies a theory, and if AI is a science, then according to Hempel each modification will make the program (theory) more complex, and eventually the program (plus theory) will be rejected in favour of a simpler (program plus) theory.

This then raises the question of how complexity of AI programs - and theories - can be measured. For instance, if AI programs are no different from conventional computer programs, then the full force of software engineering techniques currently applicable to conventional computer programs can be applied to AI programs also. Such techniques would include a rigorous functional specification of the problem to be tackled, a clear and detailed modular design, followed finally by implementation and maintenance. It will be during the rigorous functional specification of the problem that measures of complexity can be used to identify the scale of the problem and its associated solution. However, there is a school of thought which claims that AI problems are different from conventional ones (and that AI programs are different from conventional programs). For instance, Partridge writes:

> Software engineering problems are a subset of AI problems: the subset of well-defined problems. Well-defined is not in fact sufficient to characterize the class of non-AI problems. Many complex games are well-defined; they are also AI problems - chess is one popular example. (Partridge, 1986, p. 19)

Later, he writes:

> I have made a fundamental claim that AI and traditional software engineering problems are different classes of problems. While it is true that progress with certain AI problems may well reduce them to traditional software engineering problems, and that restricted versions of AI problems may be successfully treated as traditional software engineering problems, a non-trivial set of AI problems will always remain. ...I should like to make two points about this irreducible set:

(a) The problems that it contains are not amenable to computerization using the usual software engineering program development strategies.

(b) These residual problems are not just 'academic' problems that we can successfully ignore for all practical purposes. ...Problems such as sophisticated natural language communication, complex planning and decision making in the empirical world ...are in this set.

(Partridge, 1986, pp. 21-22)

Partridge then goes on to identify an AI development cycle called RUDE - *run, debug, edit* - which provides the basis for an AI *programming* methodology. Instead of starting with a rigorous specification of the problem, the AI researcher starts with an incomplete (perhaps always incomplete for certain problems) specification, constructs what might be called an 'AI prototype' program, runs it, observes its performance, and edits the program accordingly. As a descriptive, as opposed to prescriptive, method, RUDE is accurate with respect to the way that a number of AI programs have been, and will be, developed.

We can now ask how such a view of AI programming methodology fits in with AI as a science or study of the mind, in that an AI program embodies, or implements, a certain way of theorizing about mental states and processes. Any change in the program, apart from the obvious ones of correcting run-time errors, should lead to changes in the theory also, but this is to assume that somehow there is some correspondence between theory and program. Asking for an *exact* correspondence could be too strong a requirement. For instance, the theory may be expressed in English, and the program in LISP. Even if there is some mapping available between program and theory, there is still the difficulty of identifying when the theory needs to be modified: when changes are made to the program, some may affect the theory, others may only be with respect to the program. What we need here is a clear categorization of which edits lead to 'theory edits', as opposed to being program edits only. It is currently not clear, in the AI literature, how such a categorization might be achieved. AI currently does not have the sort of complexity measure which would help identify when the theory, as opposed to the program, should be jettisoned in favour of another theory.

In any case, even if a criterion of complexity for AI programs (theories) can be found, there still remains the suspicion that no criterion exists or can exist for determining whether an AI theory is true or accurate. It is probably this suspicion which has led many AI researchers to adopt the stance that their theories represent 'possible worlds' rather than 'actual worlds', that an AI program represents a possible description or explanation of mental faculties rather than an actual one. This sounds attractive until one begins to delve more deeply into the logic of possible worlds. As we saw in Chapter 4, in modal logic the following equivalences are valid:

x *is necessary* is equivalent to *it is not possible for x to be false*

x *is possible* is equivalent to *it is not necessarily the case that x is false*

These equivalences hold for individual propositions. But from these basic equivalences we can build the notion of worlds. A proposition is necessarily true if it is true in every possible world. A proposition is possibly true if it is true in some possible world. Possible worlds are usually interpreted to mean conceivable worlds, states of affairs that can be envisaged. (See Chapter 4 for further details on possible world semantics.)

There are many different ways of looking at possible worlds, but one logical fact is clear: even within a possible world certain propositions can be said to be true or false. That is, even a possible world has certain fundamental principles concerning the truth and falsity of propositions, and these principles can be shared across possible worlds. If AI researchers are to talk of their theories representing possible worlds, they still need to have criteria of truth and falsity in their worlds. Until AI researchers who claim that their theories represent possible worlds can provide such truth criteria which allow propositions in their own worlds to be true or false (which may be possible if the notion of 'model' is made more sophisticated), the suspicion remains that the notion of possible worlds is being used to disguise the self-perpetuating and essentially irrefutable nature of AI research, when it is assumed that AI programs are implementations of theories in some sense.

The arguments so far presented deal with the question of whether AI is a science, or study. Let us now turn our attention to the view that it does not really matter whether AI is a science or not: the important question concerns whether AI is producing the results. That is, many AI researchers may claim that the above discussions on scientific methodology count for nothing as long as AI can be measured by its achievements. They may point to past and current work in AI as demonstrating that AI is progressing and is actually producing the desired results, science or no science.

There are very many AI projects now under way in universities and industrial institutions around the world, and new AI systems are appearing fairly regularly. Some of these systems are called 'AI systems' because they use a few principles which, for historical reasons, are considered to be AI principles (e.g. alpha-beta pruning, search strategies). Others adopt an AI programming language, such as LISP or Prolog, and also use knowledge representation techniques, such as semantic networks, scripts and production rules. Still others distinguish between AI programs and conventional programs on the basis of the type of problem that the former, but not the latter, tackle. But although there may not be clear criteria for distinguishing AI programs from non-AI programs ('AI programs are those which embody AI techniques', for example), what criteria could we use for deciding that AI is making progress?

If AI *were* a science, we could use such concepts are 'greater explanatory power', 'more generalized and simple', 'is consistent with a larger body of facts', and 'greater predictive power' to judge whether one AI theory is 'better' than another. If AI theories are replaced by better ones, we would have grounds for saying that AI is making progress. But given the above comments, it appears that there can, currently at least, be no scientific reasons for claiming that one AI theory is better than another and that AI is making progress, simply because the conceptual tools for measuring one theory against another, and so for measuring the progress of AI, are missing. Answers to such basic questions as:

What are the objectives of AI?

What methods exist for achieving the objectives of AI?

What exactly is the relationship between an AI theory and a mental faculty?

Does the theory model, or describe, or explain the faculty?

How exactly can the model, or description, or explanation be evaluated?

How will one know that the objectives of AI have been reached?

are not forthcoming from many AI researchers because, one suspects, they currently do not know. And for an AI researcher to claim that such questions are unanswerable leads to the idea (which AI researchers may like to

promulgate) that AI as a science will develop as results start to flow in and
theories and methods are induced from these results. But this is precisely
the notion that both Popper and Hempel agree is wrong. That is, they
both disagree with 'the narrow inductivist conception of scientific enquiry',
but this conception is precisely that which is being appealed to by those AI
researchers who adopt the 'wait and see' attitude mentioned earlier.

But if AI is not a science, then how is progress in AI to be measured?
By faster programs, speedier results, the use of parallel, distributed architectures? None of these would appear to give us grounds for claiming that
AI is progressing, since they depend only on factors outside AI and not
within, i.e. on hardware and software developments in computer engineering
and computer science. Just because the technology on which AI depends
improves, that does not necessarily mean that AI itself is improving: it is
the *use* to which the technology is put that must function as a criterion of
improvement in AI.

One popular view is that AI is throwing up some 'completely surprising'
results, as if the function of surprise is somehow part of the measuring tool.
That is, it could be argued that the 'ability' of an AI program to surprise
its user with unexpected, but correct, results can be measured and somehow
used to determine whether AI is progressing. This sort of tool would probably be most useful for deciding whether expert systems are progressing. In
a sense, this is a return to the argument originally proposed by Turing in
response to Lady Lovelace's Objection, where he states that he is constantly
surprised by the results thrown up by a computer. (See Chapter 1.)

Let us relate a little story here. Once upon a time, in a certain university
AI research laboratory, a researcher wrote a natural language parser for a
subset of the Arabic language. He used Prolog as the programming tool.
His supervisor looked over the researcher's shoulder as the system was fully
demonstrated for the first time. The first two or three Arabic sentences were
parsed uniquely and the results, which consisted of categorising each word
in the Arabic sentence into its syntactic role (e.g. determiner, noun, and so
on) as well as gender (male, female) and number (singular, dual, plural),
were exactly those expected. Then one particular Arabic sentence was input. Whilst the researcher and supervisor waited for the system to respond
(about 20 seconds), the researcher confidently predicted what would happen. Sure enough, the result of the parse was consistent with his prediction.
The Prolog interpreter being used was such that every time a result is found
the interpreter displays it, then waits for the semicolon key to be pressed

as a 'continue' key so that it can find more answers to a query (very useful for database retrieval work). The researcher pressed the continue key, confidently expecting there to be no more answers. He was surprised to find the system returning exactly the same answer. He looked at it and then said: 'Yes, of course, I'd forgotten that this sentence can be parsed in two ways, depending on whether you assume the subject or object noun comes first.' He pressed the continue key again, and to his surprise a 'third' parse was found. He looked at it closely, and then he said: 'Yes, the sentence has a third reading, because the verb has more than one sense. I hadn't realised the system could do that.' He pressed 'continue' and again the same line was displayed. By now, he was becoming as sceptical as the supervisor had been since the first duplication. Whilst the researcher was using all his Arabic knowledge to provide a fourth reading, the supervisor leaned forward and pressed 'continue' a few times. Each time, the same line was displayed. It was now obvious that the system was in a loop and that the same result was being displayed over and over again because of this loop and not because of a backtracking process discovering alternative solutions.

The point of the above story (and AI researchers will know that this story, whilst there may be differences in content, describes a frequently occurring aspect of applied AI research) is this: surprise is a very dangerous criterion to use for measuring AI progress as long as an appropriate AI methodology is lacking. Without such a methodology, it may be very difficult, if not impossible, to separate genuine 'surprisability' from programming error. It is the theory that must surprise us, in terms of its predictive and explanatory ability, not the program. The minimum step must be proving AI programs somehow to be a correct implementation of the theory, 'correct' in some sense of the word so that 'surprising' results cannot be caused by a bug in the program. But again, few AI researchers seem to be interested in the highly important area of AI software engineering. (But see Partridge (1986) for a detailed examination of the relationship between AI and traditional software engineering.)

7.8   AI AS TECHNOLOGY?

It may not necessarily be disadvantageous if AI is not a science. If we consider AI to be a *technology* rather than a science, many of the more mind-expanding claims for AI can be discarded. AI technology is the use of AI techniques and tools in real world applications. AI techniques and tools are techniques and tools proposed by researchers who believe that they are providing the means whereby computers can be made to behave (not think) like humans. This constrained view of AI, which may well be attractive to those researchers who 'get their hands dirty', has some severe implications for the AI academic community.

First, there may be nothing in common between one AI project and another. For example, two different expert systems may have absolutely nothing in common except a name. No underlying principles of knowledge representation and inference need be shared between the two expert systems. No attempt need be made to relate expert systems with human experts. Expert systems are judged individually on the results they produce, and these results need not be judged against human experts' results. Similarly, with natural language parsers, computer-aided instruction packages, vision systems, and so on. A system will survive if it finds a niche in the marketplace, otherwise it soon is forgotten. So, no attempt is made to relate AI with explaining real-world phenomena; no attempt is made to look for underlying scientific principles.

Secondly, if AI is mere technology, any attempt to pursue AI research for the sake of science will not succeed. Much has been made of the dangers of AI to mankind. If AI is a science, AI researchers can ignore these dangers by claiming that science has to be pursued for science's sake, in the same way that scientists working on nuclear fission and fusion argue that their science has to be pursued. But if AI is a technology, it can be held accountable and can therefore be constrained. (See, for instance, Whitby (1988) for a variety of critical arguments based on the premiss that AI is a technology.) Few people would argue that nuclear reactors had to be built for the sake of building nuclear reactors simply because nuclear reactors are a technology. Before a nuclear reactor can be built, a lengthy process is usually entered into whereby the electricity generating board responsible for proposing the reactor need to argue their case in the public eye. Local inhabitants and environmentalists can spell out the dangers of the new technology, economic forecasters spell out the financial advantages and disadvantages in comparison with other proposals, and typically an independent panel or someone in the chair of the enquiry decides, after which the decision is passed to government for approval.

Imagine what would have to be case if this model were applied to AI as technology. Before a company could launch an AI project which might have severe implications for employment and human self-esteem, it would have to to submit its proposal for vetting. The public could raise objections, and a panel would decide. On no account would the argument that the project should go ahead because AI is a science and so needs pursuing at all costs be allowed.

One other implication of AI being a technology, rather than a science, is that it can fail or succeed depending on how many people buy it. No one can do much about electricity that is generated by nuclear reactors, because typically the electricity generating board holds a (virtual) monopoly on electrical power generated from all sources. But we can decide whether we want to buy AI goods or not, and what sort, as long as AI technology is not monopolised by central government.

Fanciful as these ideas may be, they do demonstrate the implications to be taken into account by an AI researcher who claims that AI is a technology. It is no longer socially acceptable to propose a technology and then hide behind the skirts of a science. If AI is a technology, then it must conform to all the criteria and standards society currently expects of a socially-aware technology. It is debatable whether AI researchers want to go so far down the road to social accountability, not because they are unwilling to do so (which may be true or false) but because there is a lingering suspicion that AI is more science than technology. That is, the suspicion remains that AI somehow is contributing to unravelling the workings of the human mind. But that leaves us with a problem of how such a contribution can be measured in terms which have some claim to objectivity and which therefore contribute to 'achievements' of the sort used by Kuhn to characterize a paradigm.

7.9 MARR'S LEVELS

We now turn our attention to the views of a vision researcher - David Marr - which have major implications for AI methodology. Marr's best known contribution this subject is contained in one chapter of a book called *Vision* (Marr, 1982).

Marr (1982) introduces his book on vision with a chapter called 'The philosophy and the approach', in which he provides a brief historical survey of research progress in vision. He distinguishes between three approaches. The first is based on 'psychophysics', in terms of which perception is broken down into more specialized parts, or independent modules (e.g. for dealing with stereo matching), which can be treated and studied separately. The second is based on representations, in terms of which mental processes (e.g. mental rotation of objects) can be described. And the third arises out of electrophysiology, in terms of which the physical aspects of perceived objects can be mapped onto nerve fibre signals. This last approach has now evolved into a neurophysiological approach, where questions of physiological interest to vision researchers can be explained by neurophysiological experiments.

Marr himself admits that he was, during the 1960s, in the grip of the neurophysiological approach: all that was required was a thorough, *functional* analysis of the structure of the nervous system:

> Psychophysics could tell us what needed explaining, and the recent advances in anatomy ... could provide the necessary information about the structure of the cerebral cortex. (Marr, 1982, p. 14)

But then Marr relates how during the 1970s he began to have doubts about this approach. Even if cortical structure could be understood in functional terms, it did not say very much about *how* to go about programming a vision system in a robot:

> Suppose we found the apocryphal grandmother cell [i.e. a cell which fires only when one's grandmother comes into view]. Would that really tell us anything much at all? It would tell us that it existed ... but not *why* or even *how* such a thing may be constructed from the outputs of previously discovered cells .... If we really knew the answers ... we should be able to program [the cells] on a computer. But finding [such cells] certainly did not allow us to program one. (Marr, 1982, p. 15, stress supplied)

Marr identifies the crucial point as follows:

> The key observation is that neurophysiology and psychophysics have as their business to *describe* the behaviour of cells or of subjects but not to *explain* such behaviour. What are the visual areas of the cerebral cortex actually doing? What are the problems in doing it that need explaining, and at what level of description should such explanations be sought? (Marr, 1982, p. 15, stress supplied)

This led Marr to examine research in other areas, particularly in AI, and to the following conclusion:

> The message was plain. There must exist an additional level of understanding [i.e. between the functional and neural descriptions] at which the character of the information-processing tasks carried out during perception are analyzed and understood in a way that is independent of the particular mechanisms and structures that implement them in our heads. This was what was missing - the analysis of the problem as information-processing task. Such an analysis does not usurp an understanding at the other levels - of neurons or of computer programs - but it is a necessary complement to them, since without it there can be no real understanding of the function of all those neurons .... (Marr, 1982, p. 19)

Following on from this, Marr then makes a highly pertinent point, given our earlier comments on methodological criteria for AI:

> [T]he important point is that if the notion of different types of understanding is taken very seriously, it allows the study of the information-processing basis of perception to be made *rigorous*. It becomes possible, by separating explanations into different levels, to make explicit statements about what is being computed and why and to construct theories stating that what is being computed is optimal in some sense or is guaranteed to function correctly. The *ad hoc* element is removed, and heuristic computer programs are replaced by solid foundations on which a real subject can be built. (Marr, 1982, p. 19, stress supplied)

That is, Marr appears to be adding weight to the view that, if *implementability* is to operate as a methodological criterion for AI, then the notion of implementability should be rigorously described in terms of what can and cannot be implemented correctly or optimally. Marr then introduces the term 'representation', which is

> ...a formal system for making explicit certain entities or types of information, together with a specification of how the system does this. And I shall call the result of using a representation to describe a given entity a *description* of the entity in that representation .... (Marr, 1982, p. 21, italics supplied)

For instance, the number, i.e. numerical entity, '37' can be represented in three different ways in the Arabic, Roman and binary numeral systems. In the Arabic notation is the set of symbols $0, 1, 2, 3, 4, 5, 6, 7, 8, 9, 0$; the rules for constructing the description of a particular integer n consist of decomposing n into a sum of multiples of powers of 10 and uniting these multiples into a string with the largest powers on the left and the smallest on the right. So, '37' is represented as $3 * 10^1 + 7 * 10^0$, and this is the *description* of the entity '37' in the Arabic numeral system. According to binary and Roman numeral systems, the same entity would be represented as (i.e. would be given descriptions) 100101 and XXXVII, respectively. Marr summarizes his appeal to formal systems, or schemes, as follows:

> The phrase "formal scheme" is critical to the definition .... The reason is simply that we are dealing with information processing machines, and the way such machines work is by using symbols to stand for things - to represent things, in our terminology. To say that something is a formal scheme means only that it is a set of symbols with rules for putting them together - no more and no less .... [T]he notion that one can capture some aspect of reality by making some description of it using a symbol and that to do so can be useful seems to me a fascinating and powerful idea. (Marr, 1982, p. 21)

When Marr then looks at the term 'process', his methodological framework starts to take shape. He restricts processes to mean the sort of tasks executed by information-processing machines. He uses a cash-register at the checkout-counter of a supermarket as a way of developing the concept of process:

> There are several levels at which one needs to understand such a device, and it is perhaps most useful to think in terms of three of them. The most abstract is the level of *what* the device does and *why*. (Marr, 1982, p.22, stress supplied)

The *what* part of understanding is taken care of by declaring that the device carries out arithmetic. Therefore, a theory of addition is required. The way of expressing arithmetic processes is by means of, say, mappings between pairs of numbers by means of the '+' symbol, e.g. $+(3, 4) \rightarrow 7$. By means of this functional notation, various formal properties can be defined, e.g. associativity and commutativity in addition. These properties are part of the *theory* of addition and are independent of the formal scheme used for representing numbers, e.g. in binary or Arabic notation, and independent of how the addition process is executed in the notation.

The *why* part of understanding at this abstract level, e.g. *why* does the device perform addition rather than multiplication?, is taken care of by providing *constraints* such as:

> the order in which items are presented to the cashier should not affect the total (i.e. commutativity); and

> arranging the goods in two piles and paying for each pile separately should not affect the total amount you pay (i.e. associativity).

Of such constraints, Marr says:

> It is a mathematical theorem that [such constraints] define the operation of addition, which is therefore the appropriate computation to use. ...This whole argument is what I call the *computational theory* of the cash register. Its important features are (1) that it contains separate arguments about what is computed and why and (2) that the resulting operation is defined uniquely by the constraints it has to satisfy. (Marr, 1982, p.23, italics supplied)

Marr then turns his attention to the next level of understanding:

> In order that a process shall actually run, however, one has to realize it in some way and therefore choose a representation for the entities that the process manipulates. The second level of analysis of a process, therefore, involves choosing two things: (1) a *representation* for the input and for the output of the process and (2) an algorithm by which the transformation may actually be accomplished. For addition, of course, the input and output representations can both be the same, because they both consist of numbers. However, this is not true in general. In the case of a Fourier transform, for example, the input representation may be the time domain, and the output, the frequency domain. (Marr, 1982, p. 23, stress supplied)

In other words, this second level of understanding specifies *how* the abstract processes at the first level are to realized. For instance, in the case of the cash register we may decide to use binary representation for representing the numbers, and the algorithm for the process of addition may require addition to start with the rightmost bits of two binary representations, adding these and using 'carry' if the sum is greater than 1. Marr notes that there will be a variety of representations available for describing entities of the computational theory, and also that the choice of algorithm often depends critically on the particular representation which is employed. Also, it is possible for there to be a variety of different algorithms for the same, chosen representation. The choice of one over another might depend on a number of factors, e.g. efficiency, robustness and amenability to parallel processing.

The final, and third, level of understanding processes takes us to the level at which the processes are *physically* realized. An algorithm can be physically realized differently with different entities. For example, although a child and cash-register may both add binary representations in the same way (e.g. from the leftmost bits and using 'carry'), the physical realization is obviously very different in the two cases. In the case of the child, we are looking at neural processes, whilst in the case of the cash register we are looking at electronic processes.

This gives rise to the following three-level framework within which any machine carrying out an information processing task is to be understood:

> **Computational theory** (Level 1): What is the goal of the computation, why is it appropriate, and what is the logic of the strategy by which it can be carried out?

> **Representation and algorithm** (Level 2): How can this computational theory be implemented? In particular, what is the representation for the input and output, and what is the algorithm for the transformation?

> **Hardware implementation** (Level 3): How can the representation and algorithm be realized physically?

So, at the top level we have precise mappings from one kind of information into another, with the appropriateness and adequacy for the task in question being demonstrated. In the middle is the choice of representation for the input and output as well as the algorithm for transforming input into output. And at the bottom are the details of how the algorithm and representation are physically realized. Marr goes on to say:

These three levels are coupled, but only loosely. The choice of an algorithm is influenced for example, by what it has to do and by the hardware in which it must run. But there is a wide choice available at each level, and the explication of each level involves issues that are independent of the other two. (Marr, 1982, p.25)

Each of these three levels of description has its place in the complete understanding of information processing tasks, and

...of course they are logically and causally related. But an important point to note is that since the three levels are only rather loosely related, some phenomena may be explained at only one or two of them. (Marr, 1982, p. 25)

For instance, an explanation concerning afterimages (after looking at a lightbulb) may be available only at the level of physical mechanisms of vision, whereas many optical ambiguities (e.g. a two-dimensional representation of a cube which can be interpreted three-dimensionally in two different ways) require both a neural explanation (in terms of a bistable neural network - see Feldman and Ballard (1982)) at the level of the brain as well as an explanation at the level of representations. Marr writes:

[I]f the idea that different phenomena need to be explained at different levels is kept clearly in mind, it often helps in the assessment of the validity of the different kinds of objections that are raised from time to time. For example, one favourite is that the brain is quite different from a computer because one is parallel and the other serial. The answer to this, of course, is that the distinction between serial and parallel is a distinction at the level of algorithm: it is not fundamental at all - anything programmed in parallel can be rewritten serially (though not necessarily vice versa). The distinction, therefore, provides no grounds for arguing that the brain operates so differently from a computer that a computer could not be programmed to perform the same tasks. (Marr, 1982, p. 27)

Marr stresses the importance of the top level - that of computational theory - in his framework:

[A]n algorithm is likely to be understood more readily by understanding the nature of the problem being solved than by examining the mechanism (and the hardware) in which it is embodied. (Marr, 1982, p. 27)

He then goes on to draw various inferences, given his framework:

(a) Specialized empirical disciplines of the neurosciences have failed to appreciate the absence, in their approaches, of computational theory;

(b) Early developments in AI also failed to appreciate the importance of computational theory;

(c) Failure to recognize the distinction between *what* and *how* hampered communication between the fields of AI and linguistics in that, whereas, for instance, Chomsky's transformational grammar (Chomsky, 1965) was a true computational theory, some researchers criticized Chomsky on the basis of difficulty in implementing the theory on a computer.

With regard the second point, Marr writes (pertinently, from our point of view):

> For far too long, a heuristic program for carrying out some task was held to be a theory of that task, and the distinction between what a program did and how it did it was not taken seriously. As a result, (1) a style of explanation evolved that invoked the use of special mechanisms to solve particular problems, (2) particular data structures ... were held to amount to theories of the representation of knowledge, and (3) there was frequently no way to determine whether a program would deal with a particular case other than by running a program. (Marr, 1982, p. 28)

7.10   IMPLEMENTATIONALISM

Given these comments by Marr and his three-level framework, we now have a different way of describing the debate between classical cognitive scientists and connectionists. Fodor and Pylyshyn (1988) write:

> A recurring theme [in their critique - see the previous chapter] is that many of the arguments for Connectionism are best construed as claiming that cognitive architecture is *implemented* in a certain kind of network. ...Understood in this way, these arguments are neutral on the questions of what the cognitive architecture is. (Fodor and Pylyshyn, 1988, p.64, stress supplied)

That is, all the implementation properties associated with a particular realization of algorithms that classical theorists happen to propose are irrelevant to the psychological theory; only the algorithm and the representations on which it operates are intended as a psychological hypothesis. But this implies that connectionism, as implementation theory, is neutral about the nature of cognitive processes:

> In fact, [Connectionist models] might be viewed as advancing the goals of Classical information processing psychology by attempting to explain how the brain ...might realize the types of processes that conventional cognitive science has hypothesized. (Fodor and Pylyshyn, 1988, p. 65)

This is a similar point to that raised by Broadbent (1985) when he comments on a paper by McClelland and Rumelhart (1985) on representing general and specific information in a distributed memory system. In his paper, Broadbent, whilst welcoming the general approach adopted by McClelland and Rumelhart, claims:

> [I]t is unfortunate that the evidence to which [McClelland and Rumelhart] appeal is from a different level of explanation, and therefore irrelevant to the undoubted merits of the distributed approach. (Broadbent, 1985, pp. 191-192)

That is, Broadbent argues that because the distributed model is a theory *below* Marr's computational level, in that it is a theory of how memory is implemented at a physiological level, and because psychology is concerned with computational level, McClelland and Rumelhart are wrong in claiming that their model has implications for psychology: whatever claims are made for the distributed model have relevance only at the implementational level and not at the computational/psychological level.

Rumelhart and McClelland (1985) reply that, whilst they have reservations about Marr's three levels of explanation, Broadbent is wrong on two counts. First, Broadbent has ignored the level of algorithm and representation - the intermediate level between the computational and the implementational levels; and secondly, whilst psychology is properly concerned with all three levels, the *information processing approach* to psychology is primarily concerned with the level of algorithm and representation. They write:

> We believe that our [model] is stated primarily at the algorithmic level and is primarily aimed at specifying the representation of information and the processes and procedures involved in storing and retrieving information. ...[According to Marr's analysis] ...no particular level of description is independent of the others. There is thus an implicit computational theory in our model as well as an appeal to certain implementational (physiological) considerations. ...Broadbent's failure to consider the algorithmic level is crucial ...because this is the very level at which information processing models ...have been stated. Computational models, according to Marr, are focused on a formal analysis of the problem the system is solving - not the methods by which it is solved. (Rumelhart and McClelland, 1985, pp. 193-194)

Rumelhart and McClelland's reply, therefore, is that Broadbent has misidentified the level of psychological explanation with regard to information processing models when he claims that psychology is concerned with the computational level:

> It is the algorithmic level at which we are concerned with such issues as efficiency, degradation of performance under noise or other adverse conditions, whether a particular problem is hard or difficult, which problems are solved quickly, which take a long time to solve, *how information is represented*, and so on. These are all questions to which psychological inquiry is directed and to which psychological data is relevant. ...At the computational level ...it does not matter how long the computation takes, or how the performance of the computation is affected by performance factors such as memory load, problem complexity, and so on. It does not matter how the information is represented, *as long as the representation is rich enough, in principle, to support computation of the required function.* (Rumelhart and McClelland, 1985, p. 194, stress added in both cases)

We have stressed two parts of the above quotation in order to provide one of the motivating factors behind Fodor and Pylyshyn's critique (as described in the previous chapter): if Rumelhart and McClelland themselves claim that connectionist models are pitched at the algorithmic and representational level and not at the computational level, and they make this claim in the belief that connectionist models are on par with information processing models operating at the second level, then any successful critique of connectionism as representational will, by default, imply that connectionism, far from providing explanations at the representation and algorithm level, must be implementational (if one ignores the question of whether connectionist models are pitched at the computational level). One of the aims of Fodor and Pylyshyn's critique was, of course, to provide such an attack, and that is why a substantial part of their paper is devoted to aspects of representation and to providing arguments intended to demonstrate that connectionist 'representations' cannot be interpreted as representations, *in the classical sense*.

Interestingly, Rumelhart and McClelland then go on to offer their own critique of Marr's three levels. Whilst accepting that his three levels at least 'specify the boundaries of of psychological enquiry' (Rumelhart and McClelland, 1985, p. 196), they nevertheless write:

> [T]here is more twixt the computational and the implementational than is dreamt of, even in Marr's philosophy. ...There is still another notion of levels that illustrates our view. This is the notion of levels implicit in the distinction between Newtonian mechanics on the one hand and quantum field theory on the other. [This analogy was suggested to us by Paul Smolensky.] (Rumelhart and McClelland, 1985, pp. 195-196)

What Rumelhart and McClelland have in mind is the idea that Newtonian theory is a theory at the *macro*scopic or *macro*structural level, in that it deals with entire objects and ignores much of the internal structural properties of the objects:

> However, in some situations the Newtonian theory breaks down. In these situations, we must rely on the *micro*structural account of quantum field theory. Through a thorough understanding of the relation between the Newtonian mechanics and quantum field theory we can understand that the *macro*scopic

level of description may only be an approximation to the more *micro*scopic theory. Moreover, in physics, we understand just when the *macro*theory will fail and when the *micro*theory must be invoked. We understand the *macro*theory as a useful formal tool, by virtue of its relation to the *micro*theory. In this sense, the objects of the *macro*theory can be viewed as emerging from interactions of the particles described at the *micro*level. (Rumelhart and McClelland, 1985, p. 196, stress added in all cases)

Connectionist explanations are of course claimed to be at the microlevel, where the explanations are couched in terms of a microstructure *theory*.

There are three points worth highlighting here. First, Rumelhart and McClelland's claim is that just because there is a level of explanation below that of the macrolevel that does not mean that explanations at the lower level are necessarily explanations concerned with implementation aspects. In fact, the lowest level in Rumelhart and McClelland's hierarchy would still consist of an implementational level, but any implementation would be of a microstructure theory at the next level up, and it is with microstructure theory that connectionists are concerned. It is this claim which justifies the common subtitle to the both the PDP volumes (Rumelhart, McClelland and the PDP Research Group (1986) and McClelland, Rumelhart and the PDP Research Group (1986)): explorations in the *microstructure* of cognition.

The second point concerns their view of the relationship between macrotheory and microtheory. Rumelhart and McClelland believe that, far from there being a causal and logical relationship between macrotheory and microtheory, in the direction of *macro to micro*, there is instead, if anything, a form of causal and logical relationship between the two levels in the reverse direction, i.e. from *micro to macro*. That is, properties at the macrolevel somehow, causally and logically, emerge out of the properties of the microlevel. And this is because properties at the macrolevel can only be, at best, approximations of the truth, concentrating as they do on whole objects rather than on the structure of objects and how structure causes various connections with other objects via various structural properties.

And the third point concerns what exactly Rumelhart and McClelland mean by a macrolevel theory. They accept that the computational and implementation levels specify the boundaries of psychological research. This implies that at least Rumelhart and McClelland are willing to accept, with Marr, that there is a computational level, where relationships are characterized functionally, above the macrolevel. They then appeal to various entities such as 'logogens' (Morton, 1969), 'schemata' and 'prototypes' as constructs of macrolevel descriptions. These constructs are *representational* and algorithmic constructs (using Marr's terminology for characterizing level 2) and therefore not part of level 1. Rumelhart and McClelland therefore seem to accept that there could be a separate computational level. Similar reasoning implies that they would also accept that there could be a separate implementational level. They then write:

> Marr's computational and implementation levels specify the boundaries of psychological inquiry. In between, at what Marr calls the algorithmic level, lies the heart of our concern. However, our examination of analogies to computer science and physics suggests that we may well need to consider many sublevels of analysis *within* the algorithmic level. (Rumelhart and McClelland, 108, p. 196, stress added)

Rumelhart and McClelland here are arguing for a more complex analysis of level 2 - the level of representation and algorithm - within which there is a distinction to be made between macrostructures and microstructures. Furthermore, it appears that the mapping between microstructures and macrostructures, since this mapping takes place within a level and therefore counts as an explanation at the algorithmic level, can be made independently of the other two levels.

Let us leave Rumelhart and McClelland for the moment and look at another researcher who expresses dissatisfaction with Marr's hierarchy, albeit for very different reasons.

7.11 PEACOCKE'S LEVEL 1.5

Peacocke (1986a) believes that current accounts of what explanation consists of in the domain of psychology omit a significant level of explanation. With reference to Marr's three-level categorization, he writes:

> David Marr's classic statement distinguished three levels of description of a computational psychological process .... The first level states which function is computed and why; the second states which algorithm computes the function; and the third

$$
\begin{array}{cccc}
P_1 n_1 & P_1 n_2 & \cdots & P_1 n_{10} \\
P_2 n_1 & P_2 n_2 & \cdots & P_2 n_{10} \\
\cdots & \cdots & \cdots & \cdots \\
P_{10} n_1 & P_{10} n_2 & \cdots & P_{10} n_{10}
\end{array}
$$

Figure 7.1

states how the algorithm is realized in hardware. The level with which I will be concerned does not lie within one of Marr's levels. It lies between his first and second levels; for this reason I will dub it 'level 1.5'. Level 1.5 *states the information on which the algorithm draws*. (Peacocke, 1986a, p. 101, stress added)

Peacocke uses a finite, artificial language to provide an example of what he means. Imagine we had a language with ten distinct property names (monadic predicates), $P_1 \cdots P_{10}$, and ten distinct proper names, $n_1 \cdots n_{10}$, resulting in a language of 100 distinct sentences (*Figure 7.1*). According to Peacocke, there are two ways of dealing with how a 'speaker' of this language *understands* sentences in this language:

> the speaker understands each of the 100 sentences because he or she understands the meaning of the individual components of a sentence and through a form of compositional rule thereby understands the sentence as a whole; or

> the speaker understands each of the 100 sentences, not because he or she understands that each sentence is structured according to some form of compositional syntax and semantics, but because each sentence has associated with it a pointer of some sort to another table where the meaning of that sentence is provided in full and independently of all the other sentences.

If a truth-conditional semantic theory is assumed, and if there are, for the sake of the example, two subjects, S and U, where S understands each of the sentences of the language because he or she understands the meaning of their components, and where U understands each of the sentences as unstructured, then

> ...[t]he appropriate truth theories for the languages of S and
> U will be correspondingly different. The truth theory for S's
> language will give denotation axioms for the proper names and
> satisfaction axioms for the monadic predicates, and the truth
> conditions for whole sentences will follow from these axioms;
> the appropriate truth theory for U's language will list the truth
> conditions for whole sentences outright, rather than relying on
> derivations from axioms about the sentences' parts. [It is surely
> right to say that] there is a common component in the expla-
> nation of S's understanding of all sentences containing a given
> proper name: and that this is not so for U. More particularly, I
> would say that the algorithms and mechanisms in S have access
> to information (or misinformation) about the semantical prop-
> erties of the given proper name. The algorithm or mechanism
> draws upon this information when operating to produce under-
> standing of the sentences in which the name occurs. No such
> information about the individual name is drawn upon by the
> mechanisms operating in U. (Peacocke, 1986a, p. 102)

It is important to note that, whilst Peacocke admits that he is personally
committed to a form of truth-conditional semantic theory for natural languages, this is not the point at issue: *any* semantic approach could be
adopted. However, no matter what semantic approach is adopted, Peacocke's claim is that the algorithms which are proposed for achieving language understanding are *causally influenced* by the choice of a common
semantic theory or approach. It is *this* point which he believes is overlooked
by Marr's three-level approach. Pursuing his personal commitment to a
truth-conditional approach, he writes:

> Now the common informational element in the explanation
> of S's understanding of all sentences containing a given name is
> not captured at Marr's level 1. The level 1 function from whole
> sentences to their meanings, specified by their truth condition as
> given in a metalanguage ..., is the *same* function in extension
> for the language of S and U .... In identifying the informa-
> tion on which the mechanisms in S draw, are we then offering
> a specification at Marr's level 2, *i.e.*, stating which algorithm is
> used? We are not: several different algorithms are compatible
> with what has been said so far about the nature of structured
> understanding. (Peacocke, 1986a, pp. 102-103, stress supplied)

That is, once it has been decided that a truth-conditional semantic approach is the choice, there will be several different ways of realizing the truth-value of a sentence, given the common idea that the truth-value of a sentence is computed as a function of the truth-values of individual elements in the sentence. The choice of a truth-conditional approach does not in any way commit us to a particular algorithm. Instead, what a *class* of algorithms may have in common is the requirement that they compute a truth-value of a whole sentence from the truth-values of individual items in the sentence. It therefore follows that the states through which an algorithm proceeds are somehow dependent on this common information element:

> The idea of an algorithm or mechanism drawing on information, as I understand it, is a partially causal notion. It requires that a state which carries the information drawn upon is causally influential in the operation of the algorithm or mechanism; indeed it requires that the algorithm or mechanism produce states with the content they do in part because of the content of the information-carrying state. (Peacocke, 1986a, p. 102)

Peacocke provides two further justifications for his proposal of a level 1.5. First, he notes that just as there is a one-to-many mapping between Marr's original levels 1 and 2, and between levels 2 and 3 (in that for every computational specification at level 1 there will be many algorithms at level 2 which realize that specification, and similarly for every algorithm at level 2 there will many physical realizations of that algorithm), so also is there a one-to-many mapping between level 1 and level 1.5, and between level 1.5 and level 2:

> Just as two different algorithms may compute the same function, so two different algorithms may draw upon the same body of information. ...Equally, one and the same function may be computed by drawing on different bodies of information; there is a one-many relation between level 1 and level 1.5. The pattern of one-many relations which holds between Marr's levels persists when we insert level 1.5. (Peacocke, 1986a, p. 107)

Secondly, just as descriptions and explanations at each level in Marr's original hierarchy have their own distinctive facts to account for, so do descriptions and explanations at level 1.5. Peacocke writes:

> Explanations at level 1.5 have several distinctive characteristics. In discussing these, it will be helpful to draw a distinction. There is a distinction between theories which state that mental states and structures have contents, and theories which do not. We can call the former *content-using* theories. ...What matters for the status of a theory as content-using is just that it ascribes states with contents, where the contents (or their components) refer to objects, properties, relations or magnitudes. It is not always simple to tell from the informal exposition of a theory whether it is content-using or not. On the other hand, a theory which is not content-using may be given a heuristically useful exposition by identifying, by means of content-involving descriptions, states which are not strictly asserted in the theory to have contents. (Peacocke, 1986a, pp. 107-108, italics supplied)

One feels that Peacocke here is trying to distinguish between 'Classical Cognitive Science' theories (as later expressed by Fodor and Pylyshyn - see the previous chapter) on the one hand, and 'Connectionist' theories on the other, but it is not absolutely clear that he has this sort of distinction in mind. What he does say, though, is:

> Both kinds of theories are surely legitimate and intelligible: they just have different goals. But what matters for present purposes is that explanation at level 1.5 must be by content-using theories. In identifying the information drawn upon, a theorist has to mention contents; and usually the general facts to be explained at level 1.5 concern content-involving states as described. (Peacocke, 1986a, p. 108)

If Peacocke indeed intends to distinguish between classical cognitive theories and connectionist theories, then his claims are that connectionist 'explanations' *per se* (i.e. connectionist statements which make no explicit reference to the information being handled or drawn upon) are not explanations at level 1.5. If that is indeed his intention, it is not entirely clear *whether* Peacocke would allow these connectionist statements in principle to be provided with some form of bridging statement to make clear what information is being drawn upon or handled, in which case such statements could then attain the status of being level 1.5 explanations, or *how* such bridging statements could in principle be provided for all connectionist statements.

Peacocke does not tackle this question openly in his paper, although to be fair to him this is not his main objective. However, it does look as though he identifies a position very similar to that adopted by Fodor and Pylyshyn a couple of years later concerning the lack of 'representationality' in connectionist statements.

Peacocke provides answers to two objections he predicts will be leveled against him. In general, both these objections are concerned with the following point: interesting as level 1.5 may be, there is the issue of whether level 1.5 is even psychological. That is, whilst level 1.5, from a *computational* point of view, may be of use to computer scientists when they design and develop computer systems, what is the significance of level 1.5 from a *cognitive* or *psychological* point of view?

Peacocke first tackles the objection that he is committed to a *language of thought* in which the information (at level 1.5) which is drawn upon by the algorithm (at level 2) is expressed or written out. Such an appeal to a language of thought, whilst it might at first satisfy the requirement for cognitive or psychological reality of level 1.5, may lead to circularity (e.g. what is the functional specification of such a language? what representations does it use? what are the algorithmic processes involved in such a language? how is such a language physically realized?) or vacuity. Peacocke denies that such a commitment is necessary. Instead, what is required is that the information at level 1.5, no matter how it is represented or expressed, to have causal influence on the algorithms ('psychological mechanisms' (Peacocke, 1986a, p. 111)) at level 2, in that the algorithms be causally dependent on the information at level 1.5. For example, the information at level 1.5 could be expressed in terms of a semantic theory where the meaning of a sentence is derived form the meaning of individual items in the sentence, and the semantic theory will causally influence the algorithms 'empirically involved in understanding' (Peacocke, 1986a, p. 111). Causal influence is achieved by the organism going through various states, where states realize their having the information that such-and-such in a variety of ways. It is these ways which are causally influenced by the semantic theory:

> This causal dependence is what matters for level 1.5 explanations of structured understanding .... On the account just given, that a state has certain causal powers will indeed be implicit in the claim that it realizes the subject's possession of certain information (or misinformation). But this does not make explanation at level 1.5 vacuous or circular: for the statement that there are

> in an organism states with such-and-such causal powers remains
> as empirical as can be. (Peacocke, 1986a, pp. 111-112)

The next objection which Peacocke faces is whether all he has done is come up with a way of distinguishing between different *classes* of algorithm and has elevated the distinguishing criteria into a level in their own right, namely, level 1.5. Peacocke replies in three ways. First, this objection could also be leveled against Marr's level 1, where computational specification, it could be argued, delineated different classes of algorithms at level 2; Marr nevertheless recognized level 1. Secondly:

> [W]hat justifies recognition of a new level is that it has a distinctive fact explained by truths at that level. I have argued that level 1.5 meets this condition. (Peacocke, 1986a, p. 112)

And thirdly, if it is further objected that all that is required is to interpret Marr's second level more flexibly, in that describing an algorithm also means including a reference to the information on which the algorithm draws, then according to Peacocke this is to make the same point concerning the need for a level 1.5 but in a different terminology.

Peacocke concludes his paper by applying his proposed modification to Marr's hierarchy to recent writings in the philosophy of language. Some commentators on Peacocke's proposal have concentrated on this latter part of his proposal (Schiffer, 1986; Soames, 1986). Higginbotham (1986), however, raises two methodological points concerning level 1.5. First, he asks what exactly is meant by an algorithm drawing on certain information. For example, if two algorithms compute $x^2 - 1$ for input x, where the first algorithm squares x and subtracts 1, whereas the second algorithm subtracts 1 from x, stores the result, and then adds 1 to x and multiplies by what is stored (i.e. the second algorithm calculates the answer by multiplying $x - 1$ with $x + 1$), does the second algorithm draw upon the further information that $x^2 - 1 = (x - 1)(x + 1)$? And how does the second algorithm differ from a third algorithm which explicitly *transforms* the given problem into multiplying $x - 1$ by $x + 1$ and so uses the information directly?

The point of this example is to raise the question of what exactly the status of the information is which is drawn upon, and furthermore what form the information takes. Higginbotham himself distinguishes two senses of what it is for an algorithm to draw upon certain information. The first, or *weak*, sense requires that for the algorithm to work the information drawn upon must be true, although the representation of the original information need not be involved in the computation. In this weak sense, the second and third algorithms can be classified together since they both calculate $(x-1)(x+1)$, the equivalent to $x^2 - 1$, the original information, which is not represented or involved in the computation. The second, or *strong*, sense requires that a representation of the original information be involved in the computation directly. Hence, the first algorithm, which calculates $x^2 - 1$ by squaring x and subtracting 1, draws upon the information in a strong sense. (Higginbotham in fact appears to confuse the strong sense with the weak sense when classifying the three algorithms - a point picked up by Peacocke (1986b). We have presented a simplified version of Higginbotham's objection which we believe is accurate with respect to his main point.)

Higginbotham then asks in what sense Peacocke requires the algorithm to draw on information. He argues that it cannot be in the strong sense, since Peacocke himself appears to rule out the requirement that the information should be explicitly involved:

> Specifically, [Peacocke] wishes to reject the idea that a statement that characterizes such a thing as the meaning of a word must explicitly appear as a piece of subpersonal propositional knowledge in the repertoire of the linguistically competent. (Higginbotham, 1986, p. 359)

But the weak sense may be too weak in that, if level 1.5 is psychological, it is not clear how information at that level could be used cognitively by speakers of a language: all we may have is a specification of a semantic theory which has no psychological or cognitive reality for the speaker.

Higginbotham's second objection is that Peacocke has focused on *perception* problems in language and has ignored aspects of *production*. If Peacocke claims that the same underlying semantic theory can cope with both perception and production, in that the same semantic information states causally influence two distinct sets of algorithms - one for perception, the other for production - then Peacocke's level 1.5 appears to be very similar to the Chomskyan notion of 'competence' - an abstract, ideal specification of the native speaker's *tacit* knowledge. And if that is the case, Peacocke is then left with the task of showing how his level 1.5 (competence) is psychologically relevant, or real. This could be a difficult task, especially when competence theorists themselves claim that psychological relevance and psychological reality are aspects of *performance*, i.e. the application of the 'ideal' grammar in the real world. Peacocke's level 1.5 may have no psychological plausibility or relevance at all.

Peacocke's answers (Peacocke, 1986b) to these objections are interesting. He admits that he needs to provide clarification concerning the psychological reality of level 1.5 information:

> Suppose that, in a description of linguistic competence, a certain piece of information is said to be tacitly known. What is required for this description to 'have psychological reality'? I suggest (as a second shot) that the requirement is a general one, concerning all of the performances or abilities said to be explained by that tacit knowledge. What is required is that each such performance or ability have a suitable explanation at level 1.5, an explanation which cites the fact that the given piece of information is drawn upon. It is the *same* piece of information which is drawn upon by all the different mechanisms which produce the performances, or ground the abilities. So, for instance, if a description of an Italian as tacitly knowing that 'Roma' denotes Rome is to have 'psychological reality', then this condition must be met: the information that 'Roma' denotes Rome is drawn upon both by the algorithms which explain his hearing sentences containing 'Roma' as meaning something about Rome, and by the algorithms or mechanisms which compute that one way to say something about Rome is to utter a sentence containing 'Roma'. (Peacocke, 1986b, pp. 388-389)

For Peacocke, a piece of information is psychologically real if both perceptual and productive algorithms, in their own way, draw upon the information. However, this raises another objection. If, for example, the algorithm we are concerned with is perceptual and has the task of parsing input strings as well as at the same time building up a semantic interpretation of the strings, we can ask what would happen if the algorithm could not terminate in its attempt to characterize (syntactically and semantically) one particular string. That is, if the language we are dealing with is one described by a Type 0 grammar (see Chapter 2, Section 10), the resulting algorithm may not be able to identify, for all strings which are non-sentences of the language, whether they are non-sentences. However, the algorithm, in its (infinitely looping) attempt to characterize the string as a sentence or non-sentence, may nevertheless draw upon the information concerning the meaning of individual words in the string. According to Peacocke, since the algorithm is drawing upon the semantic information at level 1.5, the semantic information is psychologically real. But what of the algorithm at level 2? Is such an infinitely looping algorithm also psychologically real?

Peacocke could reply that a more constrained interpretation of 'algorithm' is required here, namely, one which is an effective procedure, i.e. it guarantees to terminate for all input. This in turn would constrain the type of language which psychologically could be processed by such algorithms. However, this raises two further points. First, Peacocke's notion of information at level 1.5 causally influencing algorithms at level 2 needs to be tightened up considerably, so that causal influence now includes the requirement that the resulting algorithms be effective procedures. But this may mean that the type of semantic theories allowed at level 1.5 also needs to be constrained, e.g. semantic theories of Type 0 languages which contain one-to-one projection rules from the syntax of the language may not be allowed.

And secondly, it now appears that it is the nature of the algorithm which is causally influencing the nature of the information, and not the other way around. That is, we may have a causal influence from level 1 (the problem domain) to the level of algorithm (how the problem is to be tackled), and then from the level of the algorithm to the level of information (what information structures there are for the algorithm to work on).

7.12 CONCLUSION

What is interesting about Peacocke's views on the one hand, and Rumelhart and McClelland's on the other, is the different way they identify problems associated with Marr's original proposal and the method used for dealing with those problems. Peacocke can be interpreted as taking a radical computationalist view (see the last chapter) with regard to the role of representations (minus algorithms) and justifies his proposed level 1.5 - the level of representation without algorithm - by appealing not just to examples and computationalism but also to the method by which Marr himself justified his three levels. Rumelhart and McClelland can be interpreted as taking a radical neurocomputing view concerning the role of representations and algorithms also, but argue for a more complex level 2, thereby claiming that connectionist theories are theories *within* the representation and algorithmic level and therefore not theories or explanations which lie *between* levels 2 and 3. However, whereas Peacocke justified his level 1.5 by invoking the one-to-many relationship between levels 1 and 1.5, and similarly with levels 1.5 and 2, Rumelhart and McClelland appear to have no such justification in mind when proposing a hierarchy *within* level 2, yet appear to be happy with levels 1 and 3. Presumably, Rumelhart and McClelland would therefore be happy with a one-to-many relationship of some sort between their version of level 2 and level 3. But the question now arises as to which sublevel within their level 2 they regard as the candidate for a one-to-many relationship with level 3, and which sublevel within level 2 is the level on the receiving end of the one-to-many relationship between levels 1 and 2. If it is the *macro*scopic level of level 2 which is on the receiving end of the one-to-many relationship between levels 1 and 2, and the macroscopic structures are logically and causally related to level 1 in that they are dependent logically and causally on level 1 specifications and functions, how can this be reconciled with Rumelhart and McClelland's view that these macroscopic structures somehow *emerge* out of the interaction of deeper *micro*scopic structures?

Rumelhart and McClelland may claim that it is the *micro*scopic level which is at the receiving end of the one-to-many relationship between levels 1 and 2, and that the interaction of these microscopic structures gives rise to the various emergent macroscopic structures and properties favoured by computationalists. Furthermore, they may claim that it is the level of microstructure which has a one-to-many relationship with implementations at level 3, not the level of macrostructure. But this may then lead to an irreconcilable difference between computationalists and neurocomputing researchers on the status of such macroscopic structures, with computationalists unwilling to let go of the Marr-based idea that a level 1 computational specification maps onto many *macro*scopic level 2 structures, and neurocomputing researchers unable, and perhaps unwilling, to provide an account of the role of macrostructures as anything other than emerging out of interactions of microstructures.

Such reasoning leads to the conclusion that, despite efforts on the part of researchers with a foot in both camps to make peace between computationalists and neurocomputing researchers, the difference of opinion concerning the status of so-called macroscopic structures may well prevent any lasting collaboration. It is therefore possible that, whilst there may well be some unifying framework within which computationalists and neurocomputing researchers can work together happily to some degree, this will only be possible because they decide beforehand on which levels of the framework they are separately, but interdependently, concerned with for that one project. However, the implication is that the fundamental difference of view concerning the status of macroscopic structures will eventually surface when it come to assigning psychological reality and neural plausibility to the macroscopic and microscopic structures, because at that stage the two sets of researchers will have to go beyond their particular, joint project and look at wider issues of description and explanation. And this may not be a difference which can be resolved empirically.

We are not claiming that the above discussions demonstrate that AI is not a science, or that it cannot be a science, because it has no agreed methodology. Rather, one aspect of the above discussions is that they demonstrate that AI is a young science which is going through the usual problems that a young science does. From our point of view, however, the important lesson to learn is that, using Marr's framework, even if there is agreement on what intelligence consists of at the computational/functional level (and this is a point we have not even got round to discussing) there may nevertheless be deep differences in the way intelligence is approached from an algorithmic (and hence representational) point of view. Crudely put, intelligence may have to be viewed either as a macroscopic property or as a microscopic property, but not both.

With this in mind, Turing's original formulation of the Imitation Game requires some rephrasing. Whereas Turing was quite happy to use the notion of observable behaviour (in particular, answering questions in an intelligent way) in order to come up with a different way of putting the question, 'Can machines think?', this is no longer acceptable from the viewpoint of AI. That is, because of developments in our understanding of mental events, mental processes, and cognition in general, the Imitation Game needs to be rephrased in such a way that the *internal processes* of the machine must not only be taken into account but also, if we are to remain true to the spirit of the original version of the Imitation Game, provide the main justification for ascribing intelligence and thought to the machine. We do not have to look very far for a suitable statement which expresses this requirement: Searle's version of *strong AI* would appear to be an ideal candidate for a modern version of the Imitation Game, i.e.

> [T]he appropriately programmed computer with the right inputs and outputs literally has a mind in exactly the same sense that you and I do. ... [I]f you have the right program with the right inputs and the right outputs, then any system running

that program, regardless of its chemical structure ... *must have* thoughts and feelings in exactly the same way as you and I do. And this is because that is all there is to having a mind: having the right program. (Searle, 1987, p. 210, stress supplied)

The twist in the tail, as we have seen, is that there are two competing approaches to what constitutes the 'right program': the computationalist approach, and the neurocomputing approach. That is, what it is for a program to be a right program can be unpacked by appealing to various properties of intelligence which can be assigned *either* at a macroscopic level (by, for instance, the use of appropriate macroscopic-based representations using logic, scripts or schemas), *or* at a microscopic level (by, for instance, the use of appropriate distributed representations and neural mechanisms). Ideally we should like, and demand, both types of description and explanation, but given the various philosophical views on the nature of the relationship between the mind and the brain (some of which we have already examined in these two volumes) it is unlikely that we shall get both such that they are compatible with each other. The only hope is that the computationalist versus neurocomputing issue will transcend the mind versus brain issue, and if it does this may well be the long-lasting contribution that AI makes to philosophy.

References

Ayer, A. J. (1936) *Language, Truth and Logic*. Gollancz. (The page reference is taken from the Pelican edition of the book published in 1971.)

Bobrow, D. G and Hayes, P. J. (1985) Artificial intelligence - Where are we?, *Artificial Intelligence*, 25.

Boden, M. (1977) *Artificial Intelligence and Natural Man*. Harvester Press.

Broadbent, D. A question of levels: Comment on McClelland and Rumelhart, *Journal of Experimental Psychology: General*, 114, 2, pp. 189-192.

Cendrowska, J. and Bramer, M. (1984) Inside an expert system: a rational reconstruction of the MYCIN consultation system, in O'Shea and Eisenstadt (1984).

Charniak, E. and McDermott, D. (1985) *Introduction to Artificial Intelligence*. Addison Wesley.

Chomsky, N. (1965) *Aspects of the Theory of Syntax*. MIT Press.

Feldman, J. A. (1985) Response to Question 5 in a questionnaire distributed by D. G. Bobrow and P. J. Hayes, in Bobrow and Hayes (1985), p. 376.

Feldman, J. A. and Ballard, D. H. (1986) Connectionist models and their properties, *Cognitive Science*, 6, pp. 205-254.

Fodor, J. A. and Pylyshyn, Z. W. (1988) Connectionism and cognitive architecture: A critical analysis, *Cognition*, 28. Reprinted in S. Pinker and J. Mehler, J. (eds.) *Connections and Symbols*, Bradford Books/MIT Press, 1988.

Hayes, P. J. (1984) On the differences between psychology and AI, in M. Yazdani and A. Narayanan (eds.), *Artificial Intelligence: Human Effects*, Ellis Horwood.

Hempel, C. (1966) *Philosophy of Natural Science*. Prentice Hall.

Higginbotham, J. (1986) Peacocke on explanation in psychology, *Mind and Language*, 1, 4, pp. 358-361.

Hofstadter, D. R. (1979) Gödel, Escher, Bach: An Eternal Golden Braid. Harvester Press.

Kuhn, T. S. (1970) *The Structure of Scientific Revolutions*, 2nd Edition. The University of Chicago Press.

McClelland, J. L. and Rumelhart, D. E. (1985) Distributed memory and the representation of general and specific information, *Journal of Experimental Psychology: General*, 114, 2, pp. 159-188.

McClelland, J. L., Rumelhart, D. E. and the PDP Research Group (1986) *Parallel Distributed Processing: Explorations in the Microstructure of Cognition. Volume 2: Psychological and Biological Models*. Bradford Books/MIT Press.

Marr, D. (1977) Artificial intelligence: a personal view, *Artificial Intelligence*, 9, pp. 37-48. Reprinted in J. Haugeland (ed.) *Mind Design: Philosophy, Psychology, Artificial Intelligence*, MIT Press (1981). The page references are taken from the 1981 reprint.

Marr, D. (1982) *Vision*. Freeman.

Minsky, M. L. (1968) *Semantic Information Processing*. MIT Press.

Morton, J. (1969) Interaction of information in word recognition. *Psychological Review*, 76, pp. 165-178.

Nilsson, N. (1985) Response to Question 5 in a questionnaire distributed by D. G. Bobrow and P. J. Hayes, in Bobrow and Hayes (1985), p. 376.

O'Shea, T. and Eisenstadt, M. (eds.) (1984) *Artificial Intelligence: Tools, Techniques and Applications*. Harper and Row.

Partridge, D. (1986) *Artificial Intelligence: Applications in the Future of Software Engineering*. Ellis Horwood.

Peacocke, C. (1986a) Explanation in computational psychology: language, perception and level 1.5, *Mind and Language*, 1, 2, pp. 101-123.

Peacocke, C. (1986b) Replies to commentators, *Mind and Language*, 1, 4, pp. 388-402.

Popper, K. (1959) *The Logic of Scientific Discovery*. Hutchinson.

Popper, K. (1965) *Conjectures and Refutations*. Routledge.

Popper, K. (1972) *Objective Knowledge*. Clarendon Press.

Rumelhart, D. E. and McClelland, J. L (1985) Levels indeed! A response to Broadbent, *Journal of Experimental Psychology: General*, 114, 2, pp. 193-197.

Rumelhart, D. E., McClelland, J. L. and the PDP Research Group (eds.) (1986) *Parallel Distributed Processing: Explorations in the Microstructure of Cognition. Volume 1: Foundations*. Bradford Books/MIT Press.

Searle, J. R. (1987) Minds and brains without programs, in C. Blakemore and S. Greenfield (eds.) *Mindwaves*, Blackwell.

Schiffer, S. (1986) Peacocke on explanation in psychology, *Mind and Language*, 1, 4, pp. 362-371.

Sloman, A. (1985) Response to Question 5 in a questionnaire distributed by D. G. Bobrow and P. J. Hayes, in Bobrow and Hayes (1985), p. 377.

Soames, S. (1986) Peacocke on explanation in psychology, *Mind and Language*, 1, 4, pp. 372-387.

Whitby, B. (1988) *Artificial Intelligence: A Handbook of Professionalism*. Ellis Horwood.

Part IV

EPILOGUE

Chapter 8

AI and philosophy

8.1 SUMMARY

In Chapter 1 we argued for a particular *reinterpretation* of the Imitation Game. According to this reinterpretation, what Turing was doing was asking the question as to whether *it was possible for us to imagine* that an intelligent computer could be of the same type as ourselves, namely, of a type to which (the full range of) states of consciousness and intentional predicates could be ascribed. We then introduced the various objections which Turing himself predicted would be raised against his Imitation Game. Our task in this work has been almost always to *rephrase* the original objections not as statements against the possibility of thinking machines but as further questions implied by our reinterpretation of the Imitation Game. The exception to this was with the Argument from Continuity in the Nervous System, where the disagreement in approach between computationalists and neuro-computing researchers led us to rephrase the original objection by means of two different assertions.

In order to come up with contemporary versions of the original objections, we looked at various post-1950 developments in computation, logic, semantics, theories of consciousness, neurocomputing and methodology. In examining these developments, we also provided ways in which contemporary AI researchers would now tackle the objections (i.e. would now answer the implied questions).

In Chapter 2, we examined the relationship between AI and computation, specifically to recast the original version of Lady Lovelace's Objection. This objection was expressed in the following way:

> Machines can do only what they are told or programmed to do and so cannot do anything new or creative. Since the results of a computation cannot be original, machines cannot think.

Various aspects of Searle's Chinese Room Argument were presented as modern counterparts to Lady Lovelace's Objection, and we pointed out ways in which contemporary AI researchers would answer these modern counterparts, from the viewpoint of computation. We rephrased Lady Lovelace's Objection as follows:

> Are there appropriate rule systems and rule formats, and can intelligence, understanding and creativity be subcategorized appropriately, such that the following of one sort of rule as opposed to another gives rise to, or is equivalent to, intelligence, understanding or creativity in the one case but not the other?

In Chapter 3 we examined the Mathematical Objection, which originally was expressed in this way:

> In a formal system of a sufficiently powerful kind, there will be formulae obtainable which cannot be both true and derived. If thinking machines are (somehow) formal systems, then it follows that thinking machines are restricted in that when asked a certain question (for instance, concerning whether another computer will always return a truthful answer to every question put to it) in the Imitation Game, they will give a wrong answer or not answer at all. But we humans, because we are not formal systems, are not subject to this limitation. So, there will always be something that we humans can do (intellectually) which machines cannot. Therefore, machines can never fully replicate human thought and so cannot think in the way we humans do.

In order to cast this objection in a modern way, we looked at the relationship between AI and logic, specifically the relationship between the formal concepts of consistency and completeness, on the one hand, and intelligence on the other. We noted that the relationship usually consisted of some assumption concerning the *instantiation* of a formal system on a computer. Again, we presented various ways in which contemporary AI researchers would answer this objection, and this led us to recast the original objection as follows:

> What precisely is the relationship between formal systems or theory, on the one hand, and the computer or program that is supposed to be an instantiation of it, on the other, and are the formal constraints of the formal systems and theories necessarily also constraints of the computer or program?

In Chapter 4, we examined the Objection from Informality of Behaviour, which originally was expressed as follows:

> The behaviour of a machine is determined by instructions and rules which it must follow. We humans are not governed by such rules. Therefore, we cannot be machines.

In order to tackle this objection in a modern way, we looked at the relationship between AI and semantics (specifically, formal semantics), and the relationship between rules and *intensions*. This led us to an examination of a logical mechanism for ascribing mental predicates (originally proposed by Strawson (1959)) and we noted that, on certain assumptions, it could be argued that machines could have a limited number (limited through type) of mental predicates ascribed to them. But this argument depended on some definition or characterization of consciousness. The Informality of Behaviour objection was rephrased as follows:

> Is it the case that solely in virtue of running a computer program of the appropriate sort a machine can be said to think, understand or have experiences?

In Chapter 5, we examined the Argument from Consciousness objection, which originally was phrased as follows:

> No machines can have emotions, experiences or thoughts, i.e. no machines can have consciousness. Without consciousness, emotions, experiences and thoughts are impossible. Therefore machines cannot think.

We claimed that this was too simple a description of what is in fact a complex question. In order to identify the complexity, we examined in detail the views of three contemporary philosophers of mind (Dennett, Searle again (but this time his positive thesis), and Davidson) whose common link is an appeal to some form of 'mind-game' in which an 'intelligent' machine is constructed. This led us to rephrase the original Argument from Consciousness as follows:

> What precisely is the relationship between the concepts of thinking, understanding and experiencing, on the one hand, and the concepts of mental events and processes on the other? Furthermore, what exactly is the relationship between mental events and processes, on the one hand, and consciousness, on the other? Finally, what are the implications of proposed relationships (first, between mental concepts - thinking, understanding, experiencing - and mental events or processes, and secondly between mental events or processes and consciousness) for the notion of 'intelligent machine'?

Chapter 6 was concerned with the Argument from Continuity in the Nervous System, which originally was expressed as follows:

> Machines are discrete devices having separate, identifiable states, whereas the (human) nervous system is continuous. Since we cannot mimic the behaviour of the nervous system with a discrete-state system, and since thought and intelligence are based on a continuous system, machines cannot think or be intelligent.

In order to rephrase this objection in a modern way, we looked at the developments in neurocomputing since 1950, especially in one form of neurocomputing called connectionism. We contrasted neurocomputing with computationalism, and whilst we must keep in mind various reservations about such a gross division of cognitive science and AI research the division helped us identify two different, modern forms of the original objection. First, we had the following rephrasing, in the eyes of neurocomputing researchers:

> An understanding of mental and psychological concepts is not possible, and explanations of such concepts cannot be adequately provided or evaluated, unless, or until, the underlying models and simulations of the nervous system on top of which such concepts can be posited are *brain-like, brain-derived,* or *brain-based.*

And secondly, from a computationalist as well as anti-AI viewpoint, we have the following version:

> Even if various *brain-like*, *brain-derived*, or *brain-based* techniques can be successfully used for constructing models of the nervous system or machines which simulate the nervous system, that does not mean that machine intelligence and thought are possible.

In Chapter 7 we examined the second rephrasing above, which boils down simply to the objection that neurocomputing models, descriptions and explanations are at the wrong level of analysis as far as AI and psychology in particular, and cognitive science in general, are concerned. This led us to an examination of existing methodological frameworks (from philosophy of science as well as AI and cognitive science) and the claim that, in addition to the objections as originally expressed, Turing's original formulation of the Imitation Game also required some rephrasing. The rephrasing we proposed paid greater attention to the internal processes of the machine at the expense of observable behaviour. We used Searle's statement of strong AI in order to provide a modern version which, we claimed, was closest in spirit to Turing's original intentions:

> The appropriately programmed computer with the right inputs and outputs literally has a mind in exactly the same sense that we humans do. If there exists the right program with the right inputs and the right outputs, then any system running that program, regardless of its chemical structure, must have thoughts and feelings in exactly the same way as we humans do. And this is because that is all there is to having a mind: having the right program.

What it is for a program to be a right program can be unpacked by appealing to various properties of intelligence which can be assigned either at a macroscopic level or at a microscopic level.

This takes us full circle. Whilst Turing's original starting point was that the question, 'Can machines think?', contained too many loaded terms and could be usefully replaced by the Imitation Game, our claim is that the Imitation Game, even in its modern, strong AI guise (see above), also suffers from the same problems, from a contemporary viewpoint. That is, the objections Searle directed at strong AI (as well as the 'responses' he predicted to his objections) show that our modern version of the Imitation Game is no less free of confusion and controversy than the original version. Developments in related areas of AI, specifically computation theory, logic, semantics, philosophy of mind, neurocomputing and methodology, necessitated a thorough reappraisal of not just the original version of the Imitation Game but also the modern version. We have argued that the best way of carrying out such a reappraisal was to *reinterpret* the Imitation Game - both in its original and modern guises - in a way more abstract and philosophical than is usually the case in the literature. Our reinterpretation of the Imitation Game was as follows:

> Is it possible for us to imagine that an intelligent computer be of the same type as ourselves, namely, of a type to which (the full range of) states of consciousness and intentional predicates can be ascribed?

We provided some evidence that such a reinterpretation may even have been implied by Turing. With this reinterpretation, we examined the more relevant objections originally proposed by Turing to his Imitation Game and brought them up to date, mainly as questions. Along the way, we provided some indication of how the questions are, or could be, tackled.

Whilst this section is called 'Summary', it is now necessary to continue with a brief analysis of our reinterpretation of the Imitation Game, i.e. 'Is it possible for us to imagine that an intelligent computer be of the same type as ourselves, namely, of a type to which (the full range of) states of consciousness and intentional predicates can be ascribed?' If we were not to perform such an analysis, the motivating force behind our concern at keeping *rephrasings* separate from *reinterpretations* could not be brought out into the open. Let us first say something about bats.

8.2 NAGEL AND BATS

In 1974, Nagel (1974) published a paper entitled 'What is it like to be a bat?', which attempts to justify his claim that the nature of consciousness is ignored by most reductionist viewpoints. Nagel argues that although it is difficult to say in general what provides evidence of consciousness in organisms other than man,

> ...the fact that an organism has consciousness *at all* means, basically, that there is something it is like to *be* that organism (Nagel, 1974, p. 166, stress supplied)

in that an organism has conscious mental states if and only if there is something that it is like to be that organism - something it is like for that organism. According to Nagel, intentionalism, functionalism, physicalism, as well as reductionism, all fail to capture this subjective character of experience:

> [The subjective character of experience] is not analyzable in terms of any explanatory system of functional states, or intentional states, since these could be ascribed to robots or automata that behaved like people though they experienced nothing. (Nagel, 1974, p. 167)

Nagel argues that the essence of the belief that bats have experience is that there is something that it is like to be a bat. That is, although we may not be able to say precisely what it is like to be a bat, we do not doubt that there is *something* that it is like to be a bat and that this particular something is experienced by the bat. Bats perceive their external world by means of sonar, and bat sonar is not similar to any sense that we possess:

> This appears to create difficulties for the notion of what it is like to be a bat. We must consider whether any method will permit us to extrapolate to the inner life of the bat from our own case, and if not, what alternative methods there may be for understanding the notion. (Nagel, 1974, p. 169)

Nagel makes it clear that he is *not* asking *us* to imagine what it would be like for us to be a bat:

> [T]hat is not the question. I want to know what it is like for a *bat* to be a bat. Yet if I try to imagine this, I am restricted to the resources of my own mind, and those resources are inadequate to the task. ...So if extrapolation from our own case is involved in the idea of what it is like to be a bat, the extrapolation must be incompletable. We cannot form more than a schematic conception of what it *is* like. (Nagel, 1974, p. 169, stress supplied)

This means that we are compelled to recognize the existence of facts without being able to state or comprehend them:

> If anyone is inclined to deny that we can believe in the existence of facts ...whose exact nature we cannot possibly conceive,

> he should reflect that in contemplating the bats we are in much
> the same position that intelligent bats or Martians would occupy
> if they tried to form a conception of what it is like to be us. The
> structure of their own minds might make it impossible for them
> to succeed, but we know that they would be wrong to conclude
> that there is not anything precise that it is like to be us ....
> (Nagel, 1974, p. 170)

All we may be able to do is to form a *schematic conception* of what it is like
to be a bat, and it is this schematic conception which allows us to believe in
such facts. Yet we may not be able to conceive of the exact nature of such
facts because our schema does not provide us with the precise concepts for
representing and comprehending them. But that does not mean that our
schematic conception does not allow for the existence of such facts:

> My realism about the subjective domain in all its forms im-
> plies a belief in the existence of facts beyond the reach of human
> concepts. (Nagel, 1974, p. 171)

By using the phrase 'realism about the subjective domain', Nagel escapes
from the charge that he is an idealistic monist. He goes on:

> Reflection on what it is like to be a bat seems to lead us
> ...to the conclusion that there are facts that do not consist in
> the truth of propositions expressible in a human language. We
> can be compelled to recognize the existence of such facts without
> being able to comprehend or understand them. (Nagel, 1974, p.
> 171)

Nagel stresses that he is not advocating the privacy of experience to its
possessor but is asking what would be left of what it was like to be, say, a
bat, if one removed the viewpoint of the bat. In addition to its subjective
character, experience has an objective nature that can be comprehended
from many different points of view:

> [I]f the facts ...about what it is like *for* the experiencing or-
> ganism ...are accessible only from one point of view [i.e. the sub-
> jective], then it is a mystery how the true character of experiences
> could be revealed in the physical operation of that organism. The
> latter is a domain of objective facts *par excellence* - the kind that

> can be observed and understood from many points of view and
> by individuals with differing perceptual systems. (Nagel, 1974,
> p. 172, stress supplied)

The primary role of schematic conceptions in our understanding of the world
is further emphasized in the following quote:

> Lightning has an objective character that is not exhausted by
> its visual experience, and this can be investigated by a Martian
> without vision. ...In speaking of the move from subjective to
> objective characterization, I wish to remain noncommittal about
> the existence of an end point, the completely objective intrinsic
> nature of the thing, which one may or may not be able to reach.
> (Nagel, 1974, p. 173)

Just like Davidson (see Chapter 5), Nagel is critical of reductionist approaches, but he has his own reasons for disagreeing with reductionism:

> We appear to be faced with a general difficulty about psy-
> chophysical reduction. In other areas the process of reduction is
> a move in the direction of greater objectivity, towards a more ac-
> curate view of the real nature of things. This is accomplished by
> reducing our dependence on individual or species-specific points
> of view towards the object of investigation. ...Experience it-
> self, however, does not seem to fit the pattern. The idea of
> moving from appearance to reality seems to make no sense here.
> ...Certainly it *appears* unlikely that we will get closer to the real
> nature of human experience by leaving behind the particularity
> of our human point of view and striving for a description in terms
> accessible to beings that could not imagine what it was like to
> be us. If the subjective character of experience is fully compre-
> hensible only from one point of view, then any shift to greater
> objectivity - that is, less attachment to a specific viewpoint - does
> not take us nearer to the real nature of the phenomenon: it takes
> us farther away from it. (Nagel, 1974, p. 174, stress supplied)

That is, if we are concerned with the objective aspects of objects or events,
we are in effect leaving behind the subjective viewpoint:

> Members of radically different species may both understand
> the same physical events in objective terms, and this does not

> require that they understand the phenomenal forms in which
> those events appear to the senses of members of the other species.
> Thus it is a condition of their referring to a common reality that
> their more particular viewpoints are not part of the common
> reality that they both apprehend. The reduction can succeed
> only if the species-specific viewpoint is omitted from what is to
> be reduced. (Nagel, 1974, p. 175)

This has certain implications for reductionist approaches, which Nagel is
quick to draw:

> Most of the neobehaviorism of recent philosophical psychol-
> ogy results from the effort to substitute an objective concept of
> the mind for the real thing, in order to have nothing left over
> which cannot be reduced. If we acknowledge that a physical
> theory of mind must account for the subjective character of ex-
> perience, we must admit that no presently available conception
> gives us a clue how this could be done. The problem is unique.
> If mental processes are indeed physical processes, then there is
> something it is like, intrinsically, to undergo certain physical pro-
> cesses. What it is like for such a thing to be the case remains a
> mystery. (Nagel, 1974, p. 175)

Nagel concludes by accepting that his thesis rests on the nature of imagination, whereby one is asked to take up the viewpoint of the experiential
subject. His hope is that a new method, an *objective phenomenology* that is
not dependent on 'empathy' or imagination, could be developed to describe
partly the subjective character of experiences in a form comprehensible to
beings incapable of having those experiences.

8.3 THE NAGEL TEST?

There are two reasons why we introduced Nagel's views. First, he provides a
method for dealing with *possibility* which is very different from the possible-
worlds approach we looked at in Chapter 4. The logical semantics approach
of dealing with possibility is in terms of objects and facts (via, ultimately,
denotations) and for this reason exemplifies the *objective* approach whereby
commonly accepted and agreed aspects of objects and events (and also behaviour) are used in order to ground the meaning of words and phrases.

However, Nagel is arguing that such an objective approach leaves behind the *subjective* viewpoint, especially when considering the nature of consciousness. The main targets for Nagel are, of course, the philosophical doctrines of behaviourism, reductionism, functionalism and physicalism. Nagel goes on to offer his 'test' of consciousness, which is that there must be something that it is like for an entity to be a conscious entity. He stresses that he is not asking *us* to imagine what it is like to be that entity. Instead, he is asking us to imagine what it is like *for that entity* to be a conscious entity. By implication, if we conclude that there is indeed *something* that it is like for that entity to be a conscious entity, then we have succeeded in attributing consciousness to it.

The second reason is that Nagel's views explicitly question one of the fundamental assumptions we have made all along in this work, namely, that the notion of 'intelligent computer' is the notion of a type of entity which is of the same type as ourselves, whereby all the predicates of consciousness and intentionality are equally applicable, with identical meaning, to instances of the same type. We made that assumption in order to convey (in post-1950 terms) what we felt was Turing's intention in replacing the question, 'Can machines think?', with his Imitation Game. But we must now question this reinterpretation.

Bearing in mind our reinterpretation of the Imitation Game ('Is it possible for us to imagine that an intelligent computer is of the same type as ourselves, namely, of a type to which (the full range of) predicates of consciousness and intentionality can be ascribed?'), which in turn is a reinterpretation of the question, 'Can machines think?', we should now see that Nagel may well be offering us methods, subjective as they may be, for analyzing these questions. That is, given the sort of Strawsonian-ascription mechanism we looked at in Chapter 4, we can now, along Nagelian lines, subsume 'Can machines think?', the Imitation Game, our subsequent modern rephrasing of the Imitation Game (along strong AI lines), and our own reinterpretation of the Imitation Game, all under one general question:

> Is there something that it is like to be a computer which ascribes states of consciousness to others on the same basis that we ascribe states of consciousness to it?

By implication (given a Strawsonian framework), for an entity to ascribe states of consciousness at all requires that the entity does *not* ascribe states of consciousness to itself in the way that it ascribes states of consciousness to others. Instead, the entity is required to have states of consciousness which are *experienced*, rather than ascribed. By posing the question this way we include the requirement that the intelligent computer has states ascribed to it which are similar in type to the states of consciousness that we humans have (so that it cannot be argued that the words signifying states of consciousness mean something different when applied to computers than when applied to ourselves). Let us, *pace* Searle, call this the *strong AI$_\phi$* thesis (for *strong AI (philosophy) thesis*).

However, there is another way to subsume the various rephrasings and interpretations, given Nagel's 'test', and this is to question our fundamental assumption that intelligent machines must be intelligent (have thoughts, experiences and understanding) in the same way as ourselves. For instance, we could ask:

> Is it possible for there to be something it is like to be an intelligent computer?

That is, we could invoke Nagel's argument that we are compelled to recognize the existence of facts without being able to fully comprehend them:

> If anyone is inclined to deny that we can believe in the existence of facts ... whose exact nature we cannot possibly conceive, he should reflect that in contemplating the bats we are in much the same position that intelligent bats or Martians would occupy if they tried to form a conception of what it is like to be us. The structure of their own minds might make it impossible for them to succeed, but we know that they would be wrong to conclude that there is not anything precise that it is like to be us .... (Nagel, 1974. p. 170)

And later:

> Members of radically different species may both understand the same physical events in objective terms, and this does not require that they understand the phenomenal forms in which those events appear to the senses of members of the other species. Thus it is a condition of their referring to a common reality that their more particular viewpoints are not part of the common reality that they both apprehend. The reduction can succeed

> only if the species-specific viewpoint is omitted from what is to
> be reduced. (Nagel, 1974, p. 175)

Given a Nagelian viewpoint, it is certainly possible to argue that there is no requirement, as far as consciousness is concerned, that the entity in question should be conscious in the same way as ourselves, i.e. that the entity belong to a type to which the full range of predicates of (human) consciousness, as well as (human) intentional predicates, should be ascribed. Let us call this, again *pace* Searle, the *weak AI$_\phi$* thesis.

We now have two different philosophical theses concerning the goals of AI. According to *strong AI$_\phi$*, the question 'Can machines think?' can be answered positively if, and only if, there is something it is like to be a computer which is conscious in the same way as we humans are. According to *weak AI$_\phi$*, the question 'Can machines think?' can be answered positively if, and only if, there is something it is like to be a (conscious) computer: there is no requirement that the computer be conscious in the same way as ourselves. Advocates of Nagel's approach who claim that here is a different sort of test to the Turing Test would, strictly speaking, be bound by the *weak AI$_\phi$* thesis, and their aim would be to demonstrate (philosophically) that there is something that it is like to be an intelligent computer. Nevertheless, *strong AI$_\phi$* advocates could argue that Nagel's test is too weak if it does not include the requirement that an intelligent computer be intelligent in the same way as ourselves. (This does not exclude the possibility, of course, of an intelligent computer being super-intelligent, i.e. far more intelligent than any human. What is required by *strong AI$_\phi$* advocates is that the state of being intelligent, or super-intelligent, is the same for a computer as it is for a human should there be, for example, a super-intelligent human or super-intelligent computer.) It is only be adopting the *strong AI$_\phi$* thesis that the processes which give rise to intelligence (and so thought, emotions and understanding) in humans as well as computers (or any other type of entity) can be studied not just philosophically but also scientifically. Otherwise, *strong AI$_\phi$* advocates may argue, AI becomes at best subjective and at worst metaphysical. At least the *strong AI$_\phi$* thesis stands a chance of being wrong, may run the argument, and if it is we shall still have learned something about human intelligence if not computer (or other entity) intelligence.

Advocates of *weak AI$_\phi$* can counterargue that it is not the abstract processes of intelligence *per se* which need philosophical and scientific study ('abstract' in that intelligence is not constrained to a particular entity), but what allows us to say of other entities that they are conscious or intelligent.

Each entity which we want to test for consciousness may be conscious (and therefore intelligent) in different ways from ourselves, and the best way to tackle the question of whether such entities are indeed conscious is not to place them in the same category as ourselves, which after all may be too strong a condition for the entity in question to meet, but to use whatever knowledge we have of our own mental life in order to gain an understanding of the mental life, different as it may well be, of the entity in question.

In terms of schematic conception, this debate boils down to whether *one* schematic conception, based on what we know of ourselves, is sufficient for testing for intelligence and consciousness in other entities ($strong AI_\phi$) or whether we need to *construct* different schematic conceptions for different (conscious) entities ($weak AI_\phi$) by, for instance, mapping from the concepts of intelligence and consciousness that we know about (because they belong to the schematic conception we have of ourselves) onto concepts of intelligence and consciousness belonging to schematic conceptions we have of other entities. Such mappings for $weak AI_\phi$ are, of course, not one-to-one in number or type. Rather, the research programme implied by $weak AI_\phi$ would consist of formulating such mappings in order to demonstrate the feasibility of constructing schematic conceptions we may have of other entities.

The above discussion should give a flavour of the sort of discussion that can be entered into when tackling the question of whether an intelligent entity must be intelligent in the same way as ourselves. What we now need to do is examine how such schematic conceptions (either one global schematic conception for all intelligence and consciousness, or several schematic conceptions for a variety of entities) can be constructed at all. This will allow us to return to the above debate and place the issues in a more general framework. We shall see that the terms $strong AI_\phi$ and $weak AI_\phi$ represent two extreme views between which lie a variety of different approaches. We shall also outline a *final* version of the Imitation Game which will then carry us through to our conclusion.

8.4   ON CONCEPTUAL SCHEMES

What we shall now try to do is demonstrate what should go into a schematic conception (to use Nagel's terminology), or conceptual scheme (to use Strawson's terminology), such that concepts of intelligence, and consciousness in general, can be linked together in order that they form a network of interrelated conceptual constructs which, in some sense, leads to an 'understanding' of what intelligence and consciousness consist of in relation to the entity, or entities, of which the conceptual scheme is a scheme. Our fundamental assumption here is that at the heart of such schemes will be an ascription mechanism which allows us not just to ascribe states of consciousness to others but also to justify such ascriptions according to some criteria inherent in the conceptual scheme.

Our starting point is Dennett (1981), especially where we left off in Chapter 5, Section 7. There is no doubt that Dennett is onto *something* when he claims that we can ascribe intentional terms to objects in order to provide explanations and predictions (whatever they mean). Also, there is no doubt that in the domain of AI we need some mechanism which allows us to evaluate the claims various researchers make for their theories and programs. At first glance, the intentional stance appears to have a lot going for it (including its name), so let us see whether there is another way of unpacking what is involved when we ascribe intentional terms and mental predicates to others.

We identified one weakness in the original version of Dennett's thesis as consisting of the appeal to a Strawson-type ascription mechanism in the second condition, when consciousness does not play a full part in Dennett's ladder of personhood until the sixth condition. This led Dennett to propose that terms which have implications of consciousness have two uses: one at a high level in his ladder of personhood, where the terms do indeed convey their full implication of consciousness on the part of that to which they are ascribed (i.e. persons), and another at the lower level of the intentional stance, where the terms do not convey their full implication of consciousness on the part of that to which they are ascribed. The latter use is, according to Dennett, justified by the intentional stance, whereby such terms are used depending on a stance we adopt towards the entity in question. What we tried to do in Chapter 5 was to point out that this required Dennett to separate the logically necessary implication of consciousness on the part of that to which such terms are ascribed, as demanded by a Strawson-like account, from the terms themselves, leaving Dennett to justify the 'ascription' (whatever this means when the logically necessary implication is removed) of such terms without this logically necessary implication. We showed how Dennett attempted this by means of an appeal to a restricted notion of explanation and prediction (unjustified, as we saw, in fact and in theory) whereby the behaviour of an entity was expressed in terms of rationality and belief, both of which in turn had (indeed, must have) no implications of consciousness.

Somehow, such a view, although a possible one, does not seem quite to conform to the way we use intentional terms when referring to the behaviour of entities which are not human. For instance, 'x believes, or thinks, or concludes that y' does usually convey some implication of consciousness on the part of x, as a Strawson-type account confirms, irrespective of anyone adopting a stance of any sort with respect to 'entity x' and even if the implication is one of a restricted form of consciousness. It is not just the ascription of one such term which matters but the implications for a host of other intentional predicates related in some sense to the ascribed term which could also be usually ascribed. To the question of how such terms are related to each other at the lower levels of his ladder of personhood Dennett offers no answer. Our overall conclusion is that Dennett has correctly identified the problem as consisting of how, and why, the logically necessary implication of consciousness can be separated from mental, intentional and psychological terms, but that he went down a path which, because of its behaviourist direction, led him to a propose an answer which sheds little light on this question.

We now want to ask the same sorts of questions as Dennett but this time follow the implications through as neutrally as possible. Our starting point is not to baulk at the prospect of using a Strawson-like mechanism, with all the implications that such a mechanism has for ascribing mental, intentional and psychological terms. So, what would happen to the 'intentional stance' if we went along with a powerful ascription mechanism as part of the lower-level conditions of personhood?

One immediate implication is that if we allowed the full force of a Strawsonian mechanism (but perhaps not Strawson's actual mechanism) to be used where Dennett has his second condition, that not only removes the *necessity* of conditions four and five in Dennett's ladder (although these conditions may *possibly* play a part, as we shall see) but also results in a very different conceptualization. We stress that we are concerned here with an AI approach to the question of intentional stance.

What is missing from the picture so far is some reference to *representations*, so let us start with that. *One* way to specify representations is along the lines that Dennett originally followed with regard to rationality, that is, by invoking some appeal to forms of rule following (either implicit or explicit). Whereas Dennett used rule-following as a basis for rationality, we must exclude all reference to intentional terms at this stage, otherwise we shall end up with circularity. So, we shall not include terms such as 'belief' and 'rationality' with regard to representations.

This reference to representations *per se* can be used for distinguishing the behaviour of entities which are essentially 'rule-governed' (however that is defined) from those that not. For instance, this type of reference would allow us to say, for instance, that computers are rule-followers (rules given by the programmer, of course), as are also cats, dogs, fish and humans, but perhaps clocks and typewriters are not. It is not important to us how such a distinction is to be made; rather, what is important is that such a distinction is possible, and that a representation has attached to it some criteria for making this distinction. We must assume therefore that the formulation of such criteria is possible without an appeal to intentional terms.

The reference to representations here deals with the status of rules and their relationship to behaviour, without any appeal to intentionality. In this type of reference, representations for automated theorem proving, natural language understanding, vision, formal semantics, connectionism, and robotics, to name just a few areas where representations are important, could be included. Attached to the representation will be intentionality-free criteria, explicit or implicit, for distinguishing entities whose behaviour can in some sense be 'subsumed' under, or 'explained by', the representation from those that cannot.

Given this reference to representations, we can describe a *representational stance* as consisting of the application of terms, taken from a particular representational framework, to entities such as computers, dogs, cats, clocks, typewriters, and so on. For instance, the sentence 'x decides where to sit in the restaurant' is unpacked as an example of a representational stance towards x, where the behaviour of x at a particular moment is claimed to be such that a term from a representation of some sort is applicable to x. The word 'decide', which usually has intentional sense, is used in the representational stance sentence without that intentional sense, provided that it is made clear that what is being appealed to is some representation where the term 'decide' has a particular technical or theoretical meaning. That is, the term 'decide' is grounded not in our usual understanding of the term but in some representation of it, where the representation has lost the intentional sense but has some sense according to the representation. In the above example, the sentence may have used a term which is taken directly from the representation (a script, for instance, or at least some abstract representation of one). However, it is also possible to use terms in such sentences which do not appear directly in the representation. For instance, the sentence, 'x is taking a long time to decide on its next chess move', is an example of the representational stance where the term 'decide' could be *derived* from the terms used in the representation. The chess-playing program may contain no reference to 'decide' anywhere, yet the behaviour of the program is such that the term 'decide' has been derived somehow by the person who has adopted the representational stance.

We can now unpack also the notions of explanation and prediction, with restricted senses, with regard to the representational stance. We can say, in the case of a direct term, that the representational stance sentence is an *explanation* (*prediction*) provided that the adopter can ground the term in some representation which includes that term as one of its terms, with the implication that the behaviour of the entity *is* (*will be*) subsumed in some sense by that representation. In the case of a derived term, we can say that the representational stance is an explanation (prediction) provided that the adopter can somehow *substitute* some feature of a representation (e.g. another term, some control structure, some design feature) for that term, with the implication that the behaviour of the entity is (will be) subsumed in some sense by that representation. In both cases, it is important to note that the appeal to a particular, pre-existing representation need not be necessary for the adoption of a representational stance. That is, someone could use a term in a representational stance which cannot then be grounded or derived because no appropriate representation exists, or the adopter is not aware of one. Nevertheless, the *justification* for, and not explanation of or prediction from, the representational stance sentence can be expressed along the lines that the adopter implies (in the sense of 'presupposes' or 'assumes') that there *may* be some representation available which provides an explanation for, or predictions from, terms used in the sentence which usually have intentional sense but in this case do not. For instance, 'My car is reluctant to get going this morning' is an example of the representational stance where the adopter may have no particular representation in mind but nevertheless is making the claim that, if there is one, a grounding or substitution can be made.

What we are trying to do is to capture the intuitive appeal of sentences which use intentional terms but where there may be no serious commitment to ascribing consciousness on the part of that to which they are ascribed. The representational stance, as we have characterized it, is appealing to a simpli-fied form of *conceptual scheme* which embodies a representation, either real or hypothetical, where the representation is not making claims concerning the possession of consciousness on the part of entities who or which appear in the scheme. The important point to note is that the representational stance is in some sense 'removed' from the representations themselves, but at the same time requires them in order to fulfil its explanatory and predictive roles.

Such use of intentional terms is to be distinguished from their use where some commitment to consciousness is implied (in the sense of being presupposed or assumed). This brings us back to *ascription mechanisms*, in their more powerful version, where consciousness on the part of entities to whom or which intentional terms and mental predicates are ascribed is implied (presupposed, assumed). Hence, we are dealing with ascription mechanisms of various sorts where what is being referred to is the nature, and degree, of consciousness that is be bestowed on, or assumed of, entities which already (logically) possess consciousness. Ascription mechanisms will be characterized according to the type and range of mental predicates and intentional terms they ascribe to a variety of entities, all of whom or which are implied or assumed to have consciousness. It is through these terms and predicates that the nature and degree of consciousness to be implied or assumed of an entity will be identified.

We can therefore state that *the ascriptional stance* (or redefined intentional stance) consists of issuing sentences where intentional terms and mental predicates are ascribed to entities by means of a certain ascription mechanism. The sense of the terms and predicates will be fixed by the ascription mechanism which in turn will probably be grounded in some theory of consciousness.

The point of the ascriptional stance can now be simply put as follows. Whereas the representational stance could not care whether the representation is used for representing the behaviour of humans, machines, dogs, cats, and so on, since it is only the behaviour of the entity (as it 'conforms' in some sense to some representation) which is under examination, the ascriptional stance has precisely the effect of *separating* such entities and classifying them according to the success or otherwise of the ascription. Moreover, ascription mechanisms could use the same intentional term or mental predicate with different meanings. For instance, the sentence 'x decides where to sit down in the restaurant' could mean something very different when used with regard to a human, a robot, and a dog, i.e. there could be three different ascription mechanisms. Therefore, *the purpose of the ascriptional stance is to identify what are the appropriate ascription mechanisms to use with regard to various entities which have claims of consciousness of various sorts attached to them.* By an 'appropriate ascription mechanism' we mean the identification of types of intentional terms and mental predicates, together with their meanings, which are to be ascribed to entities which are in some sense 'subsumed' under that ascription mechanism. An ascription mechanism is therefore a sort of function, *either* taking types of predicate and bestowing consciousness of various degrees to a variety of entities, *or* taking entities who possess various degrees of consciousness and providing justifications for the ascription of various predicates, or both, depending on the nature of the ascription mechanism.

Just as we did with the representational stance, we can unpack the notions of explanation and prediction, with restricted senses, with regard to the ascriptional stance. We can say, in the case of a mental predicate or intentional term, that the ascriptional stance sentence is an *explanation (prediction)* provided that the adopter can ground the term in some ascription mechanism which includes that term as one of the terms it can ascribe, with the implication or assumption that the consciousness of the entity is such that other mental predicates or intentional terms which belong to the same type or to other types, as specified by the ascription mechanism, *can be (will be)* ascribed by the same ascription mechanism. Again, in both cases, it is important to note that the appeal to a *particular*, pre-existing ascription mechanism need not be necessary for the adoption of an ascriptional stance. That is, someone could use a term in an ascriptional stance which cannot then be grounded (or derived, but that aspect will be ignored since it is relatively simple to add) because no appropriate ascription mechanism exists, or the adopter is not aware of one. Nevertheless, the *justification* for, and not explanation of or prediction from, the ascriptional stance sentence can be expressed along the lines that the adopter implies (in the sense of 'presupposes' or 'assumes') that there *may* be some ascription mechanism available which provides explanations for, or predictions from, terms used in the sentence which have intentional sense. For instance, 'My car is reluctant to get going this morning' is an example of the ascriptional stance where the adopter may have no particular ascription mechanism in mind but nevertheless is making the claim that, if there is one (i.e. if there is some ascription mechanism), a grounding can be made.

One interesting characteristic of both the representational and ascriptional stances, as now portrayed, is the way they can be adopted *hypotheti-*

cally. For instance, 'My car is reluctant to get going this morning' is, with regard to the ascriptional stance, essentially of the form: 'If there is some ascription mechanism for ascribing intentional terms and mental predicates to cars, then I am somehow justified in claiming that it is reluctant to start.' That is, the claim is that the term 'reluctant' is one of the terms that can be applied by the ascription mechanism, if there is one.

The important point here is that AI researchers who want to ascribe something more than representations to entities such as computers must be careful that methodological 'begging the question' does not arise, where for example they use a term in a way that assumes one type of ascription mechanism (say, a type of restricted-human ascription mechanism) in order to ascribe that term to a computer, then use the implication of consciousness on the part of the computer to ascribe a variety of different mental predicates and intentional terms on the basis of another type of ascription mechanism (say, a full-fledged human ascription mechanism). Another, and perhaps more common form of methodological 'begging the question' can also be trapped. This is where an AI researcher uses the representational stance in order to *apply* a theoretical or technical term based in a representation to a computer (or program) and then, wrongly, uses the same term (or terms related to it by an ascription mechanism) as if the terms can be *ascribed* by some form of ascriptional stance, thereby bestowing, by a sleight of hand, some degree of consciousness on the part of the computer (or program). The ascriptional stance, as now defined, can prevent such tricks by requiring that all ascription mechanisms be classified according to the type (however defined) to which it belongs, and that once one particular ascription mechanism is used the same one (or one related somehow in type) must be used for the other mental predicates and intentional terms falling under that type. Under no circumstances would terms from the representational stance be used as if they meant the same as similar-looking terms of the ascriptional stance. This is because all one can do at the representational level is *apply* the theoretical and technical representational terms, whereas at the ascriptional level one *ascribes* the term. Ascription of terms is therefore distinguished from application of terms, according to our framework, in that ascription necessarily bestows some degree of consciousness on the part of that to which they are ascribed (the precise nature and content of consciousness is a matter for the ascription mechanism, not *whether* the entity is conscious), whereas application makes no such bestowal. But we must not forget that, just as with the representational stance, the ascriptional stance is separate from the ascription mechanisms but nevertheless depends on them for fulfilling its explanatory and predictive role.

What we are trying to do here is capture the intuitive feeling that when we ascribe an intentional term or mental predicate deliberately to another entity whose nature and degree of consciousness is in doubt, we are somehow experimenting with theories of consciousness to see how far our language can be pushed without breaking down.

Going back to Dennett's six original conditions, we can see that his first and second - rationality and intentionality - now belong to ascription mechanisms; and his third - stance - is split up between representations (physical and design stances) and ascription mechanisms (intentional stance). That leaves two remaining conditions to be examined, reciprocity and verbal communication, assuming that the sixth condition of consciousness now belongs to ascription mechanisms. We *could* allocate these two remaining conditions to ascription mechanisms also, but that would be to ignore the more general claims of these two conditions. So far, we have avoided stating whether representations are at level one and ascription mechanisms at level two in some hierarchy or other: we have been content to talk of representations and ascription mechanisms as constituting different spheres of activity. We can assume that these two spheres of activity are indeed hierarchically organized, so that representations are at a level below ascription mechanisms, although we shall not be concerned here to demonstrate the necessity or even plausibility of such a hierarchical organization. Nevertheless, for the remainder of the chapter, let us assume a level one of representations with a level two of ascription mechanisms.

8.5   THE IMITATION GAME - FINAL VERSION

We now ask whether we need a level *above* the level of the ascriptional stance. So far, we have been concerned with entities with *individual* ascription mechanisms using possibly different types of mental predicates. The third level logically should therefore concern itself with evaluating different *types of ascription mechanism*. If this third level exists, the *meta-ascriptional* level, it would consist in part of the meta-activity of examining and identifying similarities and differences between ascription mechanisms. One task at this level would be to identify the implications of adopting one type of ascription mechanism that is used for one type of conscious entity with another type of conscious entity. Similarly, we can imagine that another task would be to identify the implications of adopting one type of ascription mechanism with regard to two different types of conscious entity. These tasks would have many implications for the relativity of conceptual schemes, the substance of reality including individuals and events, the nature of truth and justification, and the role of language, for instance. But it would be at this level that we could measure the degree of overlap in the application of a mental or intentional predicate to two entities belonging to two different types (e.g. human and computer).

Here would seem to be a good place to locate the remaining two conditions of Dennett's original ladder: reciprocity and verbal communication. Namely, it is likely that one of the ways that we can *evaluate* ascription mechanisms at the second level is, from a level above, to look for abstract features such as reciprocity and what is involved in ascribing language terms to others, as well as to ourselves. Although a Gricean (1957, 1968) formulation may not be *necessary* at this level, something like it is certainly possible, provided it is accepted that consciousness is already introduced at the lower level. At this level also we can place general theories of consciousness, such as Searle's, where the claim is that, no matter which ascription mechanism is chosen at the second level, they all share the common property that justification for the ascription of intentional and mental predicates is based on neural and biological considerations.

Let us therefore assume that the third level exists and provide yet another interpretation of the Imitation Game, this time from the viewpoint of the redefined hierarchy and the modified view of stance:

> The question, 'Can machines think?', is now a question at the third level, asking whether there is a level two (ascriptional) stance of a certain type which can be used for the ascription of mental predicates to computers of a certain type.

The reason why this is a third level question is that it can be answered in several ways. In outlining these ways, we shall see that our previously-introduced terms, *strong* and *weak* AI_ϕ, stand for two extreme answers:

(a) looking at a variety of level two ascription mechanisms, we see that humans and a certain type of computer have the same type of predicates ascribable to them, hence all the predicates ascribable to humans are ascribable to computers of that type (*strong* AI_ϕ);

(b) looking at a variety of level two ascription mechanisms, we see that there is some overlap between humans and a certain type of computer which allows some mental predicates to be ascribed to one but not the other;

(c) looking at a variety of level two ascription mechanisms, we see that *certain* predicates can be equally ascribed to entities belonging to a variety of types (including humans and computers); and

(d) looking at a variety of level two ascription mechanisms, we see that there is a certain type of predicate which can only be ascribed to one type of entity (*weakAI$_\phi$*).

The reason why Turing considered the original question 'too meaningless to deserve discussion' can now be hypothesized to be that, with so many possible answers available, some level three (meta-ascription) descriptions were required in order to cut down on the number of possibilities at level two. His reformulation of the question, the Imitation Game, can be interpreted as an attempt to provide an indication of what particular level two (ascriptional) stances would look like once humans, and computing machines of a certain type, were hypothesized *at the third level* to be of the same type with regard to predicates of intelligence. His 'Objections' can then be interpreted as attempts to provide greater detail, at the second level, of how predicates of intelligence could be applied to computing machines in the first place.

These attempts had different degrees of success. For instance, the Mathematical Objection, the Argument from Consciousness, Lady Lovelace's Objection and the Argument from Informality of Behaviour are essentially arguments of the form: if this objection can be raised against ascribing consciousness to computing machines, then it can be raised against ascribing consciousness to humans also. Here, it can be interpreted that Turing was mainly concerned with level two, i.e. the setting up of individual ascription mechanisms for two types of entity, ourselves and computers, but his argument forms are only positive with regard to the latter by implication. The Argument from Various Disabilities is the objection, at level three but also with implications for level two, that it may not be possible for all the mental predicates we ascribe to humans to be ascribed to computers also. However, we can now say that even if this were the case some degree of consciousness is being ascribed by, or through, other mental predicates when ascribed to computers of a certain type at level two. Finally, the part of his paper which deals with the notions of Turing Machine and quintuples is an attempt to provide, at level one, some indication of the formalisms and representations necessary for describing the rule-following behaviour of machines.

Nothing in what we have said implies that the hierarchy must be adhered to in a 'bottom-up' or 'top-down' fashion. For instance, instead of providing some bottom-up account of how a representation at level one could give rise to, or was logically necessary or sufficient for, or was just logically possible for, consciousness, Turing's own approach relied on the general notion of effective computation, where his level three *thesis* (AI version, as provided by Hofstadter (1979)) was that mental processes of any sort at level two can be simulated by a Turing Machine at level one. It was this notion that gave his Imitation Game its originality and also, as we now perceive given our reformulation of the intentional stance into an ascriptional stance, its weakness, since according to this thesis a clear level two account concerning what is involved in ascribing mental predicates to humans on the one hand, and to machines on the other, can be omitted altogether. Fine as this may have been back in 1950, developments in philosophy of AI since then have been such that a level two account can no longer be omitted from any attempt to explain how it is that machines can be intelligent or can think.

8.6 CONCLUSION

Let us tie up the various threads. We have argued for a three-fold classification of how we talk about intelligent, thinking entities. At one level - the level of representations - we can adopt a representational stance which, whilst allowing us to talk about an entity in terms which are theory-bound, i.e. terms which have a particular technical meaning given a certain representation, bestow no implication of consciousness or thought on the part of the entity to which such terms are applied. The justification for the application of terms at this level will usually be in the form of demonstrating how the application of the terms is warranted because of the nature of the representation as well as, typically, the internal processes and outward behaviour of the entity. Also, the representational stance can be adopted on the basis of a hypothetical representation, i.e. a representation which may or may not exist. We argued, along Dennett lines, that the adoption of such a stance at this level leads to a limited form of prediction and explanation.

At another level - the level of ascriptions - we can adopt an ascriptional stance which, whilst allowing us to talk about an entity in terms which imply consciousness and thought, i.e. terms which have a particular intentional or mental sense given a certain ascription mechanism, does not necessarily bestow the same degree of consciousness to that entity as for a person (in Strawson's sense). The justification of the application of terms at this level will usually be in the form of appealing to a particular theory of consciousness, in which the ascription (rather than application) of such terms is warranted because of the nature of the theory of consciousness as well as, typically, the way that internal processes and outward behaviour of the entity can be described. Also, the ascriptional stance can be adopted on the basis of a hypothetical ascription mechanism and hypothetical theory of consciousness which may or may not exist. We argued, again along the lines of Dennett, that the adoption of such a stance at this level leads to a limited form of ascriptional prediction and explanation.

At the third level - the level of meta-ascriptions - we are concerned with what particular ascription mechanisms at the second level look like, e.g. what they have in common, what the assumptions concerning the degree of consciousness implied are, and what various intentional and mental terms have in common. One question which arises at this level concerns the different ascription mechanisms implied by a particular theory of consciousness, as well as a particular ascription mechanism shared by different theories of consciousness.

We can relate our three-fold classification to Marr's three-level framework as follows. Following Rumelhart and McClelland's suggestion (see the last chapter) that the *information processing approach* to psychology is primarily concerned with Marr's level 2 of algorithm and representation, we claim that, as far as AI is concerned, the *representational stance*, as we have defined and described it, is tied in with Marr's level of algorithm and representation. That is, neither the computational level (level 1) nor the implementational level (level 3) are the appropriate *foundational* levels for AI work (although it *could* be argued that functional specifications are AI specifications; this is a radical view which we shall not pursue here). We can state that one way of separating AI work from traditional computational work is that there is some degree of overlap between terms used in the representation and various mental or intentional terms. That is, if a computational representation does not include terms, even with restricted representational sense, which also occur at the ascriptional level with fuller sense, we do not have an AI representation. Hence, one way of separating AI work from traditional computational work lies in the choice made by the researcher deliberately to use at least one term with narrow representational sense which, at the ascriptional level, has intentional or mental sense. If this seems too strong a criterion, we may allow the *derivation* of a term from a representation with a narrow representational sense where the term derived is the same as one used, with intentional and mental sense, at the ascriptional level. Once we move onto this representational level, we have as a point of reference the level of ascription mechanisms, each of which is underpinned by some theory of consciousness. An AI representational researcher need not move onto this ascriptional level, as long as there is some commitment to a theory of consciousness, even hypothetical, which can be made on the part of, or on behalf of, the AI representation. For instance, an appeal can be made to a behaviourist theory of consciousness at the ascriptional level, or a phenomenological theory of consciousness at this level. The ascriptional level leads on to the third, or meta-ascriptional level, where particular ascription mechanisms, and particular theories of consciousness, can be compared and constructed. For instance, our earlier categorization of $strong AI_\phi$ and $weak AI_\phi$, as well as various theses in between, is a categorization made at the meta-ascriptional level.

What we have done is provide an indication of how a general framework for AI research can be started. We have also shown how it may be possible for $strong AI_\phi$ as well as $weak AI_\phi$, in addition to various approaches in between, to be subsumed under the same general framework. Our claim is that the construction of such a framework in this way justifies to some extent Nagel's appeal to an *objective phenomenology*, but we do not claim that ascription mechanisms are all there is to an objective phenomenology. No doubt much more is required, and our only claim is that ascription mechanisms will certainly be involved, centrally. All of this, in turn, justifies to some extent an appeal to a Nagel test at the expense of the more behaviourally-oriented test implied by the Imitation Game. The advantages of adopting a Nagel test are, first, it seems to allow a variety of different philosophical approaches to the question of whether machines can think to be subsumed under one general umbrella (with all the advantages that such subsumption bestows in terms of commonality of methodology, evaluative criteria and research focus), and secondly it appeals to a certain intuitive view that, ultimately, it is we who are the judges of whether intelligence and consciousness are or can be bestowed on entities of various types (which means that somehow the understanding we have of what it is for us to be intelligent and be conscious must be mapped onto an understanding of what it is for other entities to be intelligent and conscious, even if the mapping is a sketchy one).

Let us continue our comparison with Marr's three-level framework further. We *could* say that the design, specification and construction of such conceptual schemes, which will include the topics of stances, ascription mechanisms and whatever else is considered to be part of an 'objective phenomenology', belong to an area which in principle can be encompassed within Marr's three-level framework. The area *could* be at what we can call Marr's 'level 0', i.e. a level above Marr's level 1 or level of computation. Using a form of Marr's argument, it could be argued that one conceptual scheme, or theory of consciousness, or ascription mechanism, or whatever, will give rise to many different computational specifications at level 1. For instance, given a certain level 0 construct, there may be a variety of ways of computationally specifying that level 0 construct. First order predicate calculus could be used at level 1 to specify, computationally, the circumstances under which, for example, it is possible to infer the ascription of one predicate given the satisfiability of another, where both predicates are shown to be conceptually linked together by a certain ascription mechanism at level 0. Some computational specifications will be approximations to what is proposed at level 0, others will be functional subsets of a level 0 proposal. The claim here is that a level 0 is needed in order to make clear the implications that subsequent level 1 computational specifications have with regard to the ascription of mental terms, and these implications carry all the way down the various levels.

It can be further argued that a computational specification at level 1 will in turn have many algorithmic and representational realizations at level 2 (irrespective of whether we need a level 1.5). These in turn will be worked on, probably independently, by computationalists and neurocomputing researchers, who in turn can provide many level 3 implementations of a level 2 realization.

This is certainly one line of argument. Another is that the design and construction of conceptual schemes play no part in a Marr-like hierarchy as such but somehow lie in the *background* to such hierarchies. Therefore, the argument here is that AI researchers are bounded at one extreme by something like Marr's level 2 (that of representation and algorithm) and should not be bothered unduly as to what the computational and implementational specifications are. However, this is not to deny that at some stage such researchers may have to move out of a Marr-like level 2 when asked to justify the appearance of terms which, when used by persons with respect to other persons, imply the possession of consciousness on the part of that to which such terms are ascribed.

In both cases, what is being proposed is a distinction between computer science research, psychology research, and AI research. Computer science research, which arguably can be correctly characterized along the lines of Marr's original proposal in that a programming solution consists of a specification of the problem (at level 1), the design and implementation of various data structures and algorithms (at level 2), and the physical realization of such data structures and algorithms on machines (at level 3), makes no claim for plausibility - philosophical, psychological, or neural. Yet such research appears to conform nicely with the hierarchy proposed by Marr. We also saw how Peacocke (Chapter 7) had some difficulty in attaching psychological reality to his proposed extension to Marr's hierarchy. Typically, the psychological relevance of Marr's hierarchy is accepted to lie with level 2 - the level of algorithms and representations where psychological concepts and mechanisms are introduced. But it was not clear where AI fitted into such a hierarchy. If AI is different from psychology and computer science, then it must be characterized as something more than, or at least something different from, psychology level 2 accounts and computer science 'all-levels' accounts. Our task in this section has been to argue that AI work starts at Marr's level 2 but then moves out of Marr's three-level classification altogether.

In summary, our proposal for distinguishing AI from these other two, related disciplines is to argue that in AI research, whilst it is possible that there is, in principle, a level 0 above Marr's level 1 and that AI specification takes place at this level 0, much can be gained philosophically by moving to an area outside Marr's three levels, an area which makes clear the *philosophical* implications of proposed representations: in traditional computer science and psychology research there is no such commitment in principle to such a level or area.

The point of the above discussions therefore was not to propose a Nagel test as somehow superior to a Turing test but to point out that both tests ultimately have to address the central questions of mental events and processes, on the one hand, and the ascription of mental terms and predicates on the other. These are questions at a level higher than, or in an area other than, functional or computational specification. What separates AI from the mainstream of philosophy (particularly philosophy of language and philosophy of mind, both of which also address these questions) is that AI explicitly offers the challenge of how well any account of mental events and processes or of ascription mechanisms sits with regard to the idea of an intelligent, conscious machine. Even if the idea of an intelligent, conscious machine is considered to be a contradictory one, if the proposed accounts of mental events and processes or ascription mechanisms nevertheless can be somehow applied successfully to such a contradictory idea, that acts as a form of evaluation of such philosophical accounts. In the years to come, it may be impossible to do philosophy of mind and philosophy of language without taking this idea (contradictory or not) of a thinking machine into account, either formally or informally. Also, more contentiously, it may be impossible to do AI without some commitment, again formally or informally, to a certain philosophical stance concerning the role and status of mental events and processes and of what can be said of such events and processes (at what might be called level 0 in a Marr-type framework).

It is these points which substantiate the general one raised in the preface to the first volume, namely, that the idea of overcoming the formal constraints of computer science and philosophy, and of identifying the manner by which such constraints are overcome with a methodology and the subject matter of AI proper, has not been seriously explored. The task of this work has been to demonstrate how, in AI, it is perfectly possible and highly desirable that formal theories be augmented by non-formal, yet rigorous, models and approaches. These augmentations will take place at a level, or in an area, removed from functional specification, and it is at this level or in this area that philosophy of artificial intelligence has its place.

References

Dennett, D. C. (1981) *Brainstorms*. Harvester Press.

Grice, H. P. (1957) Meaning, *Philosophical Review*, LXVI, 377-388.

Grice, H. P. (1968) Utterer's meaning, sentence meaning, and word-meaning, *Foundations of Language*, 4, 225-242.

Hofstadter, D. R. (1979) *Gödel, Escher, Bach: An Eternal Golden Braid*. Harvester Press.

Nagel, T. (1974) What is it like to be a bat?, *Philosophical Review*, LXXXIII. Reprinted in *Mortal Questions*, Cambridge University Press, 1979, from where the page references are taken.

Strawson, P. F. (1959) *Individuals*. Methuen.

Index

rationality, 17, 20, 21, 23, 28, 34, 37, 38, 73,
    229–231, 236
real constituency, 125, 126
realistic monism, 63
reasoning, 139–142
reciprocity, 17, 18, 25, 28, 236, 237
reductionism, 114, 134, 221, 223, 225
reflective self-evaluation, 28, 29, 38, 39
refutations, 169
representation, 88, 90, 133, 139, 143, 146,
    186–190, 194, 195, 204, 206, 230–
    232, 235, 239–242
representational level, 235
representational stance, 231–233, 235, 239
representationalism, 120, 133
Robot Reply, 42
Rosenblatt, 93, 112
RUDE, 179
rule-explicitness, 132
rule-implicitness, 132
Rumelhart, 94, 97, 98, 101–141, 157, 193,
    195–197, 206, 207, 240
Russell, 62, 63, 67

schematic conception, 221, 222, 228
Schiffer, 203
Searle, 16, 40–56, 74–76, 79, 138, 177, 208,
    216, 218, 219, 226, 227, 237
second-order desires, 29
second-order intentional system, 26
second-order intentions, 26
second-order volitions, 29
self-consciousness, 29
semantic level, 127
semantic representations, 145
sensible properties, 61
seriality, 149
Shahan, 76
Shannon, 85
Simon, 41, 85
Skinner, 119
Sloman, 156
Smolensky, 139, 195
Soames, 203
societies of networks, 147
society of mind, 147, 148
software engineering, 178, 179, 183
stance, 17, 21, 23, 31
states of consciousness, 22, 35, 215, 220, 225,
    229
Stich, 24, 37
stimulus equivalence, 116, 117
Strawson, 15, 22, 34–36, 38, 79, 217, 225,
    228–230, 240, 245
strong AI, 40, 41, 54, 208, 219, 225
structure sensitivity, 122, 127, 128, 143, 144

substance, 61, 64
supervenience, 58, 59, 69, 75
symbolic level, 131
symbolic structures, 122, 143
systematicity, 129, 130, 142
Systems Reply, 42

test implications, 165–167
testability, 167, 171
the material, 61
the mental, 61
theory of types, 67
third-order intention, 27, 28
token, 67, 69, 99, 100
token-token identity, 54, 69
token-type relationship, 99
top-down organization, 102
Turing, 16, 30, 77, 78, 81, 84, 157, 182, 208,
    215, 219, 220, 238, 239, 243
Turing Machine, 16, 33, 118, 119, 121, 132,
    238
Turing Test, 227
type, 66, 67, 99, 100
Type 0 grammar, 205
type-token distinction, 68
type-type identity, 54, 65, 67, 69

utterer's intentions, 28

verbal communication, 18, 26, 236, 237
veridicality, 89
Von Neumann, 85, 95, 97, 129
Von Neumann machines, 119, 121

wanton, 29
weak AI, 54, 177
Whitby, 184
Winograd, 87, 89, 90
Wirth, 66